White Guys on Campus

The American Campus

Series editor, Harold S. Wechsler

The books in the American Campus series explore recent developments and public policy issues in higher education in the United States. Topics of interest include access to college, and college affordability; college retention, tenure, and academic freedom; campus labor; the expansion and evolution of administrative posts and salaries; the crisis in the humanities and the arts; the corporate university and for-profit colleges; online education; controversy in sport programs; and gender, ethnic, racial, religious, and class dynamics and diversity. Books feature scholarship from a variety of disciplines in the humanities and social sciences.

White Guys on Campus

Racism, White Immunity, and the Myth of "Post-Racial" Higher Education

NOLAN L. CABRERA

Rutgers University Press

New Brunswick, Camden, and Newark, New Jersey, and London

Library of Congress Cataloging-in-Publication Data

Names: Cabrera, Nolan L., author.
Title: White guys on campus : racism, white immunity, and the myth of
    "post-racial" higher education / Nolan L. Cabrera.
Description: New Brunswick : Rutgers University Press, [2018] | Series: The American campus |
    Includes bibliographical references and index.
Identifiers: LCCN 2018008417| ISBN 9780813599076 (hardback) | ISBN 9780813599069
    (paperback) | ISBN 9780813599083 (E-pub) | ISBN 9780813599106 (Web PDF)
Subjects: LCSH: Racism in higher education—United States. | Discrimination in education—
    United States. | Educational equalization—United States. | Whites—Race identity—
    United States. | Post-racialism—United States | BISAC: SOCIAL SCIENCE / Discrimination &
    Race Relations. | EDUCATION / Inclusive Education. | EDUCATION / Higher. |
    EDUCATION / Multicultural Education. | SOCIAL SCIENCE / Gender Studies. |
    SOCIAL SCIENCE / Men's Studies.
Classification: LCC LC212.42 .C35 2018 | DDC 379.2/60973—dc23
LC record available at https://lccn.loc.gov/2018008417

A British Cataloging-in-Publication record for this book is available from the British Library.

www.rutgersuniversitypress.org

Manufactured in the United States of America

For Joaquín

Those who profess to favor freedom and yet depreciate agitation, are men who want crops without ploughing the ground; they want rain without thunder and lightning; they want the ocean without the roar of its many waters. The struggle may be a moral one, or it may be a physical one, or it may be both. But it must be a struggle. Power concedes nothing without a demand. It never did and it never will. Find out just what any people will quietly submit to and you have found out the exact measure of injustice and wrong which will be imposed upon them, and these will continue till they are resisted with either words or blows, or with both.
—Frederick Douglass

Saying I'm obsessed with race and racism in America is like saying that I'm obsessed with swimming while I'm drowning. It's absurd.
—Hari Kondabolu

Contents

Preface

When I began conducting scholarly work on racism, I thought it might be a laudable long-term goal to write the first book on Whiteness in higher education. I quickly realized that book has been written several times under such titles as *What Matters in College* (Astin, 1993), *How College Affects Students* (Pascarella & Terenzini, 2005), and *Leaving College* (Tinto, 1987). This is not meant as a jab at the foundational texts of the field of higher education. Rather, I wanted to highlight the strong vein of Whiteness that each one of these "seminal books" has embedded within it. For example, Tinto (1987) conducted a critical synthesis of the higher education scholarship to identify the factors that contribute to students leaving college. However, the bulk of the scholarship he reviewed relied on samples that were disproportionately White, and his theorizing has been critiqued for this (e.g., Tierney, 1992). Instead of calling his text *Leaving College for White Students,* Tinto universalized his language and spoke of "college students," rendering omnipresent Whiteness invisible.

This is a simple example of how Whiteness is embedded into the very structures of society. It did not take Tinto overtly trying to prioritize White experiences to make Whiteness a central component of his theorizing. Racism is so engrained in the fabric of U.S. society that Bonilla-Silva (2006) argued we live in a country of *Racism Without Racists*. That is, it does not take intentionally racist actions to perpetuate racism, as the normality of Whiteness will do. This normality is precisely why engaging issues of race and racism is so difficult. In order to address this issue, one has to be able to first name the problem. When Whiteness is named, there is a predictable response—a lot of White outrage (e.g., "White Fragility"; DiAngelo, 2011). This anger tends to become more intense when people agitate for racial equity because, as the internet philosopher Anonymous offered, "When you're accustomed to privilege, equity feels like oppression."[1]

This dynamic is precisely why, when writing this book, the image of the Fighting Whites mascot[2] was a perfect visual metaphor for the work, but a little history is necessary. In Colorado, the mascot for Eaton High School was the Fightin' Reds. When some Native students at Northern Colorado University said the mascot was stereotypical and offensive (e.g., misshapen nose, loin cloth, and eagle feather), they were told by White school officials and community members that there was nothing racist about the Fightin' Reds (Johansen, 2010). Within this context, the students created the Fighting Whites mascot for their university intramural basketball team (Klyde-Silverstein, 2012). If there was nothing wrong with a stereotypical Native mascot, it should be acceptable to have a stereotypical White mascot, correct? Wrong! The outrage and backlash were swift. The same people who found nothing racist about the Fightin' Reds mascot were fiercely critical of the Fighting Whites, ignoring the fact that the latter was satirizing the former (Johansen, 2010). That is, they were more upset at a critique of racism than at actual instances of racism. This dynamic was present throughout my research for *White Guys on Campus*. The large bulk of White guys I spoke with were more upset about imagined racism against White people than about actual racism against People of Color.

This work is more than scholarship. I am constantly reminded that the normality of Whiteness has real, everyday consequences. While editing this book, I took a break to run to my local Walgreens. Dressed in shorts, a T-shirt, and flip-flops, I walked into the store and immediately heard over the intercom, "Security to the front please." I thought, "No way they're talking about me," and I went about my business. Soon, I realized there was a White store manager staring at me as I was pricing toothpaste. She asked me, "What are you doing?" I replied, "Shopping." She gave me some space but continued to surveil. After about five minutes, I approached her and said, "That's really messed up. I literally did nothing wrong and you're accusing me of stealing." She replied, "You're right, I should have just followed you instead." That was not much better. I put down the items I was going to purchase, left the store, and have not returned. Evidently, being a Brown man with a ponytail in Arizona means I am under suspicion while buying toiletries. It was a relatively minor incident, but still keeps me on my toes—reminding me that this work is not simply an academic exercise but rather is rooted in one of our most pressing and difficult social problems to address: racism.

This book uses a critical lens to take an unapologetically radical approach to the study of Whiteness. *Radical* colloquially is framed as a pejorative, but I use it as originally intended. *Radical* derives from the Latin root *radix*, which means "root." Frequently, analyses of diversity in higher education ignore root causes of racial stratification, which is akin to trying to kill a thistle with a weed-whacker. The root structure is still in place, and the thistle regrows. In contrast, this book presents a radical analysis of racism in higher education, seeking to get to the root of this social problem—identifying how institutions of higher education and individuals within them both contribute to systemic racism and sometimes can be vehicles for social change. So, let's get to the root of it, shall we?

1

The Unbearable
Whiteness of Being

White Male Racial Immunity
in Higher Education

On November 8, 2016, demographobia (Chang, 2014)—or the irrational fear of demographic population shifts—reared its ugly head and the Forty-Fifth was elected president of the United States. He won overwhelmingly with White people, in particular non-college-educated White people. Analyses of this trend tended to fall into tired old stereotypes of "good" (non-racist) versus "bad" (racist) White people. Implicitly, this let college-educated White people off the proverbial hook for their own racism. After all, it was the uneducated, racist, "hillbilly" "rednecks" who turned over the country to the Forty-Fifth, right? To quote the Forty-Fifth, "Wrong!" Many common and insidious manifestations of contemporary racism occur on college campuses, as I will elaborate later.

Additionally, some of the most headline-making racial controversies involve institutions of higher education. For example, Dr. Lee Bebout, a White professor at Arizona State University, offered a graduate seminar on "Racial Theory and the Problem of Whiteness." Only knowing the reading list and having no testimonies from inside the classroom, *Fox News* immediately deemed this course racist against White students.[1] That was interesting considering the reading list included Nobel laureate Toni Morrison's *Playing in the Dark*. The public outcry was swift, and while the class was still offered that semester, threats against Bebout and his family poured in and neo-Nazis flyered his home neighborhood labeling him "anti-White" (Lemons, 2015). This example proved to be so controversial that an Arizona law was recently introduced to outlaw university teaching of *social justice* in public educational institutions throughout the state, and this class was one of the central illustrations of the "need" of the legislation (Polleta, 2017).

Consider also that Boston University professor Dr. Saida Grundy tweeted, "Why is White America so reluctant to identify White college males as a problem population?" (Jaschik, 2015). From an empirical standpoint, this question makes a lot of sense. On college campuses, White men are disproportionately responsible for code-of-conduct violations, sexual assault, and alcohol abuse, among many other antisocial behaviors (Boswell & Spade, 1996; Capraro, 2000; Harper, Harris, & Mmeje, 2005). Given this context, why would this statement be deemed controversial? Instead of engaging Grundy's message, the news coverage tended to frame her as the problem, asking questions such as:

- Why is it acceptable for her to be racist against White people?
- How can *she* teach White men?
- Would this Tweet be acceptable if it was a White professor making a similar statement about Black students? (Cabrera, Franklin, & Watson, 2017, p. 16)

Dr. Grundy, a first-year assistant professor, had to publicly apologize, and Boston University's central administration openly condemned her tweet (Jaschik, 2015). What is going on here? How is it possible that these two events spiraled into national, headline-garnering controversies?

Both of these examples highlight an interesting trend regarding the intersection of Whiteness and higher education. The central questions and issues raised by Drs. Bebout and Grundy were not the core of the controversies. Instead, their actions were labeled "racist," when in reality their primary social crime was examining White responsibility for societal racism. That is, when racial issues arise, they tend to be framed as a minority problem—implicitly not holding White people accountable, unless it is those "bad" racist Whites (Cabrera et al., 2017). This is not a new trend. Almost a century ago, W. E. B. Du Bois was continually asked, "How does it feel to be a problem?" (1969, p. 43). Du Bois understood that Black people, like himself, implicitly owned the racial problem, maintaining the racial innocence of White people. Essentially, what Drs. Bebout and Grundy did was name Whiteness and highlight its problematic nature, and the negative public reaction was swift. They disrupted a powerful yet unspoken social norm: the invisibility of Whiteness. The fact that these instances became controversial says more about the current state of our society than the rhetoric these two professors used.

Almost paradoxically, the undergraduate years can also be a time of incredible racial growth for White students and sites of challenging contemporary racism (Cabrera, 2012; Cabrera et al., 2017; Reason, Millar, & Scales, 2005; Saénz, 2010). This book grapples with these tensions through a critical examination of White men on college campuses, unveiling the frequently unconscious habits of racism (Sullivan, 2006) as well as the possibility of developing anti-racism among White students (Reason & Broido, 2005). This is an unexplored issue for a number of reasons. First, and most fundamental, there is massive and pervasive misunderstanding about what constitutes racism. These limited definitions include the following:

- Racism is an individual fault, and not a systemic reality
- Racism requires meanness, hatred, or bitterness toward the outgroup
- Racism can occur against any racial group, including Whites (Cabrera, 2009, p. 7)

If this is the extent of contemporary racism, then it is only a minor problem. In the 1970s, it fell out of favor to publicly state that Black people are inferior people, and the overwhelming majority of Whites profess to favor racial equality (Schuman, Steeh, Bobo, & Krysan, 1997). Instead, the systemic realities of racism persist, but overt expressions of racism are frequently driven underground (Bobo, Kluegel, & Smith, 1997; Bonilla-Silva, 2006; Omi & Winant, 2015). This makes racism a powerful social force. It is not only an oppressive social system but also difficult to define, and its contours become apparent only when there is a challenge to it.

Within this framework, it is critically important to explore the racial lives of White undergraduate men because they tend to be ignored when issues of racism arise. For example, a common analysis of campus racism involves microaggressions, the "everyday verbal, nonverbal, and environmental slights, snubs, or insults, whether intentional or unintentional, that communicate hostile, derogatory, or negative messages to target persons based solely upon their marginalized group membership" (Sue, 2010, p. 3). The insidious effect of microaggressions is not the isolated incidents but their cumulative impact as they mentally and emotionally wear down People of Color, frequently resulting in *racial battle fatigue* (Smith, Allen, & Danley, 2007). Microaggression scholarship, however, is very limited because, as Cabrera et al. (2017) argued, "these analyses almost always stem from the perspective of those targeted by microaggressions" (p. 36). That is, there is a microaggression enacted upon a microaggressee, but without a direct analysis of the microaggressor. There is an effect with no cause. This is the purpose of this book—to fill in this missing component on campus-based racial analysis.

Whiteness and Racism on the College Campus: Past to Present

In 2015, the University of Oklahoma's Sigma Alpha Epsilon (SAE) fraternity made headlines when a YouTube video went viral of them singing the song, "There will never be a nigger in SAE."[2] They were immediately expelled, and OU's president David Boren claimed that his university had a "zero-tolerance policy for racism." This framing views racism as the exception on college campuses, not the rule. I took issue with this stance and offered the following: "No institution of higher education in the country has a zero-tolerance policy for racism. Racial bias—much of it unconscious—is so ingrained in American society that any institution that actually enforced zero tolerance would have to expel half its freshman class before winter break. What Boren actually means is that OU has zero tolerance for overtly racist actions that are caught on camera, are posted to YouTube and embarrass the institution in the national news" (Cabrera, 2015). Essentially, racist incidents tend to be individualized, and perpetrators on college campuses are viewed as a "few bad apples" instead of a predictable outcome of two issues. First is the persistence of systemic racism in contemporary society, and our collective unwillingness to address this oppressive social force. The second is that despite being labeled "bastions of liberal indoctrination,"[3] many of the same racial conflicts that play out in the general society also occur on college campuses (Cabrera, 2009).

Institutions of higher education were not created to be racially inclusive, and they have been struggling with that legacy ever since (Cabrera et al., 2017; Cole, 2018; Geiger, 2005; Harper, Patton, & Wooden, 2009; Karabel, 2005; Mustaffa, 2017; Thelin, 2004). That is, universities are paradoxically spaces for educating the societal elite (Cabrera et al., 2017; Karabel, 2005), while concurrently aspiring to be spheres of democracy via scholarly inquiry and non-repression (Gutmann, 1999). Unfortunately, it is not possible to have an arena of democracy and non-repression if minoritized racial groups are systematically excluded, preventing equal participation (Cabrera, 2014d).[4] Given the history of U.S. higher education, it is not surprising that racism is a central and foundational component (Harper et al., 2009; Mustaffa, 2017). As Cabrera et al. (2017) offered, "It was not just that [institutions of higher education] actively recruited [White] students, but they also created exclusionary policies both implicit and explicit that excluded non-White, nonmale, and nonwealthy students from gaining access" (p. 58). Access to colleges and universities did increase substantially through the Morrill Land-Grant Acts, which started the movement toward mass higher education (Geiger, 2005; Trow, 1970). While Black students also experienced substantial gains in access, some nuance is warranted (Harper et al., 2009).

First, Black enrollments primarily rose at historically Black colleges and universities (HBCUs), a reminder that segregation was the law of the land and became further entrenched with the *Plessy v. Ferguson* (1896) ruling (Chesler, Lewis, & Crowfoot, 2005; Harper et al., 2009). Second, the quality of education at these public HBCUs tended to be substandard due to a combination of underfunding and a primary focus on vocational training. Roebuck and Murty (1993) offered a scathing interpretation of the reasons for structured inequality: "To get millions of dollars in federal funds for the development of white land-grant universities, to limit African American education to vocational training, and to prevent African Americans from attending white land-grant colleges" (p. 27). Even with a massive expansion of public higher education, there were mechanisms in place to keep Blacks in their place and preserve White racial dominance.

Some of these formal structures of explicit segregation were dismantled by the mid-twentieth century, in particular via *Brown v. Board of Education* (1954), in which the U.S. Supreme Court ruled that separate is inherently unequal. However, Derrick Bell (1979) has been highly critical of this ruling in that he did not see it as actually having the best interests of justice and Black people at heart. Rather, segregation was outlawed because it benefitted White people, or what Bell (1979) referred to as *interest-convergence*. Additionally, it is questionable how much this ruling affected higher education. In fact, Brown (2001) argued, "the mandate to desegregate did not reach higher education until one decade after Brown, when President Lyndon B. Johnson signed the Civil Rights Act of 1964" (p. 49). That is, the "all deliberate speed" clause of *Brown* did not have a meaningful impact on colleges and universities until they were threatened with the loss of federal funding if segregation persisted.

Despite this issue, patterns of higher education access substantially increased for minoritized students with the creation and implementation of affirmative action (Crosby, 2004; Harper et al., 2009). Even though affirmative action tends to be framed as a race-based program, the primary beneficiaries numerically have been White women (Crosby, 2004). Regardless, the program has been a significant driver of access for minoritized students in higher education (Chesler et al., 2005; Harper et al., 2009). However, these modest gains have eroded because of persistent attacks on affirmative action in particular and race-conscious social policy in general (Crosby, 2004; Santos, Cabrera, & Fosnacht, 2010). HBCUs have even been pressured to recruit more White students (Harper et al., 2009). Within this sociopolitical landscape, racial gaps in access along racial lines persist and have sometimes even expanded (Carnevale & Strohl, 2013; Posselt, Jaquette, Bielby, & Bastedo, 2012). However, the racial problems of higher education only begin with access. The college campus, as Hurtado (1992) argued, is a "context for conflict."

An issue that is prevalent in the larger society and very widespread on college campuses is cultural appropriation (Keene, 2015). It is not just that White students adopt cultures that are not their own, but they also do so in very stereotypical and racist ways (Garcia, Johnston, Garibay, Herrera, & Giraldo, 2011). A common way that this occurs on college campuses is in the form of racial theme parties. One example was the "ghetto-themed" party UT Austin students threw in 2007 in "honor" of Dr. King's holiday, where White students came dressed as Aunt Jemima while eating fried chicken and drinking malt liquor (Wise, 2007). Later that year, students at Santa Clara University held a "south of the border" party where the White students in attendance dressed as maids or pregnant Latinas (Georgevich, 2007).

Given the massive size of U.S. higher education, one could think that these transgressions represent the beliefs of just a few "bad apples." However, similar parties have been documented at the University of Texas School of Law, Trinity College, Whitman College, Washington University, Virginia, Clemson, Willamette College, Texas A&M, UConn School of Law, Stetson, Chicago, Cornell, Swarthmore, Emory, MIT, Macalester, Johns Hopkins, Dartmouth, Louisville, Wisconsin Whitewater, William Jewell, Oklahoma State, Auburn, UC Irvine, Syracuse, Tarleton State, Union College, Colorado, Tennessee, Arizona, Alabama, Illinois, Delaware, and Mississippi (Wise, 2007). Keep in mind this list represents only the schools where students were caught and embarrassed their institution on social media. Thus, this is simply the tip of the proverbial racial iceberg.

Parties like these have been in existence for years, but the emergence of social media has allowed them to be more publicly visible (Chesler et al., 2005, p. 48). It is a classic example of what Picca and Feagin (2007) refer to as *backstage performance*—that is, the actions of White people are markedly different in the presence of People of Color (*front stage performance*) versus among other White people (*backstage performance*). Additionally, racial theme parties and hate crimes bring an incredible amount of negative publicity to institutions of higher education, creating coercive pressure to handle these situations with minimal media attention. This is why in Hurtado et al.'s (1998) study of Texas A&M, fewer than 10 percent of racial discrimination cases on campus were actually reported.

Part of this trend is related to White racial segregation on college campuses. Contrary to Beverly Daniel Tatum's (2003) provocative title, *Why Are All the Black Kids Sitting Alone in the Cafeteria?*, it is actually White men who segregate on campus the most (antonio, 2001). Despite the empirical reality, Students of Color are continually blamed for campus segregation or balkanization (Cabrera & Hurtado, 2015; D'Souza, 1991). Also, these racially segregated environments are not innocuously "separate." Rather, they are the campus subenvironments that foster the greatest sense of "reverse racism," or the perceived racial victimization of White people. Throughout this book I present "reverse racism" in quotation marks for two reasons. First, it is an accurate description of how many White people *feel* about issues of race. Second, it has no basis in reality, necessitating the scare quotes. It represents what Feagin and O'Brien (2003) refer to as *sincere fictions*. They are sincere because White folk genuinely believe them, and they are fictions because they are not real in an empirical sense.

Returning to the college campus, the more that White students are segregated from the non-White campus population, the more they are likely to perceive a sense of "reverse racism" (Cabrera, 2014b; Sidanius, Van Laar, Levin, & Sinclair, 2004). The housed Greek system is an area of campus where segregation is particularly heightened (Cabrera, 2014b; Chang & DeAngelo, 2002; Ross, 2015; Syrett, 2009). This makes a certain amount of intuitive sense because the Greek system is one of the few areas on campus where students are able to exclude their peers from participation (Cabrera, Watson, & Franklin, 2016; Ross, 2015). This is not a new phenomenon. Astin (1993) postulated that racial insulation might be one of the driving forces behind Greek participation: "A good deal of racial strife may lead to the formation of social organizations that cater to a particular racial or ethnic group or to conservative students who want to isolate themselves from racial interaction" (p. 341). This segregation, in turn, tends to foster *backstage performance*, as Picca and Feagin (2007) described.

Specific to their study, Picca and Feagin (2007) analyzed racial journals of White college students and uncovered a disturbing trend. The journals detailed over nine thousand incidents of racism in the participants' lived experiences, and these tended to occur only among other White students. These acts of racism were largely overt, such as racist joke telling or using the n-word; however, in the presence of racial minorities, these behaviors mostly disappeared (Cabrera, 2014c; Picca & Feagin, 2007).

There is, however, some heterogeneity within the college environment. For example, Saénz (2010) demonstrated that institutions of higher education have the potential to actually break "the cycle of racial segregation" that is engrained in K–12 education. Additionally, university life has been demonstrated to be a time of great growth for some (not the majority of) White students as they work on their racial selves and sometimes become racial justice allies (Broido, 2000; Cabrera, 2012; Linder, 2015; Reason et al., 2005). By *racial justice allies* I mean White people who struggle against racism (Cabrera, 2012), and I offer more on this definition in chapter 7. Thus, institutions of higher education have an almost paradoxical relationship with systemic racism. They are, at the same time, what Carnevale and Strohl (2013) refer to as the *intergenerational reproduction of White privilege* as well as arenas for challenging racism (Cabrera, 2012; Linder, 2015; Saénz, 2010).

Within this context, it becomes critically important to explore the racial views and experiences of White male undergraduates. First, as previously discussed, college-educated White people are frequently ignored in racial discussions—not because they are less racist than poorly educated White people but because they are better at *appearing* less racist (Bonilla-Silva, 2006). Second, there is still massive misunderstanding about what constitutes racism. There is almost universal condemnation of White supremacy; even leaders of the modern-day KKK assert that they are not White supremacists. Rather, they claim they are "White separatists" seeking to advocate on behalf of the White race (Associated Press, 2016). Third, there is a tendency to individualize issues of racism. That is, people all too often locate racism within a specific person instead of seeing a structural reality. The name of that structural reality has been and continues to be *White supremacy*.

This term makes a number of people very uncomfortable, but I also think it is accurate as I elaborate in the subsequent section. Some have asked, "Aren't you going to alienate White people by using this term?" My response is as follows. First, I am not writing this book to cater to White people's racial sensitivities, or what DiAngelo (2011) refers to as *White fragility*. If one term turns readers away from my writing, they were probably not going to meaningfully engage with the text in the first place. Second, there should be many parts of this book that make White people uncomfortable, but I ask readers to explore that discomfort. Frequently this is an indication of racial growing pains instead of something fundamentally wrong with my thesis. For White people who rarely think about racism, learning about its ugly, painful, and oppressive contemporary realities can be a difficult and jarring process; however, please keep in mind that it is far more difficult for People of Color to survive racial oppression than it is for White people to educate themselves on the subject.

Whiteness, White Supremacy, and White Privilege

When asked what he thought about the current president, Representative Charles Rangel (D-NY) said, "The one good thing Trump does for our great nation is that he shatters the myth of white supremacy once and for all" (Flegenheimer & Haberman, 2017). That is, the Forty-Fifth's public buffoonery means that White people cannot continue to claim they are the "superior race." Rangel's jab, while humorous, highlights a frequent misunderstanding of the nature of racism. First, there is a tendency to individualize racism and see it as a mistaken belief in the inherent superiority of the White race over all others. Implicit in this formulation is that White supremacy derives from White supremacists. Second, this misunderstanding of the nature of racism tends to separate people into good (non-racist) and bad (racist). The nature of contemporary racism is much more complicated than this. To begin, there is an old phrase, "The whole is larger than the sum of its parts." This is an important way of framing contemporary racism because one cannot simply aggregate the racial views of people in the United States and understand racism. Instead, racism has to be understood as a *system* of racial oppression (Bonilla-Silva, 2006; Omi & Winant, 2015; Feagin, 2006) whereby actions are assessed in relation to the larger social structure. Those actions that support systemic racism are racist, and those that challenge it are anti-racist.

To further clarify this issue, allow me to offer an analogy. Capitalism is the contemporary U.S. economic structure. It sets rules and values that govern monetary exchanges, and as Cabrera (in press) argued, "In the absence of capitalism, a dollar bill is just a piece of paper." By the same token, in the absence of White supremacy, White people are just folks in need of a tan. Returning to the analogy of capitalism, given the size of my bank account and lack of stock or business ownership, it is unlikely that I could be considered a "capitalist." However, any time I go grocery shopping, I am supporting the system of capitalism. Likewise, I do not have to be *a racist* to support systemic racism. Rather, my individual actions, views, and ideologies should be judged in relation to systemic racism and assessed in terms of whether they prop up or challenge its persistence. This complicates racial analyses because racism and antiracism can be (and frequently are) enacted by the same individual (Cabrera et al., 2016). Thus, as Bonilla-Silva (2006) so succinctly argues, we exist in a social structure of *Racism without Racists*.

According to Omi and Winant's (2015) theory of racial formation, the U.S. was originally a totalitarian regime of racial stratification. That is, the dominant racial ideology was one where People of Color were naturally inferior beings, and this became the justification for their subjugation (e.g., slavery, Manifest Destiny, Jim Crow, lynchings, etc.). A significant development of the Civil Rights Movement was not just the policy shifts but the ideological ones as well. That is, one of the biggest developments of the Civil Rights Movement was the affirmation that People of Color were *actually people*. By the early 1970s, it fell out of favor to publicly state that White people were inherently superior or that People of Color did not deserve "equal treatment" (Schuman et al., 1997). Despite these important developments, racism—both individually and systemically—did not magically disappear. Rather, it was driven underground, and Whiteness was rearticulated from superior to normal (Bonilla-Silva, 2001, 2006; Cabrera, 2009; Omi & Winant, 2015).

This normality of Whiteness meant it evolved from a de jure to a de facto form. For example, the formal laws of education segregation became outlawed via *Brown v. Board of Education* (1954), but massive levels of student racial separation persist (Frankenberg & Orfield, 2012; Orfield & Eaton, 1997). Whiteness has become a more malleable form of racial oppression, but its adverse effects against People of Color remain (Omi & Winant, 2015). The normality of Whiteness also means that racial analyses tend to be extremely one-sided. For example, it is fine to discuss inner-city poverty among People of Color as long as it is not linked to the affluence of the vanilla suburbs. This is akin to saying *up* with no *down*, *good* with no *bad*, *hot* with no *cold*. Unfortunately, this is how a number of contemporary investigations of race occur—engaging racial marginalization without also analyzing advantage.

Returning to higher education, the lack of access to higher education for People of Color exists only if there is concurrently an unwarranted advantage for access to higher education that White people experience (Carnevale & Strohl, 2013). While this may seem obvious, one-sided racial scholarship is the norm within the field of higher education. In his critical review of higher education literature, Harper (2012) found that scholars in this field tended to use race in their analyses but with no consideration of systemic racism, or that they analyzed *race without racism*.

There is additional popular misunderstanding about what "Whiteness" means, often conflated with "White people." Instead, Leonardo (2009) argued, "'Whiteness' is a racial discourse, whereas the category 'white people' represents a socially constructed identity, usually based on skin color. . . . Whiteness is not a culture but a social concept" (pp. 169–170). In Leonardo's understanding, Whiteness is a discourse that serves to naturalize the existence of systemic racism. Returning to the capitalism analogy, the hegemony of capitalists naturalizes economic inequality (Gramsci, 1971). By the same token, Whiteness as a racialized discourse naturalizes the existence of systemic racism and racial inequality (Cabrera, in press). Some core components of Whiteness, according to Leonardo (2009), involve (1) an unwillingness to name the contours of systemic racism, (2) the avoidance of identifying with a racial experience or minority group, and (3) the minimization of the U.S. history of racism. Essentially, these are discursive mechanisms that deny the persistence of systemic racism. This, in turn, also serves to reify structural White advantages, which is why Harris (1993) refers to Whiteness as a form of property.

On an individual level, the result of systemic racism is the manifestation of White privilege (McIntosh, 1989). White privilege is "an invisible package of unearned assets that I can count on cashing in each day, but about which I was 'meant' to remain oblivious" (McIntosh, 1989, p. 10). Within this formulation, White supremacy is the structure, Whiteness normalizes this structure, and White privilege is the predictable output of the system. To make the "normal" visible, McIntosh listed dozens of unearned privileges she obtained because she was White in a racist society. This concept has evolved into the development of White privilege pedagogy, which seeks to educate White people of their unearned social privileges while strategizing how to disrupt and challenge racism (Kendall, 2006). While this concept has taken hold over the past decade in higher education scholarship and practice, it is also increasingly coming under scrutiny (Lensmire et al., 2013; Leonardo, 2009).

White Privilege versus White Immunity

> It's the complexion of the protection for
> the collection.
> —Paul Mooney on being White[5]

When discussing White privilege, former *Fox News* commentator Bill O'Reilly said, "I didn't experience [White privilege] when I worked in Carvel, painted houses, mowed lawns? I'm going to have to exempt myself" (Coscarelli, 2014). O'Reilly's framing of White privilege is a common response when the subject arises. There is a tendency to identify a time in one's history when either oneself personally or one's family struggled, and then ask, "How were we privileged?" Part of the problem is the implication of the term *privilege*, as many interpret it to mean a semi-charmed life or one that is defined by wealth.

Many of these critiques and misunderstandings of White privilege, like the one O'Reilly offered, willfully misrepresent the concept. That said, there is a legitimate semantic issue embedded in the term *White privilege*. Before diving into that, I think it will help to return to some of McIntosh's (1989) examples of White privilege:

- I can go shopping alone most of the time, pretty well assured that I will not be followed or harassed.
- I can be sure that my children will be given curricular materials that testify to the existence of their race.
- I am never asked to speak for all the people of my racial group. (pp. 11–12)

In many respects, these examples represent a baseline standard for humane interaction. That is, *no one* should be harassed while shopping or asked to speak on behalf of their entire racial group. Rather, systemic racism means that People of Color are not guaranteed protection from this type of disparate treatment. White privilege in this sense does not so much elevate the status of White people; rather, White people find themselves in an elevated social status because systemic racism depresses the life chances of People of Color. White people are inoculated from this disparate treatment, echoing Paul Mooney's pithy observation that White skin is the "complexion of protection."

Within this context, I prefer the term *White immunity* instead of *White privilege* as it more accurately describes this outcome from systemic racism. I understand that there are critical scholarly works that more explicitly engage systemic oppression as the source of privilege (e.g., Johnson, 2001; Kimmel & Ferber, 2017; Rothenberg, 2005, 2016). Instead, I am concerned with the frequent misuse of "privilege," such as the semantic misapplication of the term, the tendency to individualize privilege, and the subsequent loss of the critical analysis of systemic racism (Lensmire et al., 2013; Leonardo, 2009). Therefore, I use *White immunity* because it is a more accurate description of how "privilege" operates. Additionally, it more closely aligns with the way that Whiteness was formed in the U.S. context.

When Europeans first came to the "New World," they were primarily identified by their country of origin and the concept of being White did not exist (Allen, 1997; Ignatiev, 1995; MacMullan, 2009; Sacks, 1994; Takaki, 1993; Wander, Martin, & Nakayama, 2005). A combination of forces colluded to create the label *White*. First, Bacon's Rebellion highlighted for many social elites of European descent (especially in the South) that it was necessary to offer marginal incorporation of poor people of European descent into the economic system above Black and Native American people (Allen, 1997; Kendi, 2016; MacMullan, 2009). The logic was that a coalition of poor or enslaved Blacks and poor people of European descent could effectively overthrow the existing power structure, but putting the poor of European descent in charge of Blacks (e.g., as slave patrols) would preemptively quash larger rebellions. Part of this also involved articulating the ideology that White people were a superior race. This led DuBois (1935) to argue that all White people garnered the "public and psychological wages of whiteness"—that is, they may be poor and struggling, but at least they are not Black.

Additionally, there was a rampant ideology that Christianity was a civilizing religion that people from Africa and the Americas did not possess (Allen, 1997; Kendi, 2016). Soon, Christianity and Whiteness ideologically became synonymous in a racist cyclical logic: Europeans are the pinnacle of civilization. Why? Because they have Christianity. Why do they have Christianity? Because they are the pinnacle of civilization (Allen, 1997; Kendi, 2016; MacMullan, 2009; Yancy, 2012).

Finally, the implementation of racial laws was central in creating Whiteness, but it was done in a very interesting way. Instead of passing laws that elevated White people, politicians denied rights to People of Color—in particular Native Americans and Blacks (Allen, 1997; Haney-López, 2006; Wander et al., 2005)—including rights to intermarry (especially minoritized men with White women), vote, own property, and possess guns (Allen, 1997; Haney-Kendi, 2016; Haney-López, 2006; MacMullan, 2009). These laws were central in the creation of Whiteness because they defined Whiteness through negation. That is, they created the contours of Whiteness by defining what it meant to *not* be White.

Ultimately, becoming White was a twofold process. First, it required Europeans to give up their cultural heritage (Ignatiev, 1995; Sacks, 1994). Second, it required a belief in the superiority of the White race over all others. This belief was expressed in the behavior of European immigrants even into the twentieth century. As they immigrated to the United States, they concurrently learned part of *working toward Whiteness* entailed learning to hate non-Whites, Blacks in particular (Roediger, 1991). Within this context, Takaki (1993) described the visceral hatred Irish immigrants faced upon arrival and their curious response: "[The Irish] sought to become insiders, or Americans, by claiming their own membership as whites" (p. 151). This entailed the combination of losing their native culture, attacking Blacks, and assimilating into Whiteness (Ignatiev, 1995; Takaki, 1993). From this time comes an old adage that the second word European immigrants learned upon arriving in the United States was "nigger," preceded only by "okay" (Roediger, 1998).

To be clear, Whiteness in a U.S. context was created to elevate people of European descent by oppressing People of Color (Allen, 1997; Ignatiev, 1995). It had no productive value and is in many ways an empty social category. Try this quick social experiment. Ask a Person of Color what is great about being from his or her racial/ethnic group. Frequent responses include food, family, traditions, and music. Then ask a White person what is great about being White. The response is usually silence or something like, "I don't get racially profiled like Black people do." That is, usually what is great about being White is that one does not have to experience the disparate treatment that People of Color do.

This returns us to the concept of *White immunity*. The construction of Whiteness allowed a baseline standard for humane interaction to be afforded only to people of European descent, while denying this to People of Color. White as the social standard of humanity has long been established (Allen, 1997; Bacote, 2015). This is why *White privilege*, in part, has not been entirely successful at addressing racial issues from a White perspective. It implies an elevation of White people when in fact it is more about the decreased life chances of People of Color. A central facet of immunity is that it is assumed. Part of this taken-for-granted nature is that it makes it very difficult for White people to consider perspectives that are not their own (Applebaum, 2010). This White immunity was the overarching context for the interviews that are the crux of this book. However, immunity stretched beyond that of race, as all interviewees were cisgender men, the bulk of whom were also heterosexual, Christian, middle class, able-bodied, and all were university students. Therefore, their immunity encompassed protection from heterosexism, ableism, as well as religious and class-based oppression. In particular, the White guys I talked with tended to have racial views and experiences that were informed by masculinity.

Discourses of Whiteness, Discourses of Masculinity

Instead of a singular masculinity, there are multiple masculinities—or ways that male-identified individuals present and embody what it means to be a man

(Connell, 2005; Johnson, 2005; Kimmel & Messner, 2004). Among these masculinities, however, are dominant and less dominant forms. While males receive male privilege over women via structured patriarchy (Connell, 2005; Johnson, 2005; Kimmel & Ferber, 2017), there is a hierarchy within the category of "men" in terms of who is more "manly." Laker and Davis (2011) explained that there are normative social pressures that push men to conform to dominant forms of masculinity: "The underlying factor is a code that essentially says don't appear feminine: don't show emotions, don't show taste in art or music, watch how you dress" (p. 7). This is what Edwards and Jones (2009) referred to as the "man face," and it is a prevalent feature of how men develop their masculine sense of self while in college (Harper & Harris, 2010; Laker & Davis, 2011). Rarely, however, do scholars consider the intersection of race and masculinity, but when they do there are two common features. White men tend to experience frustration, framing themselves as the "true" victims of racism and sexism, while largely having a limited range of masculine-acceptable emotions to express their angst (e.g., anger) (Carroll, 2011; Kimmel, 2013).

Thus, the interviews of White guys on race were also contextualized within experiences of negotiating hegemonic masculinity. The intersection of White and male immunity meant that the White guys I talked with rarely had a marginalized social identity, did not understand oppression, framed themselves as racial (and sometimes gender) "victims," and did so through anger. I do understand, as bell hooks (1995) so succinctly defines, that we live in system of "white supremacist capitalist patriarchy" (p. 78). That is, there are multiple, mutually supportive systems of oppression working concurrently. While there are important structures beyond White supremacy and patriarchy in terms of contextualizing these White guys' narratives, I primarily focus on White and male immunity to maintain analytical focus. This is not to say that other forms of oppression are unimportant, but rather, to borrow from Jon Stewart formerly of *The Daily Show*, "If we amplify everything, we hear nothing" (Cherette, 2010).

Talking with White Guys

> It was awkward just because I've never had anybody that's asked me about race in the context of me being a White person.
> —Dwight

When I first embarked on this research, some friends and colleagues tried to dissuade me, for several reasons. Many thought there was no way that White male undergraduates would be open and honest about issues of race with a Person of Color, and this concern was partially supported in the empirical scholarship. For example, Macalpine and Marsh (2005) interviewed a number of White people on what it meant to be White in contemporary society, and their frequent response was "There's nothing I can say." Despite living in a racialized society, their participants were so unaware of how their racial/ethnic background affected their lives that they were generally inarticulate on the subject. In addition, a great deal of scholarship argues that the views of White people are markedly different in the presence of a minority versus only other White people (e.g., Picca & Feagin, 2007). As the subsequent chapters document, I do not think the participants were being reserved or "politically correct" in their views. I did ask some about how aware they were of my racial/ethnic background during the course of the interviews, and almost uniformly they said they were unaware. This largely stems from me being a light-skinned Chicano as well as being able to speak "standard" English. Essentially, my racial/ethnic background was able to fade into the background, and one participant even said, "If you were Black, I don't think I would have been so open." For more details on my methodology, please see Cabrera (2016).

In the subsequent chapters, I provide the findings from two years of interviewing White male undergraduates at two separate institutions of higher education, Southwestern University (SWU) and Western University (WU). SWU is a public Research I university in the southwestern United States that has a student population of approximately forty thousand. It is a predominantly White institution (about two-thirds of the students), practices affirmative action, but is not academically selective, as approximately 80 percent of students who apply gain admission. WU is also a Research I university, is on the West Coast, and also has a student population above forty thousand. Unlike SWU, it is academically selective (about a 20 percent acceptance rate), does not practice affirmative action, and is only about 35 percent White. I chose these two sites because I thought that the views and experiences of White students at these institutions would illuminate interesting differences in the racial experiences and views of White men. I was right and wrong with this suspicion. The participants' narratives tended to be more similar than different, but when differences arose they were really interesting, as chapter 5 illuminates.

I piloted this work in 2006 but conducted the bulk of the interviews between 2007 and 2008, prior to the elections of both President Obama and the Forty-Fifth. Over this period, many commentators professed that we were entering a "post-racial" society at the same time that racial tensions throughout the country continually escalated. Therefore, the timing of these interviews was critically important because the previous nine years have been ones of racial retrenchment, with racist politics and views moving from covert to overt. Essentially, these interviews with White male college students are as good as it gets, and as the subsequent chapters demonstrate, things were not that good to begin with. College students tend to care about societal progress and improving race relations more than the society at large (Eagan et al., 2017), and even among this segment of the U.S. population there is rampant, frequently unconscious, but still potent racism. To state the obvious, we have a lot of work to do.

There was diversity in the views and experiences among the White guys I spoke with. The bulk of them spent their interviews downplaying the relevance of contemporary racism; seeing racism as an individual defect instead of a systemic reality; existing in racially homogenous, White environments; claiming White people were the "true" targets of contemporary racism; and espousing many overtly racist beliefs. The narratives of these guys are the basis for chapters 2 through 6. Those who tended to see racism as a system of oppression, explored issues of White privilege/immunity, and took anti-racist actions are the subject of chapter 7. In previous work, I labeled these guys as "working through Whiteness" (Cabrera, 2012). This is not to say those White guys featured in chapter 7 were "good Whites" and the rest were bad, because they also had a number of racial issues they continually struggled with. They were, however, much more advanced in their views on and engagement with racism than the interviewees presented in chapters 2 through 6.

I interviewed only men as cross-gender interviews in pilots proved that it was very difficult to disentangle gender-based power dynamics from racial views and experiences. Also, as these students come from what Cabrera (2011) referred to as *racial hyper privilege* (being both male and White), they are at the epicenter of White racial immunity on college campuses. Finally, I want to be clear about one central issue. I am not interested in understanding White male undergraduate views on racism for their specific benefit or exploring their developmental opportunities. Some of the work will have implications for student development, but that is not its underlying purpose. Rather, I am concerned with how the views, attitudes, and experiences of White male undergraduates lead to the marginalization of Students of Color on college campuses and what can be done to transform this social structure/practice. Essentially, this is intended to be an analysis of Whiteness at the service of Students of Color.

Conclusion and Overview

This exploration of White immunity, White supremacy, and their occasional disruption on college campuses is the center of this book. Whiteness is a nimble form of social oppression, and the following chapters chart many of its contours. To begin, chapter 2 illustrates how most of the White guys I spoke with existed in racially homogenous, White living/learning environments. It then engages the different styles, or *semantic moves* (Bonilla-Silva, 2006), White men use to verbally dance around racism. They believed that racism continued to exist, but they concurrently downplayed its contemporary significance. They tended to individualize issues of racism, labeling people as either racist or non-racist instead of seeing it as a systemic reality. They also tended to believe that the United States is meritocratic and therefore the solution to promoting racial equity is more "hard work" by racial minorities. Finally, when discussing apparently racist events, they found ways to describe them as non-racial (e.g., "It's more an economic thing").

Chapter 3 documents White men's *sincere fictions* (Feagin & O'Brien, 2003), in particular their proclamations of "reverse racism." The White guys I spoke with did not always see themselves as racial victims. Rather, they tended to identify "reverse racism" when the normality, or hegemony, of Whiteness was disrupted in their learning/living environments. Some of these disruptions included tense cross-racial interactions (especially via race/ethnic-specific campus groups), perceived political correctness, and race-conscious social policies. During these parts of the discussions, the White guys I spoke with became particularly expressive emotionally, but they tended to be only angry, which is consistent with the range of acceptable feelings within normative scripts of masculinity (Connell, 2005; Edwards & Jones, 2009).

Chapter 4 explores the most common form of racism the participants discussed in the interviews: racist joking. This stemmed from the interview question, "Have you seen instances of racism here on campus?" And the narratives had an additional component to them whereby the students not only described telling racist jokes among their friends, but concurrently framed the jokes as "not racist." They also tended to be very direct that the jokes were almost only told in front of their White friends, similar to the work of Picca and Feagin (2007), who described this as *two-faced racism*. The students rationalized this behavior because they said that minorities were "overly sensitive" when it came to issues of race. This created a cyclical logic whereby the White guys told racist jokes in White (usually male) social environments, while concurrently believing that Students of Color are "overly sensitive" on racial issues. This perceived sensitivity then became the rationale to continue telling racist jokes in White male environments.

Chapter 5 explores one of the strangest Whiteness dynamics in the book. At the institution where affirmative action was practiced, SWU, the participants tended to be against affirmative action but did not feel oppressed or marginalized by it. The students at the institution where affirmative action was not practiced, WU, were strongly against the program and felt marginalized by it. That is, the White guys at WU tended to feel oppressed by a program that did not exist on their campus.

Chapter 6 is also unique in racial analyses because it centers the intersection of Whiteness and space. It is guided by the concept of ontological expansiveness (Sullivan, 2006) whereby White people feel that space (i.e., physical, linguistic, and cultural) should be open to them. It shows how White guys frequently viewed race-conscious campus programming (e.g., ethnic theme centers and groups) that created non-White cultural ownership over campus space, and the White guys I spoke with viewed them as being racially exclusionary to White students. This chapter also shows how the White guys I spoke with frequently entered cultural center space with a sense of entitlement (i.e., "All campus space should be open to me") and were met with some resistance, which they subsequently believed was "reverse racism."

Chapter 7 is the most promising within the book because it explores how the small but important minority of those White guys I spoke with gained racial awareness and sometimes engaged in anti-racist action. The bulk of these narratives focused on how they transformed from color-blindness to racial cognizance, particularly focused on cross-racial relationships, course content, and minority experiences (e.g., being gay in a heterosexist society). While most could not be considered racial justice allies, there were some who did take their racial awareness and translated it into action. Each one of them, however, continued to struggle with issues of race and racism.

Chapter 8 offers a brief overview of the previous seven and then centers two core questions: How are institutions of higher education responsible for the perpetuation of racism? And how can institutions promote greater social equity through the challenging and transformation of Whiteness? This includes how those who receive racial immunity bear responsibility for challenging racism, while offering guidance in terms of how to do this. Additionally, it provides analyses of the campus environment, highlighting how institutions paradoxically serve as agents of racial stratification and social change. I conclude with a discussion of the importance of continuing to study and challenge racism in ostensibly "post-racial" times.

Now then dear reader, if you will, please accompany me into the heart of Whiteness in contemporary higher education.

2

"Race Just Doesn't Matter That Much"

White Insulation, Occam's Racial Razor, and Willful Racial Ignorance

Interviewing these White men was both interesting and frustrating. It was frustrating because I told the participants that we would be talking about race and racism, yet they spent a ton of time in the interviews explaining how they viewed race as a nonissue. It was interesting examining how much time and energy they invested in developing *semantic moves* (Bonilla-Silva, 2006) to explain the racism out of situations. They reminded me of Baldwin's (1984) statement, "For there is a great deal of will power involved in the White man's naïveté" (p. 166). Essentially, it is not just a matter of racial ignorance for White men, but there is also a great energy investment required to maintain this mental state. During the interviews, I was perpetually reminded of Occam's razor, where the most simple or straightforward explanation is the most likely. When I asked these White guys for their interpretations of contemporary racial inequality, they perpetually offered complicated rationales that had nothing to do with race. Returning to Occam's razor, the most direct and simple explanation for persistent racial inequality is racism (Bonilla-Silva, 2006); however, this interpretation was rarely present.

I was also reminded of a conversation my mom and I had repeatedly when I was a child. She could not stand when I began sentences with *"Yes, but . . ."*[1]

because it was dismissive of whatever she previously said. Rhetorically, the White men in these interviews offered thoughts that functioned like a racial "*Yes, but....*" That is, they would give a token nod to the idea that racism still exists and then spend the bulk of their interviews explaining why racism was not at the core of a racial issue. Essentially, it became a dismissive mechanism regarding claims of contemporary racism. A great deal of this was related to these White men's immunities. They lived in relatively segregated environments in high school where the bulk of people were White, saw little evidence of racism in their everyday lives, and therefore thought racism was a nonissue for everyone. All of this began, however, from the racial isolation they experienced in their learning and living environments.

Whiteness, Structured Racial Insulation, and Racial Ignorance

The White guys I spoke with who are featured in chapters 2 through 6 tended to come from either racial homogenous neighborhoods or ones where they were consistently in the majority (see Appendix A). Of the twenty-seven who completed questionnaires, only five lived in neighborhoods and five attended high schools where Whites were *not* the majority.[2] These numbers do not tell the full story because as Brandon conveyed, "An interesting thing was AP classes. Like, there was maybe like one or two Black and Latino or Chicano person in those classes.... And the rest was mostly Asian and whatever White kids were left." Thus, internal segregation within Brandon's high school further exacerbated the racial separation of the students.

Trevor also believed students in his high school were separated based on race, but there was a very specific reason for cross-racial interactions: "There were a very few, small number of Black people in my school. No one interacted with them except to buy drugs." In Trevor's experience, not only did he have very few Black peers, but interactions, when they did occur, were functional (e.g., White students wanted drugs). White environments frequently persisted in college despite the differing levels of compositional diversity between WU and SWU.[3] Of the participants' three best friends in college, twenty-four of twenty-seven reported having two or more who were White. Again, their "normal" racial experience meant being in the majority. The numbers told a more promising story in terms of eating meals with and dating racial minorities. Just fewer than half of the White guys I talked with dated a minoritized person in their lifetimes, with the vast majority of these dating Latinxs. Overall, being in the numeric majority or hypermajority was a normal state of being for these White guys. Their accounting for this phenomenon utilized a range of explanations, but racism was not one of them, and this was the beginning of their rhetorical, racial *Yes, but....*

Before diving into this, I was struck by how much their White immunity insulated them from issues of race. I asked them how often they thought about issues of race and to identify examples of racism either in society as a whole or on their college campus specifically. Their answers were incredibly telling for two reasons. First, many of the White guys I talked with were able to go days, weeks, and sometimes even months without really thinking about race. Second, the White guys I spoke with had very few examples of racism they could pinpoint. For example, Kurt said that he rarely thought about issues of race and offered a pretty straightforward explanation:

N: Okay. And then you said in your survey that you don't think about race very much.[4]

K: Not really.

N: Is there any particular reason why?

K: I don't really think it's that . . . really too important stressing upon which race you identify with as far as like your status within society.

Kurt's racially segregated learning/living environments meant that he did not have to deal much with racial conflict. He (mis)understood that to mean that there was no racism in these environments. Therefore, he thought about race on only a rare occasion, which is the epitome of White immunity (Cabrera, 2017). Matt offered a similar sentiment, but was more succinct:

N: Okay. And so, you said over here in the questionnaire that you think of race maybe like less than once a year. Why?

M: Because it's a nonissue for me.

As the narratives in the subsequent chapters demonstrate, the White guys I spoke with did not always consider race to be a "nonissue." It was more that they enjoyed the calm times when they had the social luxury of not thinking about issues of race—something not afforded to People of Color but also something they felt entitled to.

It was very telling how racially insulated the White I spoke with were, and this was strongly related to their inability to identify contemporary instances of racism. For example, Jack could not give me a solid example, and he explained why, linking it to his upbringing: "Because since . . . ever since you're a little kid, when you're growing up, you're growing up, you're supposed to be. . . . You grow up with color-blindness, you're not supposed to see anything, you're just supposed to like. . . . Everybody's everybody, it doesn't matter, and I've tried to do that in my life because it's true. You shouldn't evaluate people that way, it shouldn't affect you." Jack was very direct that he learned to value color-blindness growing up, oblivious to the idea that this is actually a form of racism (Bonilla-Silva, 2006). It was also telling how Jack framed this issue. He continually used "you" and "everybody" when describing his personal experience, essentially normalizing his learned color-blindness. He saw nothing wrong with his racial ignorance and actually saw it as an attribute instead of a liability.

When the subject became the college campus, the White guys I spoke with had even fewer examples of racism to share. Most simply said that there were not *real* examples of racism on their college campus. Their descriptions were so repetitive, they bordered on boring. Here is a sample of what they offered:

> Yeah, yeah. I mean, I've seen movies like *Crash* and whatnot, but I've just really never, ever encountered it and I feel fortunate for that. (Joel)
>
> [An example] of racism? I guess not off the top of my head. (Kurt)
>
> I don't really see much discrimination. (Mark)
>
> Um, nope. I haven't. (Ryan)
>
> I don't think so. I haven't seen . . . no, not racism. (Justin)
>
> Not that immediately comes to mind. (Jonathan)

One student, Trevor, offered some further description on the subject even though his overall sentiment was the same. What was really telling was the experiences he used to justify his beliefs. "I think though, at WU in particular, I, you know, and I don't have a lot of, of uh, of Black friends. But just in the way my White friends view race. They—I don't think the discrimination people, or the obstacles, for instance, that people face, are as great here. Um, I have very little information on this. It's my feeling." Trevor's statement was telling on several levels. First, he generally prided himself on being a very analytical person, but offered in this situation, "It's my feeling." Second, his feeling was based upon his interactions with his White friends. That is, he knew very few People of Color on campus, yet he believed that the way his White friends viewed race must mean that there was minimal racism at WU. It was telling that Trevor even admitted he had "very little information" on the subject, yet he held pretty strong beliefs that WU was a racially inclusive institution. In his understanding, the bulk of racial strife on campus stemmed from racial/ethnic campus-based organizations, as I will detail in later chapters.

This racial insulation corresponded to the White guys I spoke with having a general color-blind worldview. At least they professed to have a color-blind worldview, which in practice meant downplaying racism against People of Color, as the remainder of this chapter demonstrates. They tended to have a strongly color-conscious worldview when it meant "reverse racism" against

White men as chapter 3 will detail. Regardless, their personal assessments of anti-People of Color racism in society tended to be that race is present, but it is relatively insignificant. Derek was straightforward in his assessment: "[My personal experiences] sort of solidified my views whereas race doesn't really matter." Lance elaborated a little more, but his overall sentiment was the same: "I don't think that White is much of an advantage or disadvantage. I'm just acknowledging that these sorts of things exist and perhaps through marginal extents, but maybe more so in other contexts." Lance believed that being White in contemporary U.S. society neither helped nor hindered him. This related strongly to his Objectivist views that stressed hyperindividualism, and this context is important in understanding his subsequent viewpoints.[5]

Many of the White guys I spoke with offered their rationales as to why they thought race was not an important contemporary social problem, and sometimes they related their views to their social identities as White men. For example, Jay offered: "Well, personally . . . I mean, I'm a White male so I'm kind of. . . . You know, race has either never come to the forefront or it's just something that you're taught. . . . Not bring up just because it doesn't necessarily affect you." Jay did not see racism affecting him in his everyday life, and interestingly, he tied it to him being both male and White. Martin offered a similar view when he stated, "I have not experienced what . . . at least I would not consider myself to have experienced a great deal of racism since I've been a student here on the part of anybody towards me." Again, White immunity meant Martin saw and experienced very few instances of racism targeting him personally. This then corresponded to his color-blind worldview, in which he forcefully believed that (1) race is not an issue and (2) anything color-conscious amounted to a form of racism. These professions of color-blindness strongly informed how the White guys I talked with explained contemporary patterns of racial segregation. They all acknowledged that different racial groups tended to cluster together, balkanizing the student population; however, their explanations for the phenomenon involved anything but racism.

Anything but Racism: Whitesplaining Racial Segregation

Whitesplaining refers to White people explaining the nature of racism to People of Color—frequently in a condescending way. There is nothing wrong with White people in general, or White men in particular, having views on race. However, it does become problematic when they state their views with a degree of authority when the accuracy of their beliefs does not warrant this level of self-assuredness. For example, the White guys I talked with acknowledged that a great deal of racial separation existed on their university campuses, but their explanations for this involved anything but racism. They tended to understand racial segregation as a function of either social comfort or chance, becoming a rhetorical *Yes, but* (i.e., "*Yes* there is racial separation on campus, *but* it is not related to racism"). One of the primary explanations for segregated environments focused on the issue of racial comfort. As Duncan explained, "People tend to like the company of others that share similar values, similar, I guess, life experiences as them, and it just so happens that people in your same ethnic group or racial category have similar values." To him, commonality of values led to racially homogenous environments, but what values do People of Color possess that make it difficult for him as a White man to connect with them? He did not have an answer.

Bernard focused more on social interests as he explained racial segregation, but again racism was noticeably absent from his views. In fact, he was very clear that he did not see racism as a contributing factor: "I don't know, [segregation] might have to do with, like I said, people just associate with people like themselves, and I *don't* think it's about race. I think it's more about, 'Oh, we like the same music and we like the same sports, and we watch the same thing on TV.'" Bernard specifically argued that racial clustering is *not* a function of racism but rather a manifestation of social comfort fostered through similar interests. While cultural commonality is undoubtedly a key component of racial balkanization on college campuses, an exclusive focus on this explanation overlooks the historical and contemporary legacies of racial exclusion (Chesler, Lewis, & Crowfoot, 2005; Feagin, Vera, & Imani, 1996; Ross, 2015).

Other White guys I spoke with utilized explanations that focused on racial separation being a naturally occurring phenomenon. As Matt explained, "White people flock together and people of different races flock together and they all just.... Birds of a feather flock together, so they like to hang out with people who are similar to them." Roger took a different approach, focusing on how cross-racial interactions can lead to social discomfort: "And people tend to be uncomfortable with other people that are not similar to themselves." Implicitly, these explanations assume that there is something fundamentally different between Whites and People of Color that promotes tension. This also stood in stark contrast to the White guys' previously articulated views that race is not really a prominent social force. That is, how could race be so socially impotent that it "doesn't matter" *and* so strong that it drives people of different races apart?

Trevor spoke to this issue specifically while criticizing minoritized student activists on campus: "That level of confrontation just makes White people feel really uncomfortable." To him and others, it was the racial minorities who promoted campus antagonism, and this justified the perpetuation of homogenous, White campus space. I provide more background on Trevor's interactions with campus-based minoritized student activists in chapter 6. Andy also believed that racial clustering occurred on campus, and it was primarily a function of the actions of Students of Color: "I guess one thing that I notice more on campus than really anything else in terms of racism . . . which I don't feel is evident when I walk around campus, but one thing I do notice is that most of the sort of categorized minority groups, people that fall into these groups, tend to basically form clusters with other people in their group." Again, racial clustering occurs, but it is not related to racism according to Andy. To the extent that racial segregation is problematic, Andy located the issue within minoritized communities. Noticeably absent from his discussion was the issue of White people clustering together.

Jonathan moved beyond the college campus and explored the workforce implications regarding the creation and maintenance of these racial comfort zones. He explained: "And obviously I've noticed that races are more comfortable with their own race. It's just a natural thing. So, if a particular race has all the jobs, naturally they're going to tend to give them to people they know or people they feel comfortable with." Later, Jonathan explained how racial privilege could beget racial privilege through workforce racial nepotism; he, however, viewed this cycle not as problematic because he saw it as a naturally occurring phenomenon. Matt offered a similar sentiment, refocusing the discussion on the college campus: "[Segregation is] just what people do. I don't think it's problematic. I don't think it causes any problems, it's just who people like to hang out with."

These explanations for racial segregation tended to focus on the amorphous group "people" (i.e., *people* tend to feel more comfortable with those like them). Kurt was one of the few participants who personalized the discussion of racial (dis)comfort and segregation: "I mean, personally it would probably be hard for me to approach a group [of racial minorities]. Not because of how I view them, but just because of how they might view me." This apprehension was rooted in not any specific incidents in his past but rather a general feeling. Interestingly, he had difficulty understanding that the same emotions he felt regarding homogenous groups of People of Color are also frequently experienced by minoritized people with White-dominant groups (Chesler et al., 2005).

Three of the White guys I interviewed specifically talked about their involvement in the housed Greek system and their experience with racial segregation. They were, however, slightly defensive regarding their respective fraternities:

You look at the way things are and you see all the fraternities and they're full of White guys and you. . . . I don't know, things of that nature. You get a feel there's something going on, but it's not . . . I mean, it's kind of like the status quo. (Jonathan)

I'm in a Greek fraternity, and so they tend to be really White, so they kind of self-select in their own groups. (Chris)

Um, well I mean, most of the people I interact with are in my fraternity, and most of the people in the fraternity are White. . . . Um, not necessarily that they have to be White, but that's just what most people who join fraternities are. (Ryan)

Ryan, Chris, and Jonathan explained their fraternities being overwhelmingly populated with White men as a function of chance as opposed to design, and this was a key frame for explanations of racial balkanization. Overall, the White guys I talked with tended to view existing in racially homogenous environments as natural and *not* resulting from racism. It might be a function of self-selection (Chris), the "status quo" (Jonathan), or that fraternity guys "just are" White (Ryan). None of these White guys I interviewed considered or engaged the possibility that racism was part of this social phenomenon, even though there is a strong historical legacy to support this interpretation (Ross, 2015). This did not mean they argued that racism no longer existed. Rather, they viewed racism as existing, of minimal importance, and located externally from their personal experiences. Hence, the rest of the interviews continued the aforementioned "*Yes, but* . . ." conversations.

Yes, but . . . : Anything but Racism

The White guys I spoke with offered many opinions on why racial inequality persists, and much like issues of campus racial segregation they explained these patterns in terms of anything but racism. From this orientation, I was surprised at how open and willing these White guys were to acknowledge that racial inequality persists. For example, Duncan offered: "You know, it's harder [for People of Color] to get a job. It's harder to. . . . There are certain ethnic groups that maybe are. . . . It's more difficult to get loans, but if that's something you're looking for, it's pretty easy to see at least statistically that that occurs." He subsequently downplayed the importance of racism in creating this phenomenon, "At the end of the day, I think [racism is] very small in the overall scheme of things and it's . . . I guess I would say it's statistically insignificant [in determining one's life chances]." Duncan understood that racial inequality existed, but he would not interpret this as related to racism. This was consistent with his view that racial segregation is created and maintained primarily through people seeking racial comfort (i.e., *not* racism). It was also telling that he used the term "statistically significant" when he did not offer any statistical evidence to support his claim, thereby framing his views as the result of an objective, scientific analysis. This could also be related to social norms of masculinity where men are viewed as "objective" and "rational" in their assessments, and those who disagree are "subjective" and "emotional" (Kimmel & Ferber, 2017; Laker & Davis, 2011).

Kurt was more direct in his understanding that people were racist, but he also did not see that as a potent social force. He began, "I think people are just really narrow-minded still and whether they would like to admit it or not, they still see other people as inferior just because of their race or ethnic background for, whatever reason that may be." He followed this statement with, "I don't really think [racism is] that . . . really too important stressing upon which race you identify with as far as like your status within society." By downplaying the social power of racism, Kurt like Duncan was able to explain racism as largely irrelevant in determining opportunities in contemporary society.

Justin did not offer an explanation for why racial inequality persisted. Instead, he spent the bulk of his interview describing how White people in general, and he in particular, were not responsible for the current state of affairs. He acknowledged that racism existed, but only in the past: "So, I definitely wasn't a part of the group that held the Black people down or held the Mexicans down or all these types of groups. I feel kind of like I have to accept responsibility for a group of actions in which I was. . . . I'm not responsible personally or ancestrally." Justin was very clear. When it came to issues of race, he was not responsible. Yes, he knew about the social sins of the past (e.g., slavery); however, that had no bearing on him personally. He also made the claim that his ancestors were not the White people holding Black or Mexican people down. They were, in his understanding, the "good White people" historically (i.e., not slave owners). Justin believed that he did not personally oppress racial minorities and neither did his ancestors. The primary takeaway from this narrative was that Justin individually held *no individual responsibility* for contemporary racial inequality.

Roger also gave credence to the idea that differential treatment exists along racial lines. He focused on the classroom by offering, "I think that like within classes and the way that people look at people that are different than themselves, there's absolutely a certain racism that occurs and I think it's just, it's an attitude." When asked about his explanations for contemporary racial inequality, he also focused on education but in a much different way: "And education is said to be the way that success is attained. . . . And I think that it is less emphasized in other Communities of Color." Roger began by saying that there was racism in classrooms, but interpreted racial inequality as a function of some groups valuing education (Whites and Asian Americans) and others not (Blacks and Latinxs). Racism played no role in his explanation, which served the dual purpose of both explaining racial minority educational underperformance and justifying his family's upward mobility. Being Jewish, he claimed that his culture was very "learning oriented," and this explained their successful assimilation into the U.S. mainstream. Conversely, Roger believed minoritized populations did not value education, and this led to their educational, economic, and social marginalization.

Martin took a slightly different approach and gave some credence to contemporary racism being subtler than in the past: "I have not seen a great deal of racism overtly, but it's often subtle, right. Sometimes the worst racism is not what I do with my hands or with my mouth as much as what I'm thinking." Martin was one of the few White guys I spoke with who used "I" when referring to the possibility of racist actions, but this ownership of responsibility for contemporary racism was short-lived. He forcefully believed that nothing was holding back the possibility of success by People of Color and that social welfare programs were counterproductive: "I believe that the role of the government in terms of welfare, if you will, is to defend the defenseless, to help the helpless, and just that, and people who are born to Black parents are born to Hispanic parents are not automatically helpless. Do they have two legs? Do they have two arms? Are they healthy? Are they intelligent? Are they able to function? If they are, then there's really nothing that holds them back." To Martin, opportunity is open to all who are willing to put forth the effort. He was very consistent in his opposition to anything race-conscious, equating affirmative action with racism and saying that in applications for either employment or college admissions "race should not even be a question."

The White guys I spoke with minimally acknowledged that racism existed but spent the bulk of the interviews explaining how racism is largely irrelevant or the personality defect of some "narrow-minded people." Racism, in their understandings, was intermittent not systemic, and in general opportunities were available to all. There were additional thematic means by which participants constructed rhetorical *buts* that served to undercut their acknowledgments that racism continues to exist (i.e., "*yes* racism exists, *but* it's not that important"). These *buts* included comparative suffering, pitting race against class, hard work as the answer to racial inequality, and stereotypes existing for a reason.

Yes, but . . . : I've Struggled Too

Some of the White guys I talked with used a strange rationale to undercut the importance of contemporary racism. These essentially broke down into the following: I've struggled too in my life, so People of Color should get over it. For example, George spoke of his parents' divorce: "Hardships are all kinda' relative, I think. I mean because, well, my parents get divorced, and i–, i–, it's messy, and it really sucks for me. . . . That's like, I mean just like, ripped me apart. But again, it's not as, it didn't, it doesn't sound as bad like, someone's parents being killed or being really poor. I mean, but, when you're talking about people and people's emotions, it's like, it's like—it's all relative." George did not believe it was possible to determine which is a more difficult obstacle to overcome: being a Person of Color or having divorced parents. How can one make this determination? How can, for example, admissions officers differentiate among the unique hurdles individuals have in their lives? From that perspective, George felt disadvantaged in the admissions process because he believed his campus practiced affirmative action (it did not; see chapter 5), while having divorced parents created a substantial burden for him that he felt was not considered.

Trevor brought this focus back to issues of race on campus. He read in the student newspaper that WU was considering the creation of theme houses on campus based upon race/ethnicity. The first paragraph in the article contained a quotation from a Black female student who said she can walk across campus all day without seeing another Black person, which became socially exhausting. Trevor was critical of this comment:

> I say, "Why?" Why does it have to be? I mean like races, you know, sort of . . . I mean, so like I like traveled to Zambia. [I was the] only White person around. Everyone's Black except for me. You know, the first couple of days, it was exhausting. I was like, this is intense. And even more that they're Black. It's not just that they're Black, but they don't share the same cultural background. So, like even if I were walking around Germany I would still be like, you know, exhausting. But after a while, you know, like—that's the inherent plight of being a minority, and at a certain point you've gotta say, "Hey, I'm me, and you know, you know, I'd like to know you. I'd like to know who you are." And you know, yes, there's discrimination, and people are more apt to judge you, but you know, again, it's part of life. You—ya know, you have to get over these things.

There was a strong tension in Trevor's narrative. On the one hand, he was a White man who benefited from both White and male immunity. On the other, the essence of his argument was, "That's the inherent plight of being a minority." That is, he was claiming to be an authority on what it means to be a minority, even though he was speaking from the position of being a White man. In Trevor's understanding, the student interviewed by the school newspaper was choosing to focus her attention on the negative aspects of minimal campus diversity. He was flippant regarding her claim ("it's part of life") and then reinforcing his belief through what he believed to be an analogous experience in Zambia ("Everyone's Black except for me"). In addition, Trevor saw no difference between his voluntarily entering a foreign country and adapting to Zambian culture versus being a Black student entering WU having to adapt to the collegiate environment. Within this context, Trevor was aggressively critical and dismissive of his classmate's viewpoint. In addition to using comparative suffering to undercut the significance of racism, many of the White guys I talked with argued that economics, not racism, was at the root of racial inequality.

Yes, but . . . : It's Class, Not Race

Many of the White guys I talked with claimed that issues of racial inequality were, at their source, economic. These rationales implicitly argued that racism and classism are mutually exclusive forms of social oppression/advantage. For example, Dwight articulated a form of the *declining significance of race* thesis (Wilson, 1980): "The hard part for me when race is talked about is so much currently, even more than race, is tied to a person's economic status." Dwight did not view racism as a contemporary problem. He disregarded the ways that race and class are mutually reinforcing systems of social stratification (Brown et al., 2003), and from this perspective, he was able to pit them against each other (i.e., inequality is a function of either class or race). It was questionable how much Dwight cared about class-based inequality because he tended to mention it only when he was undercutting the significance of racism. Along the same lines, Adam offered,

A: [Racial inequality is] more a problem of money . . .

N: Okay.

A: . . . than a problem of race in and of itself. And there's plenty of poor White people that are not getting very far in life. There's plenty of poor Black people that aren't getting very far.

Nick summarized these sentiments by asserting, "I mean, I'd much rather be a rich Black person than a lower income White person." All of these statements created a false dichotomy whereby one must choose between either race or class. Again, it is difficult to tell what is driving these beliefs. None of these White guys were overly concerned with class-based inequality, and it seemed more like their economic analyses were primarily methods to downplay the significance of racism.

Brandon was an interesting case because he was forceful in articulating how being White was a social advantage while also downplaying its contemporary importance. He, like the previous group of White guys, reduced racial inequality to a matter of economics. Brandon began with a very direct and somewhat surprising assessment:

N: So then, do you, in your opinion, is being White in America an advantage or a disadvantage?

B: It is an amazing advantage.

N: In what respect?

B: You're given the benefit of the doubt in many instances.

Brandon replied that this meant that he was not followed in stores or suspected when something was stolen, and his intelligence was rarely questioned in class.

Despite this depth of understanding regarding how his racial background socially benefits him, he was unwilling to view racial inequality as resulting from racism. Without the slightest bit of cognitive dissonance, he subsequently offered, "I don't blame [racial inequality] on race or anything. I just think that's a socioeconomic situation." Brandon then took his beliefs one step further, stating that opportunities were available to all people who were willing to pursue them: "I mean like [People of Color] have the same advantages in getting a job. They have the same advantages in um, where they wanna live, where they wanna go, what they want to do, what they want to pursue and accomplish." On the one hand, Brandon believed being White was an amazing social advantage. On the other, and in direct contradiction to his first statement, Brandon did not believe racism hindered the life chances of People of Color. Brandon, like Nick, Adam, and Dwight, reduced racism to an issue of economics.

It was telling not only that Brandon held these views, but also how he came to these understandings. Brandon explained that he arrived at these conclusions via experiences interacting with Black people, in particular Black people he met during his undergraduate years. To that end, he offered,

> B: Um, well, I know one, two, three, four—I know four Black people on this campus.
>
> N: Okay.
>
> B: By name. Um, I've had an actual conversation with two of them.

Brandon could count the number of Black people on campus he knew on one hand, yet he still claimed to understand the Student of Color experience. While many White guys I talked with used the "I have a Black friend" rationale to either claim expertise or gain insulation from charges of racism, Brandon was one of the few who actually counted. Interestingly, his counting tended to undercut his overall argument. If you can name the number of Black people you know, you are probably not an expert on the Black experience.

As I previously noted, the pitting of race versus class seemed like a red herring in these interviews in the sense that almost none of the White guys I spoke with were truly committed to alleviating economic inequality either. Rather, it was a convenient way to frame racial issues and essentially downplay the relevance of contemporary racism. This contextualized a number of participants who argued that the solution to racial inequality was increased effort/hard work on the part of minority groups.

Yes, but . . . : Hard Work Will Triumph

Rather than supporting race-conscious social policies, many relied upon commonsense articulations of the American Dream/Puritan ethic as their solution to racial inequality. They tended to believe that if People of Color want to succeed, they have ample opportunity as long they are willing to work hard. Martin began with a critique of what he labeled "welfare culture" that he argued is endemic in minority communities: "There's a welfare culture among some Black people for example. Not all Black people. It exists among some Hispanic people. The idea that you don't . . . lack of accountability for your actions, lack of responsibility, the idea that you don't really have to work very hard to succeed." The underlying irony of Martin's statement was that his critique centered around People of Color lacking accountability, but the implication of his statement is that he personally is not responsible for contemporary racial inequality (i.e., *he* has no accountability). As previously explored, Martin viewed racial inequality as a function of liberal social policies that undercut minority work ethic. The problem, as he understood, was a lack of responsibility that leads to laziness. To him, racism was not the issue as the U.S. system is generally open and meritocratic. It was interesting, however, that Martin thought of himself as very informed on race: "I have a Black roommate. He's a football player for [university name] and my mother has been in a relationship with a Black man for about three years." The basis for his self-ascribed authority on the situation relied on the "I have a Black friend" cliché.

Bernard also tended to believe that the social welfare programs were primarily responsible for the persistence of racial inequality. In his historical understanding, the elimination of de jure forms of racial discrimination (e.g., legalized racial segregation) meant the end of U.S. racism. Bernard was, however, very critical of the welfare state, which he saw as central to perpetuating racial inequality. "Well, after the end of slavery, there was the Jim Crow laws and segregation, what have you, which the Irish. . . . Well, the Irish did to a certain extent have to deal. . . . But there's also sort of a welfare structure in place that people. . . . Politicians get elected in order to deliver welfare to certain people and it's in their interest to keep those people receiving welfare so they're dependent on them." Essentially, Bernard, much like Martin, thought that a "welfare culture" kept racial minorities from rising in society. That is, their reliance on the government meant that they did not have to work as hard as others in society, and this kept them in a cycle of poverty. His ultimate solution was the elimination of the welfare state, which he thought would lead to increased self-reliance of People of Color and eventual racial equality.

Others were more direct about their views on work ethic as a pathway toward upward mobility. Adam succinctly articulated, "Um, if people work hard, they will succeed. I believe that. That's what I believe." For Adam, there was no need for further examination or explanation. He took it as an article of faith that hard work leads to success, and that was as far as he was willing to explore the issue. The belief that the American system is generally open to those with sufficient dedication and work ethic led to some very unique explanations for the persistence of racial inequality. For example, George explained why Latinx people are not economically on par with Whites: "[Latinx people are] probably not very, not very success-oriented. I'm sure they want their kids to be self-sufficient, but not wildly successful like they probably don't have aspirations for their children to be businessmen, doctors and stuff like that." The foundation of George's orientation was a belief in the American Dream, that the system is equitable and hard work leads to success. George elaborated, "Like success-driven cultures, like, upbringing is usually pretty similar between a White person and an Asian person. But, between a Hispanic or a Black person there's not nearly as many connections I think." George believed that if Black and Latinx people spent more time fostering a "success orientation," racial inequality would largely vanish. Noticeably absent from this belief was any mention of racism. Regardless, this discussion of a success orientation was enough for George to explain the persistence of contemporary racial inequality, and I explored this further because there was a tension in our discussion. George was talking with a Chicano PhD student from a prestigious research university about how Latinx people lacked a success orientation. When I asked him about this issue, I represented to him an exception to the rule of success orientation; I was an anomaly that did not disprove his original thesis.

The belief in the power of hard work became very personal for some of the White guys I spoke with as they explicitly used it as a justification for their privileged position in higher education. They tended to use their own success narratives as evidence that those who work hard will be successful. Jonathan and George elaborated:

> I mean, like I was, I got my way through high school and I got into WU, and, if you want to succeed that bad, you can. And you shouldn't just get a free ride because you're a minority. (George)

> In high school, I decided I was going to really work hard because I really wanted to go to WU and so I really turned it up and I pretty much busted my ass nonstop. I just worked really hard and did everything I could to hit the level that would get me accepted. (Jonathan)

Both felt their hard work led to their positions at WU, and conversely, People of Color who did not gain access did not sufficiently dedicate themselves to their studies. Again, the possibility that racism might have played a role in either People of Color's exclusion or their inclusion was either not considered or dismissed. This is a rearticulation of Sears's (1988) "symbolic racism," whereby professions of the American creed become a discursive means of insulating and maintaining racial inequality. A commonsense belief in hard work creates an uninterrogated space whereby the root cause of racial inequality, racism, is left unexamined.

To further support the view that hard work leads to upward mobility, some of the White guys explored Asian American educational success. As Andy said, "[Asian Americans] work harder, flat out." The question then became, if Asian Americans work harder than other racial minorities, what explains their drive to succeed? The answers tended to focus on their parents and culture instilling a strong work ethic in these students. Dwight highlighted how the parents of his Asian American friends were some of the hardest working people he knew: "It's definitely parent-based because all the parents that I've met of my friends that are Asian American . . . or Asian . . . their parents are all very diligent workers." This, in his mind, translated in their kids (his peers) being hard workers, which sufficiently explained inequality. There were some who worked hard and succeeded, and there were those who did not work as hard and failed.

Keith did not have as great a level of personal exposure to Asian Americans as Dwight, and instead he relied upon abstract notions of Asian American culture to support his belief: "It seems like Asian American culture just instilled hard work, like, above all, and uh, and they just use that to gain financial stability." It was strange that Keith referred to Asian American culture as an actual definable category, considering that this represents approximately twenty million people in the United States and over four billion in Asia. Regardless, he saw a unifying characteristic among Asian Americans in that their cultures fostered a strong work ethic. Earlier in the interview, Keith also referred to what he viewed as deficits in Black culture that also accounted for the persistence of racial inequality. Thus, Keith engaged in the anti-Black strategy of *racial triangulation*, whereby the relative success of Asian Americans becomes a means of blaming the Black community for their lack of economic and educational success (Kim, 1999). Functionally, it is a way of alleviating White responsibility for racial inequality by pitting Asian Americans against Blacks.

Many of the White guys referred to Asian Americans being hardworking as a "positive stereotype," but it becomes problematic for other reasons beyond racial triangulation. It overlooks the diversity embedded within the Asian American community where there are a number of Southeast Asian groups that are actually underrepresented in higher education. The educational needs of these subpopulations are frequently overlooked because the myth of the model minority homogenizes this population (Cabrera, 2014a; Chou & Feagin, 2008; Escueta & O'Brien, 1995; Museus & Kiang, 2009; Suzuki, 2002). Overall, this group of White guys held commonsense assumptions that opportunity existed for those willing to take it, and racism did not play a role in structuring racial inequality. This denial meant that some of the participants even explained racial stereotypes as socially acceptable because, in their understandings, they had some grounding in reality.

Yes, but . . . : Stereotypes Exist for a Reason

Almost all of the White guys I spoke with for this chapter explored various social stereotypes in their interviews; however, a substantial number of believed stereotypes reflected reality and were therefore not racist. Trevor explained, "Um, so, I, I think that in some ways, uh, those stereotypes have some factual basis." Many other White guys I spoke with also held this belief. For example, George began by describing a common stereotype on campus, but concluded by stating that it merely reflected an unfortunately truth:

G: Well I'm sure that a lot of people if they see some, like I said, they see some big Black guy walking up, they'd think, well, he's probably an athlete. And he's probably not that smart.

N: Okay.

G: Um, I don't necessarily think that's a bad thing. I mean, I wouldn't, I wouldn't call that, necessarily call that a negative thought.

N: Why is that?

G: Well, I guess it does kind of degrade that person, maybe it is kind of a negative thought. But to me, it doesn't really seem that negative because most of the time it's true. Unfortunately, it is what it is.

George did not find the stereotype to be problematic because, in his understanding, it reflected reality on his campus. When I looked a little closer at George's social context, some telling trends arose. By his own admission, George had not recently had a meal with a Person of Color, his three closest friends were White, and he never had a romantic relationship across race. Regardless, he was sure that his perception was a reflection of reality, and he did not understand how assuming the intellectual inferiority of Black men was racist.

Martin began his statement on stereotypes by passively condemning them, then explaining why they are not as bad as people make them out to be. Like George, he believed that they still reflected reality: "Stereotypes. . . . Yes, stereotypes are wrong . . . to assume that a stereotype is always true . . . but a stereotype exists for a reason. There is a basis for that. It's not just made up out of thin air." In Martin's understanding, there was an underlying truth to stereotypes, and even though they frequently have negative connotations, they also have some truth embedded in them. While Martin initially critiqued stereotypes as *wrong*, he spent the majority of the discussion undercutting this belief. That is, if they were wrong, why also say they exist for a reason? Is reality "wrong," or is this a means of trying to justify the use of racist stereotypes?

Like Martin, Derek believed that stereotypes have some underlying truth behind them. From this context, he had trouble negotiating the balance between fact and insult: "But there's always some truth in what people say and so it's like that stereotype does exist for a reason, so like . . . I don't know to what degree it would be like insulting." Derek tended to err on the side that stereotypes are representative of reality, and therefore socially acceptable. He then offered an example of stereotypes that he felt were relatively harmless, "Racism has that connotation where it's always going to be negative and everything, whereas there's some aspects that it's either neutral or positive, like Blacks having large penises versus Asians having small ones." Derek saw nothing wrong with either stereotype, overlooking the systematic emasculation of Asian American men in U.S. society, or what Eng (2001) refers to as "racial castration." Derek ignored the centuries of racial violence against Black men that was justified due to the myth of their hypersexuality coupled with the call to protect the "purity" of White women (Allen, 1997; Kendi, 2016). For Derek, these were relatively innocuous beliefs that for the most part were true. The other question then becomes how he personally was able to verify the accuracy of the stereotypes regarding Black and Asian American penis sizes.

There were a few White guys who did talk about the negative power of stereotypes, but they represented a minority ($n = 3$). Overall, the interviews tended to center around how the White guys who are featured in chapters 2 through 6 viewed stereotypes as benign, but they also tended to believe they represented some truth. Noticeably absent from these discussions of racial stereotypes were ones about White people in general, and White men in particular. When it came to racial stereotypes, the White guys I spoke with almost always discussed People of Color. This raises the issue of whether these White guys would believe stereotypes "reflected reality" or were "benign" if they were the targets. As some of the later chapters will demonstrate, the White guys did not handle it well when they felt that they were the ones being stereotyped.

Yes, but . . . : It's Still Racism

These White guys tended to exist in precollege environments where they were in either the majority or the hypermajority, and this persisted through their undergraduate years, even though the compositional diversity differed substantially between WU and SWU. They tended to understand this racial segregation as *natural*, and it was never viewed as something that could be informed or constructed through racism. Instead they saw it as a matter of culture, chance, or social comfort. The White guys I spoke with tended not to see racism in their lived experiences, and therefore, in their understandings, racism was not a pertinent, contemporary issue in America as a whole. They also tended to believe that the American educational and economic systems are truly open and meritocratic. Within this context, the White guys I interviewed tended to believe the primary solution to addressing racial inequality was increased hard work by racial minorities. These commonsense understandings of combating inequality were reinforced with proclamations that the participants themselves worked hard, which explained their success (i.e., White immunity was *not* a factor). It was sufficient for the participants to articulate some form of the American Dream as a solution to persistent racial inequality.

It was extremely telling how much energy the White guys I spoke with invested in explaining racial issues in non-racial terms. Most of the issues we explored in the interviews had an explanation rooted in anything but racism.

> *Yes*, the racial groups on campus are separate, *but* it has nothing to do with racism.
>
> *Yes*, racism might make life difficult for People of Color, *but* I've struggled too.
>
> *Yes*, racial inequality exists, *but* it is actually a class-based issue.
>
> *Yes*, racial inequality exists, *but* the solution to the problem is more hard work by People of Color.
>
> *Yes*, stereotypes are bad, *but* they are not really harmful and they have some basis in reality.

This rhetorical dance around racial issues became a form of *White agility*. Instead of having a meaningful discussion of race and racism, many of the White guys I spoke with avoided using these terms during these parts of the interviews. It was really interesting because as the next chapter will demonstrate, these White guys were very willing to label and decry racism as long as White people were the perceived target. Regardless of the specific manifestation, all of the *Yes, buts* . . . functioned in a similar manner: to frame contemporary racism as minimally important. Over thirty years ago, Baldwin (1984) commented on and critiqued this method of systemically ignoring the realities of oppression: "Americans, unhappily, have the most remarkable ability to alchemize all bitter truths into an innocuous but piquant confection and to transform their moral contradictions, or public discussions of such contradictions, into a proud decoration such as are given heroism on the field of battle" (p. 31). Instead of engaging the historical and contemporary realities of racism, the White guys in this chapter downplayed its significance and continually articulated that hard work would triumph because the American Dream made opportunity open to all—alchemizing bitter (racial) truths into innocuous but piquant confections.

Part of this unwillingness to engage racism might also have to do with the intersection between being White in a racist society and wanting to maintain a positive sense of self. That is, to be *a racist* is a bad thing, but they want to think of themselves as good people. As racism is a systemic reality from which White men benefit, it can start challenging this view, and as Ryan (1976) offered in his book *Blaming the Victim*, "no one [wants to think] of himself as a son of a bitch" (p. 20). Instead, it is psychologically easier to "blame the victim." This tendency to protect one's ego and avoid meaningful engagement with racism is particularly pronounced among White men (Cabrera, 2011; Unzueta, Gutiér- rez, & Ghavami, 2010; Unzueta & Lowery, 2008; Unzueta, Lowery, & Know- les, 2008). If this is correct, it has troubling implications because it means that these rhetorical *Yes, buts . . .*, which distract from the real racism discussions, exist in part so White guys can maintain a positive self-image. That is, a key barrier to racial equity is the delicate White male ego. The challenge therefore becomes to cut out these distractions and stop centering Whiteness in racial discussions.

Within this context, I return to the concept of Occam's razor as I offered at the beginning of the chapter. I am reminded of the hit television series *Scrubs*, where Dr. Cox offered a version of Occam's razor when he said, "If you hear hoof beats, you go ahead and think horsies not zebras."[6] That is, hoof beats *could* indicate zebras, but they are much more likely to come from horsies instead. By the same token, the challenge with these White guys becomes, "If you see racial inequality, you go ahead and think racism not . . . whatever else you were thinking." But how? What is at the root of these racially evasive linguistic maneuvers? Why are these young White men so reticent to meaningfully engage race? The current chapter offered a few points of speculation, and the subsequent chapters will continue to illuminate solutions to this conundrum.

3

"The Only Discrimination Left Is That Against White Men"

The Campus Racial Politics of "Reverse Racism"

> J: I think ... honestly, I think it's me putting that in the context, at least I think that's what I'm doing, because I've never really had a negative experience with racial minority groups. I mean, they always turn out to be really great, you know.
>
> N: So then where does your apprehension come from?
>
> J: I don't know. I didn't even know I had apprehension. This is ... I think it's just the fact that I feel isolated in a way if I'm the only one or one of a few in a larger group that I don't typically identify with. (Justin)

Justin never had a negative interaction with racial minorities on his campus, yet he was constantly apprehensive interacting across racial difference. When asked, he openly admitted this fear was not rooted in a tangible reality. He was very honest that prior to my question, he did not even know he held such apprehensions. This is the tension with *sincere fictions* (Feagin & O'Brien, 2003). White people really believe and feel them, but when pressed, they tend to have little basis for this racial fear. That is a consistent theme throughout this chapter. The White guys I spoke with really believed White people in general, and

White men in particular, were the "true" targets of modern-day discrimination. They generally could not point to strong evidence of this; it was more of a feeling they had.

This is part of a larger social trend. In 2011, Norton and Sommers showed how White people believe that contemporary anti-White racial prejudice is actually more prevalent than its anti-Black counterpart. While there is no empirical basis for these beliefs, and even though all evidence continues to point to massive, systemic White advantage (Bonilla-Silva, 2001; Brown et al., 2003; Omi & Winant, 2015), the myth of "reverse racism" is a powerful one. It is a potent societal fiction that at best distracts from real racial conversations and at worst becomes the basis for anti–People of Color thoughts and actions (Bonilla-Silva, 2006). Despite professions of liberal higher education indoctrinating students in political correctness (e.g., D'Souza, 1991; Greer, 2017), many of the White guys I interviewed experienced college as a time of racial regression— in particular becoming more acutely aware of "reverse racism" (see chapter 6).

In the previous chapter, White male undergraduates demonstrated how they misunderstood, avoided, and downplayed issues of racism. This was central to their White immunity—they did not have to witness the insidious effects of racism and were allowed to be blissfully unaware of how racism operates. Within that context, however, a strange psychology emerged. When this state of racial ignorance was disrupted, they continually framed themselves and other White people as the "true" victims of contemporary racism. There were two primary ways in which the White guys framed themselves as racial victims. The first was via campus racial diversity, in particular how many believed Student of Color political correctness became a form of censorship against White people. The second was through race-conscious social policies, within which there was a particular focus on affirmative action, but this was primarily expressed at WU (see chapter 5 for an extended discussion of this issue at WU).

Victimization and the Culture Wars

General Statements on Race

Several White guys I spoke with, especially when closing the interviews with their summative thoughts, offered general statements on race/racism. These frequently centered on "reverse racism" and how they viewed racism against White people to be the dominant form of racial prejudice in contemporary society; however, these views on "reverse racism" overlapped with a perception that men were also the targets of discrimination. George offered the following thought: "I mean [racial minorities] do experience some discrimination, but then again, the pendulum kind of swings back. And White males, I think, get a really raw end of the deal because nobody sympathizes with White males. Women get sympathy because they're women. Um, I mean all different races [receive sympathy] except White males.... I mean pretty much the only racism that's all right is against White males." This sentiment was very similar to the *Yes, but* ... sentiment outlined in the previous chapter, where *yes* "racial minorities do experience discrimination" *but* "the real victims are White men." George thought not only that he had to work harder because he was a White male, but also that nobody sympathized with his plight. This stemmed from both his White and male immunity. That is, due to patriarchy, he also experienced male immunity that allowed him to be ignorant to the social oppression of female-bodied individuals. These immunities created a frame of reference for him where it seemed to George that everyone except White men were being supported and helped by society.

This form of White narcissism (Matias, 2016) allowed George to center his racial experiences while downplaying the real racism People of Color regularly face. His White and male immunity helped reinforce this view that racism did not harm People of Color because he did not see many examples of racism in his everyday life. This led him to make the following summative statement: "Race helps [racial minorities] but it doesn't help us. And so that means that we need to work harder." Even though George gave a nod to the existence of racial discrimination against racial minorities, he viewed it as relatively minor and isolated instead of systemic. Conversely, race-consciousness and social policies made him have to "work harder." Therefore, he believed that "reverse racism" was the dominant form of racism in contemporary society.

Lance's views tended to align with George's, but he had a semantic issue with using "reverse racism": "So-called 'reverse racism' ... I think is a misnomer. I just think reverse racism is just ordinary racism. The reverse only applies to an inversion of the ordinary direction of racism or historically the ordinary direction of racism." Lance viewed any form of race-consciousness as a form of racism. He did not believe in the "reverse" terminology, but he did think that the dominant form of racism on college campuses stemmed from liberal administrators, professors, and racial/ethnic campus-based student groups.

Sometimes the White guys I spoke with became visibly agitated about race-consciousness and perceptions of "reverse racism." Sometimes these emotional outbursts are easy to see in the transcripts because many of the White guys cursed during the interviews. However, it was also telling when they raised their voices in frustration, which I captured with italics. Within this context, Jonathan summed up his feelings as follows:

> *It just fucking sucks that [race] is even an issue.* I just ... this is really ... sometimes it just really depresses me, it really does, just like.... It just really doesn't matter and it *bothers the hell out of me* that it just ... I don't know, that really all I'd say, *why the fuck does this matter?* It just so doesn't and I oftentimes will get pretty bothered.

A little context for this quotation is necessary. Jonathan did not think he actively discriminated against racial minorities, but also felt that he was being held personally accountable for the racial sins of his ancestors. Race-consciousness, in his understanding, amounted to a form of racism against White people, and it really upset him. He was not distressed about racism harming People of Color but only concerned to the extent that it involved White people. Again, part of his White immunity (Cabrera, 2017) coupled with his White narcissism (Matias, 2016) allowed him to ignore the racism that targets Communities of Color and then elevate his own racial angst above these realities.

Some of the White guys I spoke with took "reverse racism" to also mean that racial minorities are systematically advantaged in contemporary society. That is, instead of focusing on issues of White privilege, many focused on "minority privilege." Martin, for example, did not think that then–presidential candidate Barack Obama was actually qualified to run: "Absolutely. I also think that . . . I mean, we have to give these people credit separately as well. Barack Obama is a very intelligent man and he has a lot of capabilities, a lot of skills. So, I'm not trying to say he's not worth of it, but I'm saying it's a tough world out there and the fact that he has those things and he's Black has certainly given him a leg up." He later succinctly offered that if Obama was a White man, he would not have even made it out of the Democratic primary. In his mind, Obama being Black (technically biracial) was a substantial advantage for him. Mark held a similar view that racism did not hinder the opportunities for non-White people, again using Obama as an example: "I absolutely believe that if Barack Obama were not Black or if he did not have any Black parent, then he would not be nearly the . . . you know, the famous national figure that he is. He might do well, but not that well." In Mark's mind, the primary factor in Obama's success was his Blackness. He did not think that anti-Black racism might hinder Obama's rise, and he actually saw it as an asset. Returning to the college campus, there was a very specific issue that many of these White guys felt harmed them as White men: political correctness.

Political Correctness

Many of the White men I interviewed felt that their views on race and racism were not seen as valid due to political correctness. They were frequently afraid to express themselves in classes and on campuses, which made the interviews very interesting. First, the participants wanted to talk about race and did so freely with me because there were almost no potential repercussions to them expressing their viewpoints. Many continued talking with me well after I turned off the audio recorder, and one even followed me into the bathroom to keep the conversation going. Second, when I asked the participants where their anxiety around political correctness came from, they could not clearly identify events that led to their view. It was just a feeling—as if Reverend Sharpton was waiting in the bushes, waiting to spring out and yell "Gotcha" at the first utterance of a politically incorrect viewpoint. Dwight explained how he approached racial discussions: "I feel that at times, I'm . . . because I'm the White person in the room that I had better not say anything. You know, if there's a Hispanic person and a Black person talking about race and I'm sitting over here as the only White person, I'd better stay out of this." It was debatable how much Dwight was the "only White person" in the room given that his friendship group was White and the huge bulk of his peer interactions were with other White people. I tried to probe a little deeper on this issue to have Dwight clearly pinpoint an incident or series of interactions that led him to this conclusion. He offered,

> D: Even though I didn't [oppress racial minorities], the connotation that comes with me being a White person is difficult to deal with because all of a sudden, you know, I make a comment on race and they look at me like, "What are you talking about? Your people oppress everybody. You don't know anything about racism or anything."
>
> N: Do they actually say that to you in class?
>
> D: No, but that's how I *feel*.

Dwight began by professing his racial innocence ("I didn't oppress racial minorities"). He then moved to perceived slights by Students of Color ("You people oppress everybody"). However, when I asked if he *actually* experienced this, he responded that it was more of a hunch, a gut feeling. Dwight really did believe that he was being silenced in race-based discussions, but he could not offer a single example of where his feelings matched the reality of the interactions.

Ken offered a more philosophical perspective regarding political correctness on campus, again not rooted in any tangible experiences. As with Dwight, his perspective was more of a gut feeling. Ken described, "Political correctness I think is more or less trying to avoid offending anyone at all times via speech or actions, and I feel in a way that that kind of oppresses people and it takes away their freedom of thought, freedom of expression." It was really interesting how he framed it as infringing on constitutional rights because he could not point to specific examples of people being censored via political correctness. Rather, it was a sense he felt deeply. He was, however, very direct that political correctness "oppresses people," but there was an interesting subtext to his comment. "People" implicitly meant "White people," as Dwight discussed People of Color freely and openly having conversations about issues of race and racism.

Martin took a slightly different angle on this issue and was very explicit about the difference between what he thought and what he said publicly. He was fiercely critical of what he saw as "Black culture" and what he viewed as political correctness forcing him to embrace it: "There are a number of Black stereotypes of Black culture that I don't care for. I don't have to accept that stuff, I'm sorry. I mean, wearing bling-bling gold chains and wearing your hat backwards and baggy pants and, you know, talking unintelligently, *that's bullshit.* I'm sorry, I don't. . . . *That's bullshit. I'm not obligated to embrace that or to say that, 'That's really great. Let's accept cultural diversity.'"* Martin offered a very narrow version of what constituted "Black culture," even framing it as a stereotype, and was quick to condemn it. However, he kept his disdain to himself as Martin continued, "[When I] notice something that I don't like about the way a Black person acts, I think to myself, as much as I don't articulate, 'Oh, stupid Black person, what the hell are they doing? What a dumbass.'" Martin was frustrated because he thought that political correctness meant he had to be accepting and embracing of Black culture, and that he could not express his disdain. What was extremely telling, however, was that he kept his thoughts to himself. He wanted to be able to call some Black people "dumbasses" or "stupid Black people" for their behavior, but he felt censored. It never occurred to him that maybe it is inappropriate to call strangers stupid or dumbasses. Like so many White guys I spoke with, there was no specific incident that made Martin hold his tongue. Rather, it was just a general feeling he had.

Roger made a direct link between political correctness and affirmative action. In a subsequent section, I will more clearly detail how these White guys felt about affirmative action. For now, I will state just that Roger was relatively unique in that he believed affirmative action hires were an example of political correctness: "I think there are things that White people are in, kind of due to the political correctness phenomenon and people wanting to be politically correct. There are certainly examples of people being hired because of their color and not because of, and not because of quote-unquote merit. . . . But there are certainly obvious examples both within education admissions as well as in the job search, because of White privilege, Whites are expected to have accomplished more. And that makes it harder for Whites." Roger began by framing affirmative action as an offshoot of political correctness. This was, in his understanding, a policy response to White privilege, which he also felt was unwarranted. He then used the age-old frame of pitting diversity against merit (Crosby, 2004), as if they are mutually exclusive constructs. Roger believed that this made it structurally more difficult for White guys like him to get ahead in society.

Just like with the general statements on race/racism, those regarding political correctness sometimes made the White guys agitated. In particular, many were upset by a feeling that their views on racism did not carry equal weight to those of racial minorities. Lance was particularly mad about this because, with his Objectivist orientation, he believed that we are all individuals and racial background does not affect the validity of a viewpoint: "*I really don't give a damn what someone who thinks that my opinion is invalid because I'm White* and haven't experienced racism against Blacks as a victim. You know, someone who believes that isn't really worth my time." Lance felt his views on race were continually dismissed because he was White. The White guys I interviewed also tended to locate issues of political correctness and even campus-based racism among Communities of Color—in particular racial/ethnic-based student groups.

Cross-Racial Interactions and Campus-Based Ethnic Groups

Cross-racial interactions while in college have been shown to positively impact intellectual, social, and cognitive development (Chang, Astin, & Kim, 2004). Instead, cross-racial interactions among many of the White guys featured in this chapter tended to lead to increased racial tension and antagonism. For example, Ryan offered, "And [Black people] always introduce race into [discussions], and also having a condescending, negative connotation as being White." He felt that Black people held strongly negative views of him because he was White. Ryan was very frustrated by this because he felt he had done nothing racially wrong. His mechanism for dealing with this situation mirrored those presented in the "Political Correctness" section: "Yeah, yeah. Like there's certain things that occur, I'll keep to myself just because I think that people may assume that I'm racist." Based upon his feeling that People of Color will assume he is racist, he decided to stay silent in these situations. This was slightly different from the political correctness conversation because Ryan believed that Black people had a negative view of him simply for being White. This contrasted with the politically correct narratives where this perceived dislike was based upon what the White guys wanted to express about issues of race. A commonality between the two areas, however, was that the White guys struggled to name specific incidents that made them feel this way.

Andy expressed a similar frustration toward Students of Color on his campus. He, like Ryan, thought that he did nothing wrong but was constantly accused of being racist (although it was difficult to pinpoint specific instances). He was very direct in locating campus-based racism among Communities of Color, and in particular racial/ethnic-based student groups: "In my opinion, when I try to interact sometimes with these groups, I'm the one who's subject to racism because it's almost like they're either assuming I'm going to be racist." It was really interesting how Andy confused being called "a racist" as being a form of racism in and of itself. It was also telling that Ryan was completely dismissive of the idea that he might have said or done something racist. In a strange logic, Ryan did not believe he was a racist individual and felt that anyone who called him racist was the actual racist.

Trevor actually blamed racial/ethnic-based student organizations for inflaming racial tensions on campus. He saw them as having a primarily regressive function as they taught their members to dislike and mistrust White people: "It's important for people to get together with people who are like them culturally in order to better understand their culture and gain a better sense of pride. But what I would hope is that the extra pride they got would empower them to go out and interact with people who are different than them and sort of try to overcome the suppositions that, 'Oh, White people are discriminating against me.' So, I think a lot of times, White people are judged for being White, like, 'Oh, you're gonna discriminate me, and you're gonna have these preconceptions.'" Trevor gave a nod to the idea that people should be able to group with those who are culturally similar to themselves, but he thought that these groups essentially taught their members to dislike and distrust White people. I will explore this in greater depth in chapter 6 regarding the intersection of race and space, and in particular an incident involving Trevor. Returning to this analysis, Trevor was really interesting on a number of levels. Throughout his interview, he was strongly dismissive of minority claims of campus-based racism and therefore viewed Students of Color being wary of White racism as a form of racial paranoia. However, as I will detail in chapter 6, Trevor openly discussed engaging in racial harassment of a Chicano student on campus. Additionally, he had only a few key tense moments interacting with people from these student groups, and from that narrow sample he made this generalized statement about how they function on campus.

Lance also believed that racial/ethnic campus organizations were responsible for the bulk of campus-based racism. This was also due to his strong Objectivist orientation whereby anything race conscious was, in his (mis)understanding, racist. Lance stated, "When we get later down to racism on campus, I think most of the racism on this campus originates, um, maybe not in historical origin, but at least right now, originates from these race-based student groups that all like to group together on the basis of race and whatnot." Lance was very direct that race/ethnic-specific campus-based groups were responsible for racism at his university. He subsequently did offer a relatively unique take on campus-based racism because he suggested that White people supporting the agendas of these organizations were also responsible for racism at WU: "I've seen a lot of Whites be racist against themselves and just like. It's really funny, a lot of letters to the editor in the [student newspaper] were about race. It's like self-flagellation." Lance was hostile to anything race-conscious, dismissed the idea that he might ever be racist, and was very forceful in his condemnation of anyone who engaged issues of race on campus unless they came from an Objectivist perspective. This led him to believe that Students of Color tended to be the primary source of campus racism, and the targets tended to be White people.

Among these White guys, there was a severe lack of self-reflection coupled with their narratives of perceived racial victimization. They almost never engaged the oppressive reality of contemporary, systemic racism (Bonilla-Silva, 2006; Omi & Winant, 2015) and completely disregarded the idea that they themselves could also have racist tendencies. Instead, their White immunity allowed them to be blissfully ignorant of what it was like to actually be the target of racism, and when this ignorance was disrupted, they framed their dissonance as "reverse racism." These narratives became especially pronounced when the White guys I interviewed discussed race-conscious social policies, in particular affirmative action.

Race-Conscious Social Policy

If there was one consistent issue that these White guys agreed on, it was their view that race-conscious social policies were (1) a form of racism and (2) one of the most common forms of contemporary racism. Their views tended to be strongly rooted in *sincere fictions* (Feagin & O'Brien, 2003) whereby they truly believed they were being discriminated against (sincere) but there was no tangible basis for these views (fictions).

Scholarships, HBCUs, and Everything but Affirmative Action

A key way that the White guys I interviewed felt racially oppressed was via race-conscious scholarships. Jack felt some pressure to pay for his education, and he was frequently searching for assistance. He made the following observation about his searches: "There's just all kinds of scholarships that. . . . You know, this is for African American males going into the medical field, or whatever. I mean, you don't ever see a scholarship that says, 'This is for a blond-haired, blue-eyed, White men getting jobs in business,' or something like that." Jack did not feel that it was fair for scholarships to focus only on particular racial/ethnic groups or women, and later he said this amounted to a form of "reverse discrimination." I also asked him how widespread these scholarships were, and he thought they were extremely common, although he could not put an exact number on it. It was interesting how Jack framed this issue because White people actually receive a disproportionate share of private scholarships and racially restricted grants compose less than 5 percent of those available (Kantrowitz, 2011). Despite these realities, Jack believed that race-based scholarships were extremely common, and there needed to be more scholarships catering to people of his demographic—not realizing the overwhelming majority of them already do.

Nick explained White male angst about race-conscious social policies. He actually had some sympathy for the overall goals of programs such as bussing, but he thought they were poorly executed and became a cause of contemporary anger among White people. He offered, "I think there were some really dumb liberal policies in the realm of racial politics, one being bussing. I mean, I think that's. . . . I think in retrospect that's kind of getting hard to defend, but I think that for so many Whites . . . and I think Bill O'Reilly now typifies this the best, is that so many Whites have this feeling like all of a sudden, they were being punished for everything that happened beforehand, and for me, my roots in this country don't go back farther than 1917." It was interesting that Nick dropped in the fact that his family came to the United States only in 1917, which seemed to be a rhetorical means of saying that they (and in particular *he*) bore no responsibility for the U.S. history of racism. That is, he articulated what Pierce (2012) refers to as *racing for innocence*, where White people use different rhetorical devices to claim they bear no responsibility for racism. Regardless, Nick thought that race-conscious liberal policies were having a regressive effect and causing more problems than they were offering solutions. Interestingly, he did not propose any meaningful solutions to racial inequality, but he was quick to critique those that he felt were not working.

Jeff went so far as to claim that the existence of historically Black colleges and universities (HBCUs) amounted to a form of discrimination against White people like him. He began by misidentifying any form of race-conscious social policy as affirmative action, and then went on to critique the existence of HBCUs:

> J: Yeah, being a White male, I've always just known that affirmative action isn't on my side. I mean, I hear a lot . . . there's like over sixty only-Black colleges or all-Black colleges in country. . . .
>
> N: Do HBCUs have White students on their campuses?
>
> J: I don't know. It doesn't sound like it. I mean, I really don't know because it's . . . I'm not gonna apply to a school that claims it's all Black. I mean, but I've always heard that there's. . . . You know, proclaimed all-Black colleges in the United States and I don't like that.

Jeff was completely unaware of the widespread, systemic racism that led to the creation of HBCUs in the first place (Roebuck & Murty, 1993). Instead, he was focused only on how he as a White man might not fit into this social environment. It was also fascinating that Jeff did not want to be in the minority at an HBCU, but later in his interview he was also dismissive of minority students feeling socially isolated at predominantly White institutions (PWIs). He did not think that minoritized students experienced many racial issues at PWIs because in his view racism against People of Color was only a minor contemporary issue. Instead, he had a lot of trepidation about being in the minority among People of Color. Within this context, Jeff framed HBCUs as a form of racial segregation, and I challenged him on this assertion—that these institutions came out of a history of forced segregation and that they were more of a response than a cause of segregation (Roebuck & Murty, 1993). Jeff was relatively dismissive of this history and claimed that HBCUs were a violation of the spirit of integration and the Civil Rights Movement. He even invoked the memory of Jim Crow laws, saying that while the existence of HBCUs was a more positive form of segregation, he did not "see it as much different." Yes, he actually believed that HBCUs were the moral equivalent of Jim Crow.

There were a number of White guys who did not even like being racially identified. For example, they saw checking a box for "race/ethnicity" on an application as a form of racism. Martin provided an example: "On college applications it still asks you to put your race. I don't believe that question should even be asked, it doesn't matter. It would eliminate the entire problem." His formulation was simple: there is no more racism in society, and therefore we should stop categorizing by race and the entire problem will go away. Others did not necessarily think that problems of racism would disappear if there were no racial classification, but they did tend to think that this exacerbated the problem. Jack offered, "I'd say it is, but it shouldn't be based . . . I don't know, I don't think they should . . . I mean, college application, there should be no discussion of race, I think personally. . . . You're going to get an education, you're going to move on, and I don't think race should play into that at all." Jack did not think that race does play a role in structuring inequality, and therefore he also thought the college application should be color blind. He saw racial classification on college applications as a distraction from education. These were some of the many ways the White guys felt discriminated against as White men, but their primary source of social angst was affirmative action.

Affirmative Action

In chapter 5, I detail how the White guys I interviewed, in particular those at WU, created an imagined affirmative action. In this section, I provide an overview of how they rhetorically frame affirmative action oppressing them as White men. There is a lot of overlap between these two areas, but I think that the issue of imagined affirmative action is so unique and compelling that it deserves a chapter-length treatment. Conversely, it would be difficult to have a chapter about "reverse racism" if I did not have part of the discussion focus on affirmative action. The discussion in this section begins by offering how the White guys I interviewed defined affirmative action, then shifts to their reactions to it. The bulk of those defining affirmative action focused on it being some type of a quota system:

> The best examples I can think of are like affirmative action with the quota system to where it's forced upon different schools that so many Blacks have to be admitted, so many Latinos have to admitted, so many Asians have to be admitted and so on. (Ken)

Affirmative action is government-enforced race-based quotas in hiring and education admission standards. (Lance)

I also knew already that WU has like a certain quota of races it tries to fill when it takes in students. (Jonathan)

The bulk of the White guys I interviewed thought that affirmative action meant that a certain percentage of spots had to be allocated to different races. It was really interesting that they consistently used this framing device, since quotas in affirmative action were outlawed in 1977 (Crosby, 2004). While they based their views on a misrepresentation of the nature of affirmative action, their reactions to and feelings about affirmative action were real.

There were some who described affirmative action in more detail, and their descriptions frequently were framed as being institutionally sanctioned racism against White people. Many times, they rhetorically did this by doing small thought experiments as Martin offered: "If we're going to consider that . . . same grades, same everything. One is White and one is Black, to me it's just as racist to say, 'Well, I'm going to let the Black person into my university because they're Black and I'm going to value that for this particular thing as being better, for whatever it is I'm doing, than being White.' It's just as racist to do that as it is to do the reverse and say, 'I'm going to let the White person in because they're White.'" Martin gave no credence to the idea that contemporary racism might inequitably structure opportunity in his favor as a White man. Instead, his White immunity allowed him to ignore this reality and then subsequently frame affirmative action as racism against White people. He did this by simply switching Black for White in affirmative action and claimed the program was racist. This switch makes sense only if we completely ignore history and social context, which he was able to do based on White immunity and likely his male immunity as well.

With this as context, the White guys I interviewed were really agitated by affirmative action, and their angst tended to focus on perceptions of "reverse racism." It was fascinating how they tended to adopt the language of equal opportunity and racial exclusion to justify their beliefs, particularly because these same White guys were dismissive of these claims when People of Color made them. Justin was very direct that he believed affirmative action was a form of "reverse racism" couched in an equal opportunity framework: "I think that affirmative action, simply because Whites are excluded from that. It's almost like a reverse type of racism and we're just trying to see the logic and the equality in pointing out somebody's . . . in pointing out. . . . I think that they fail to see the logic in making . . . in trying to fix equalities by making inequality a significant factor." He felt that White people were being excluded from equitable treatment due to affirmative action. Part of his reason for "failing to see the logic" behind affirmative action was that he was ignorant, sometimes willfully so, about the realities of contemporary racism. That is, his White immunity meant he was unaware of a social context where affirmative action might be necessary, but instead of exploring his own ignorance, he believed there was something fundamentally wrong with the program.

The bulk of these affirmative action "reverse discrimination" discussions centered on issues of fairness. Ryan was direct on this point: "You're not letting people go to school just because they were born into a family that had money. Just because they were born White. And that's not fair." Ryan was both White and born into money, and he actually felt his opportunities were lessened because of this reality. It was interesting because he still gained admission to WU, but his feeling of the threat remained: "And that's not fair. It's not fair to, um, do that to the person—the White guy who worked harder and uh, had a better education, or studied more, or whatever it was that his situation is, just because he's White, he doesn't get the job, or he doesn't get to go to the school he wants to." It was interesting how Ryan framed this issue because there were a number of assumptions embedded in this statement. He began by framing Whites and wealthy people as better educated and working harder than their People of Color and working-class counterparts. Then he framed White people (in particular White men) as being hurt by affirmative action. He did not consider that his Whiteness, maleness, and financial privilege were systemic advantages for him. Instead, his White (and male and affluent) immunity allowed him to ignore structured inequality and instead paint himself as the "true" victim.

Jonathan was very similar to Ryan in his assessment of affirmative action, but his views went beyond simple fairness and included issues of freedom enshrined in the Constitution: "It makes sense that [affirmative action is] a good idea, but at the same time, it feels like it infringes *on fundamental freedoms* because. . . . So, I think it should be totally based on academic ability, off of character, off the attributes of the individual and have *nothing to do with the skin* because . . . or with their color or whatever because to me *that's just not fair.* . . . You know, you have someone who works really hard and then they miss out *because of their color.*" While Jonathan spoke abstractly about people potentially missing out on opportunities "because of their skin color," his views did not include everyone, just White people. He was only concerned with the possibility that their opportunities might be limited. He did not see racism as a very strong contemporary force against People of Color. Jonathan, like many of the White guys, focused on hard work by White people and their possible exclusion due to affirmative action. These were really interesting rhetorical devices because, again, he assumed that White people work harder and are more deserving than People of Color but were being "unfairly" excluded because of the color of their skin. The difficulty with these views is that they are the epitome of *sincere fictions* (Feagin & O'Brien, 2003). These White guys really believed their life chances were limited due to affirmative action despite the fact that all were White, most were at least comfortably middle class, and all were pursuing their undergraduate education at research universities. The White guys attending the more elite the university (WU) had much stronger anti-affirmative action beliefs despite the program not being in existence on their campus, as I will demonstrate in chapter 5.

Back to Life, Back to (Racial) Reality

The power of the White male racial imagination was on full display in the interviews that formed the basis for this chapter. While there is no meaningful empirical basis for the existence of "reverse racism," these White guys continually felt racially oppressed from a variety of sources, including political correctness, racial minorities assuming they were going to be racist, and race-conscious social policies, in particular affirmative action. The common denominator among all of these triggers was that they disrupted the invisibility of Whiteness that these White guys experienced. That is, in the previous chapter the White guys' narratives demonstrated how they rarely witnessed instances of racism against People of Color, and were able to downplay and verbally dance around its contemporary significance. In these cases, they could not avoid it and became very defensive, leading them to cry "reverse racism." This is what DiAngelo (2011) refers to as *White fragility*, and it was on full display. The young men were continually confronted with how to engage a multicultural society, and instead of exploring this terrain, they retreated to the myth of "reverse racism." Essentially, when Whiteness could not be agile (chapter 2), it became fragile (chapter 3).

The White guys I spoke with tended to be in very fragile emotional states when it came to issues of race and in particular "reverse racism," and their verbal tone helped me understand this. The White guys featured in this chapter were constantly upset about issues of race, and it showed in both their increased use of profanity and their frequently raised voices. This was really interesting because, as I will show in chapter 4, the White guys tended to view People of Color as overly sensitive on issues of race. The imagination of these White guys was impressive. They felt oppressed and their racial views suppressed by political correctness, campus-based racial/ethnic organizations, and even simple cross-racial interactions. They could not, however, identify instances when they were actually silenced or had their views restricted; they just had "a feeling."

This is really interesting because, as I have previously argued, "most of the literature in racial theory tends to rely on a cognitive framing of race/racism" (Cabrera, 2014b, p. 772). That is, racial analysis tends to examine issues of ideology (e.g., Bonilla-Silva, 2006) with little attention paid to the role that racial emotions play in perpetuating racial inequality (Matias, 2016, is a notable exception). A number of the narratives these White guys offered seemed to invert this equation. That is, instead of rational thought or ideology driving action and leading to emotional responses, it was an emotional response that led to their (mis)understandings about the role that racism plays in contemporary society. Or, to borrow from the title of e. e. cummings's classic poem (1994), "since feeling is first."

Ultimately, these White guys had a severe lack of self-reflection in their narratives. Let us temporarily assume that there were a number of People of Color telling the White guys I interviewed that they were racist. While there is not a lot of evidence this was actually occurring, these guys tended to feel that it was. If their gut feelings were correct, why would they not take that as an opportunity to self-reflect? Why would they not engage the opportunity to think about how their actions and beliefs might be racist? If all your friends tell you that you're an alcoholic, it might be time to attend an AA meeting. By the same token, if People of Color continually tell you that you are being racist, it might be time to consider how you are being racist. Instead, it was more important for the White guys I interviewed to maintain a positive, non-racist view of self than to actually engage and understand the realities of contemporary racism. The problem with this disengagement was that they not only, to borrow from Pierce (2012), "raced for innocence" but also turned People of Color and race-consciousness into racial boogiemen. The subsequent chapters will demonstrate how this then translates into some very racist actions taken against Students of Color.

Tying chapters 2 and 3 together, I am reminded of an interesting thesis that Orozco (2013) offered: that White innocence cannot exist without minority aggression. That is, in order for White people to frame themselves as racially innocent, they need to concurrently frame People of Color as the "true" source of contemporary racial oppression. While I think there are a few situations where Orozco's thesis does not entirely hold, it still provides an accurate description of the sentiment of these White guys. They could never pinpoint specifically how they were oppressed by race-consciousness, in large part because they simply were not. However, they truly felt that they were not racist but were penalized for the racism of others, in particular that of their White forebears.

One huge problem is that these White guys had no meaningful understanding of what constitutes racism. They tended to individualize racism and then dichotomize people into good (non-racists) and bad (racists). Not surprisingly, they fit into the former category with anything race-conscious in the latter. They never engaged racism as a systemic reality (Leonardo, 2009), but rather, wanted to be treated as individuals independent of social context. This might also be a function of them being White and male. That is, a core component of hegemonic masculinity is also to individualize systemic oppression (Connell,

2005). Some of the narratives the participants offered discussed being "oppressed" or having "higher expectations" because they were both White and male. Extending White immunity to gender, they were also experiencing male immunity whereby they did not have to experience or understand the systemic, disparate treatment women and gender-nonconforming people receive. Thus, their narratives were completely divorced from social context and individualized, which allowed them to create the fiction of "reverse racism."

Part of this fear might stem from these White guys' desire to protect their group positioning (Blumer, 1958; Bobo & Tuan, 2006). James Baldwin (1961) provided an incredibly insightful analysis of the U.S. racial hierarchy and how it can trigger White racial paranoia. He offered, "[White people cannot afford to lose] status on this peculiar ladder, for the prevailing notion of American life seems to involve a kind of rung-by-rung ascension to some hideous desirable state. If this is one's concept of life, obviously one cannot afford to slip back one run.... In a way, the Negro tells us where the bottom is: *because he is there*, and *where* he is, beneath us, we know where the limits are and how far we must not fall" (p. 111, italics original).

Essentially, minoritized people in general and Black people in particular tell White people where the bottom rung on the U.S. racial ladder is. It was not that the White guys in this chapter were actually struggling economically. Rather, modest disruptions in the totality of White hegemony meant they slipped one metaphorical rung on the ladder. They were nowhere near the bottom, but this modest slippage led to protestations that White people (especially White men) are the "true victims" of multiculturalism.

At times, these White guys seemed to engage in the same psychology as kids afraid of a monster in the closet. The fear is real, but all they have to do is get out of bed and turn on the light to realize the monster is not. All these White guys needed to do was start a meaningful engagement with issues of racism from the perspective of those oppressed by this systemic, contemporary reality. Instead, they stayed in their imagined reality where White people in general, and White men in particular, are the "true" targets of modern-day racism. Ultimately, this is more than simply individual psychology; it becomes the foundation for linguistic and physical violence that targets People of Color (Cabrera, Franklin, & Watson, 2017). That is, these White guys' *imagined* oppression becomes a basis for the *actual* oppression of People of Color.

4

"Why Can't Stevie Wonder Read? Because He's Black"

Whiteness and the Social Performance of Racist Joking

> I personally . . . I don't consider myself to be racist whatsoever, but I'll tell racially insensitive jokes or make comments at times, but I wouldn't consider myself a racist.
> —Jack

Frequently, stand-up comedians claim that because their job is making people laugh, their words should not be taken seriously. For example, shock comedian Lisa Lampanelli began one of her routines offering racist stereotypes of Asian Americans and Latinxs while dropping the n-word, then offering, "I love guys who can take a joke. My feeling is, this is a comedy club. If you can't take a joke, leaaaaaave!"[1] Progressive White comedians can also play this game. Moshe Kasher began his "Live in Oakland" performance by offering, "I do not give a fuck if you get offended."[2] He then followed up by stating, "Well, if it makes you feel any better, I was just kidding! The whole time . . . I think it's important to set down those ground rules at the beginning of the show because if at any time you do become offended, we've now established that's just you . . . being a bitch!" Bill Maher, from a slightly left-of-center perspective, has been on a several-year-long rant against contemporary college students being too sensitive and politically correct (or "snowflakes"), and he, Jerry Seinfeld, Larry the Cable Guy, and Chris Rock all now refuse to perform at university campuses for this reason (Ernst, 2015). These comedians essentially avoid social responsibility for anything racist, sexist, homophobic, or Islamophobic they may say. Instead, the problem lies in an "overly sensitive" audience—especially college students. Interestingly, the White guys I interviewed tended to offer similar sentiments even though, as college students and according to the previously described comedians, they should be running in horror from racist jokes instead of telling and laughing at them.

Jack's quotation illustrates how many of the White guys I talked with navigated racist jokes. He framed his joking as non-racist regardless of what he may have said. That is, he may tell "racially insensitive jokes" but that does not make him "a racist." This was an incredibly common phenomenon in the interviews. When I asked where the White guys I spoke with saw racism on their respective campuses, the number-one response was a form of racial joking, but they were also quick to downplay the racial significance because "it was just a joke." As I demonstrated in chapter 2, many of the participants' narratives evolved into a racial form of "Yes, but . . . ," and this chapter falls along these same lines. However, I think this component of their experiences warrants its own chapter for a few reasons. First, joking was the most common form of racism these White men identify in their lived experiences. Second, while the White guys I spoke with tended to tell racist jokes only among other White guys, they justified this practice because they believed People of Color were "overly sensitive" on issues of race. Third, because their sentiment was expressed in joke form, many believed they were absolved of any social responsibility for their racism. As demonstrated above, this has long been the mantra of comedians—no offense can be taken from a joke.

Since I am on a pop culture riff right now, I began thinking about Pierre Delacroix, the Black male main character in Spike Lee's *Bamboozled*. When a White man rewrote the pilot for his sketch comedy show that engaged issues of race, Delacroix was furious. The producer explained that the writer kicked it up a notch and made the skits "more funny"—which meant more overtly racist against Black people. In response, Delacroix asked the incredibly provocative question, "Funnier to who and at whose expense?" (Lee, 2000, p. 56). This is the core of my racial joke telling analysis. Telling jokes is a social performance that requires an audience, and it is important to understand the interaction of the teller and his audience (gender-specific for this analysis). These White guys did not tell jokes to themselves in the bathroom mirror while shaving.

Instead, they required an audience. If racist jokes were universally humorous, they would be told in front of everyone. As these narratives demonstrate, the racist joke telling of White male undergraduates is not for everyone, almost exclusively meant for other White males, functioning as a form of both White bonding (Sleeter, 1994) and male bonding (Lyman, 1987). Within that context, I dive into the racial joke telling patterns of White male undergraduates and the environments in which they occur.

"Dude, It's Just a Joke": The Art of Downplaying the Racism in Jokes

I asked the White guys I spoke with to identify instances of racism on their respective college campuses, and the most common example by far was racial joking. Within their racially homogenous college sub-environments, the participants reported both hearing and telling jokes about race on a consistent basis (e.g., "Q: Why can't Stevie Wonder read? A: Because he's Black"), but they then Whitesplained how the incidents were not racist ("Dude, it's just a joke"). Consider Alex's response when I asked him to identify an example of racism on campus: "Intentionally racism meant to be like cruel or demeaning, I would say no. I mean, I've seen jokes, I've heard jokes. I mean, if somebody says. . . . It's done in lighthearted good fun or whatever, it's still is said, it still has an impact. Whether the impact is as severe as if it was done intentionally, I don't know, but. . . . Just like . . . just racial jokes, like saying the n-word, things like that." This description is telling on a number of levels. First, Alex claimed that he never saw "cruel or demeaning" racism; therefore, whatever followed was not serious. Second, he framed any harm from the jokes as unintentional. Third, he offered that his friends also play with the n-word, but in his mind doing so is not racist.

Jay had a very similar experience. He was struggling to find an example of racism that he witnessed on campus, so he also turned to racist joking among his overwhelmingly White and male friends: "I don't know if you can call them racist just because they're thought to be jokes, but there's a general joke that's thrown out by someone, like an African American joke or just a religious joke or whatever, it may be that it's intended to not bring any harm." Much like Alex, Jay had trouble labeling these jokes *racist* because they were not *intended* to offend. He did offer some insight into the social environment in which he and his friends told these jokes: "It's usually not said . . . probably not said of somebody of that minority group." That is, Jay and his friends tended to tell these jokes in the absence of Students of Color. I asked Jay to describe further what he saw and experienced regarding this racist joke telling among his friendship group, and he elaborated:

It's not . . . it's an ongoing thing. It's two kids talking to each other or a group of people who. . . . Somebody just throws out a joke or will say the n-word or will say this, will say that, without even thinking about it, without thinking that it can be seen as racist when clearly it can, it's just thought to be a joke. So, most of the racism that I have been exposed to have been in joke manners. Whether they be funny or not, I think that most of them are intended to be jokes. I haven't seen any . . . well, maybe I just haven't been aware of just racism on campus.

Like Alex, Jay was keenly focused on intentionality when identifying a racist incident. He did not think that his friends wanted to hurt or offend anyone, which led him to say that he was unaware of racism on campus. This was an interesting juxtaposition because he described at one point people in his friend-ship group using the n-word, but like Alex he did not even find that to be racist.

Continuing on the theme of the n-word, Jeremy said, "Evidence of racism here on campus? People . . . I've noticed say 'nigger' lightheartedly, so in like a joking manner." Jeremy had difficulty labeling these statements as racist, in part because of the joking manner in which the epithet was said. I explored this fur-ther by asking, "Do they say [the n-word] in front of Black people?" Jeremy responded, "No. It's not like. . . . They would never. . . . The people I know and I'm talking about would never, and they're not . . . they're open-minded people, they're not prejudiced in that sense." Jeremy understood racism as a hatred of racial minorities. His friends did not fit this profile, so he did not label them racist ("they're open-minded people"). For Jeremy, it was a joke and therefore relatively harmless.

Many other White guys described hearing racist jokes while on campus, but they consistently framed the jokes as both funny and not racist:

I mean, I've heard racist jokes and things like that on campus, but nothing like kind of, you know, really racist. (Kevin)

I would say, yeah, with the intention of hurting somebody. I mean, I really don't intend to hurt somebody, sometimes [the jokes are] just funny. (Jack)

I mean, I've seen people make interracial jokes, but that's just "Ha-ha." (Ken)

For many, racist jokes were the primary examples of racism they saw on cam-pus, but they tended to frame them as not intentionally hurtful, not racist, and simply humorous. Also, the White guys I spoke with described racial jokes more objectively ("the jokes are funny") rather than from a subjective position ("I find them funny"). I probed these assertions by asking why the jokes are funny, and the responses did not lead anywhere. For example, Jack responded, "I don't know, they just are." For Jack, no further explanation was needed, a questionable assertion on his part because, like Jeremy, he said racial jokes were rarely told in front of members of the race who were the butt of the joke. Adam discussed this process: "[Racial joking] probably happens more without the [racial] group present. . . . I don't know [why], I think that when it happens, there's still the. . . . It's done with a certain level of confidence it won't be misconstrued, but there's still the possibility, so I think you just feel . . . a person feels safer knowing that it can't be misconstrued versus having the person there and it could be." According to Adam, racial minorities misconstrue issues, and thus it is socially acceptable for Whites to tell racist jokes behind their backs. Adam saw nothing wrong with racist joking, and he later explained that in his understanding, only political correctness made it improper for him to tell these jokes in mixed company.

This apprehension of political correctness as explored in chapter 3 was strong during many of the interviews. This intersection of political correctness and racist joke telling arose as some of the interviews occurred in the aftermath of the Don Imus controversy. On Imus's radio program, he was talking about the Rutgers women's basketball team and referred to this group of Black women as "nappy-headed hos." When the White guys I spoke with described this event, they did not believe Imus was being racist; Bernard was the most outspoken on the issue: "Well, what's Don Imus? There's always things in the media where people make comments that aren't explicitly racist, but then someone interprets it, when it's obviously up for debate whether it's racist or not, and they get punished for it or they're censored." Bernard felt the term Don Imus used was not racist because it referred to hair texture, but he was primarily offended that someone could be "censored" over something that he viewed as not racist. Bernard continued, blaming the "liberal media" and Al Sharpton for making a mountain out of a racial molehill, arguing they made money by stirring up controversy. He then said that on Imus's show, this kind of behavior was expected: "Well, I mean, he was generally describing them and he sort of. . . . In the context of his show, he's sort of grumpy and he's also sort of a comedian, and so he wasn't. . . . I mean, he wasn't explicitly talking about their race." Bernard used the combination of context and content to argue that Imus's remarks were not racist. He could not answer another question during the interview, however: How racially offensive do remarks have to be for them to be racist? He did not have a specific answer, but Bernard said he would know it when he heard it. Additionally, the assertion that these jokes are harmless is questionable. The White guys I spoke with consistently stated that racist jokes were told without the minority group present. If the jokes were really innocuous, why would the participants not tell them in front of Students of Color? One possible answer lies in their belief that racial minorities are overly sensitive on issues of race.

Minorities Are "Overly Sensitive"

Closely related to the theme of racial joking in ostensibly White spaces, the White guys I spoke with tended to believe that People of Color in general, and Students of Color in particular, frequently saw racism where none existed. Sometimes this directly related to questions of racist joking (e.g., believing that among White students the jokes would not be misconstrued). Other times, this was a general belief regarding issues of race. Both themes (racial joking and minority sensitivity) were strongly present in the interviews with these White guys, even when they were not directly related to each other. For example, Lance did not see racism in his experiences, and therefore he argued that those seeing racism are actually being irrational: "[Students of Color] claiming that they don't feel welcomed by Whites in college, I think that's again like seeing racists and race [issues] just everywhere. *They can only think in terms of race*, and so they draw these incorrect inferences. . . . [My minority friends] don't see racism everywhere they turn, so my impression is that [claims of racism are] highly exaggerated, if not blatantly false." Lance and his Friends of Color saw little evidence of racism in their everyday life, so in Lance's understanding there must be something wrong with people who did. Additionally, as an Objectivist, Lance saw himself as a strongly rational being, so when the reality of many Students of Color differed from his, he blamed the discrepancy on people "only [thinking] in terms of race," which leads to drawing "incorrect inferences." Lance also forcefully denied that as a White man he would have difficulty understanding racism despite the fact that he was not targeted by this oppressive system (Bonilla-Silva, 2001, 2006; Omi & Winant, 2015). Instead he framed his views as rational and objective, while those challenging racism were irrational and subjective, fighting a problem that he did not believe existed. Ironically, the inverse is actually true because Lance used his subjective experience as a White man to claim that racism is not a powerful, contemporary social force. He is objectively incorrect in this orientation (Bonilla-Silva, 2001, 2006; Omi & Winant, 2015), exhibiting the same behavior he perceived in Students of Color.

Many other White guys I spoke with offered similar sentiments. Derek was succinct in his assessment of claims of racism: "Minorities do play the race card and they are overly sensitive in some issues." Roger gave his own version of this same theme, "Like sometimes people. . . . People see things in situations that aren't there." Robert offered an example from his father's business, where a fired employee sued claiming racial discrimination, which Robert thought was absurd: "Sometimes you hear about people not getting jobs, and they immediately assume it's, uh, because of their ethnic background." Robert, Roger, and Derek all tended to cast doubt on claims of racism by arguing that minorities are too racially sensitive.

Keith also believed that minorities were too sensitive on issues of race, and he provided a specific example. He heard about Mel Gibson getting pulled over for a DUI and argued Gibson's drunken rant was not racist in any way. A little context is necessary. After being stopped, Gibson went into a belligerent tirade, including, "Fucking Jews. The Jews are responsible for all the wars in the world."[3] Within this context, Keith began with the following, "Some of the issues where some people say, it's like a racial issue where they're like being racist, I think it's overblown." Keith was frequently skeptical of People of Color claiming issues were racist, and he specifically used the Gibson arrest as an example of an issue getting blown out of proportion: ". . . like the Mel Gibson example where he said—I don't know exactly what he said, but some people were saying he said something against Jews. That the Jews were responsible for the current war, and what not. And people said that was racist. Like, the Jews took it as racist. Myself, I really didn't see it as racist because it was a war thing, not a racial thing." This was interesting because Keith said that it was acceptable to blame the Jews for causing wars because "it was a war thing, not a racial thing." Blaming an entire religious minority for contemporary wars seems to me the epitome of anti-Semitism. In Keith's understanding, the blame for wars had nothing to do with racism and was an example (tying into his first statement) of people reading too much into a non-racist situation.

Kurt also believed that People of Color play the "race card," are overly sensitive on issues of race, and are opportunistic. He began by offering the following: "Some people would try and take advantage of being a minority and that they get unfair treatment." Kurt gave some credence to the idea that People of Color experience racism and then offered, "but I think it's kind of blown of our proportion sometimes." Kurt was general skeptical of claims of racism, and gave a specific example from his life. "There's this guy I work with and it's mostly a joke, but I think deep down it's. . . . Subconsciously, it's just like, 'Oh, it's because I'm Mexican,' or whatever, all the time, nonstop . . . I don't think anyone really treats him differently. He just does it as a joke, but subconsciously he really does feel like he's being treated unfair or inferior to others." Kurt's friend always used the refrain "Oh, it's because I'm Mexican" as a "nonstop" joke at work. Interestingly, Kurt thought that there was some truth in this joke. That is, Kurt thought his coworker subconsciously did think he was be treated differently. This stands in stark contrast to so many of the narratives in this chapter. That is, when these White guys were telling racist jokes among other White guys, it was "just a joke" and should not be taken seriously. In this case, however, Kurt suspected that his coworker was expressing a deeper racial belief through joking—a belief Kurt disagreed with because he did not think his coworker was treated worse on the job due to his ethnic background.

Jonathan was not as specific as Kurt about issues of playing the "race card," but he still believed racial minorities did it on a regular basis. He was concerned that this meant People of Color did not appreciate the opportunities the U.S. economic system afforded them and instead were looking for a "free lunch": "I have had experiences where I've seen people just play the race card because they can and I think sometimes when those who are being treated unfairly are fighting for justice, others. . . . I don't know, they don't tap into the same appreciation for what's going on and instead they just see free doors or free opportunities and instead of understanding what they're doing they just. . . . You know, if there's a free lunch you try to take it." It was telling that, when pressed, Jonathan did not have tangible examples of People of Color playing the "race card." Instead, it was more of a philosophical musing on the issue that concluded with the refrain that some opportunistic minorities might ruin it for the rest of the group. His narrative also strongly tied into those of chapter 2 where the White guys I talked with continually articulated "*Yes, but . . . hard work with triumph.*" The flip side of that coin is that laziness and seeking "free opportunities" prevent racial equality from becoming a reality. Noticeably absent from either one of these narratives is the idea that perhaps racism is a powerful, contemporary social force.

Jeff also offered a version of "*Yes, but . . .*" in his assessment of playing the "race card" and People of Color being overly sensitive. Interestingly, he began by saying that even if he did not possess complete information, he tended to have a consistent viewpoint: "I mean, I'd have to know the situation, but probably. If it's completely unknown, I usually veer towards the race card idea." That is, his null hypothesis was that People of Color play the race card when racial issues arise. He was highly skeptical that racism played a large role in structuring contemporary inequality and said that he formed a lot of his opinions on race from his trips to the heavily Mexican American city of East LA with his housekeeper:

> I'm going to have say I'm pretty strong on the latter, they're playing the race card, they're. . . . I had a housekeeper who lived in East LA. We were really close friends and I'd spend a lot of time in East LA, a highly Mexican demographic. I mean, it's not the case that the kids were Mexican that bothered me. I mean, they're wearing bandanas, they're covered in tattoos. And I don't know if that's discrimination, but when you cover yourself with tattoos of skulls and guns and maybe your girlfriend too. They just don't look like respectable people. They don't present themselves well.

There were a number of layers to Jeff's narrative. First, he restated that he believed minorities played the race card. He then offered that he was uncomfortable with people in East LA not because they were Mexican, but because of their tattoos and bandanas. In his understanding, if these people would dress more "respectably," they would not experience discrimination. Ultimately, it was ironic that Jeff downplayed the power of contemporary racism while at the same time stereotyping an entire population as essentially *cholos*.

Some of the White guys I spoke with had additional theories explaining how in their minds minorities saw racism when they personally did not. Returning to Kurt, he made an analogy between seeing racism and the road game "Slug Bug" (where a rider who first spots a Volkswagen Beetle gets to punch another rider in the arm): "It's kind of like the Volkswagen Bug effect, you know, [when] you're looking for them. . . . You're looking for certain things, and you start seeing them a lot more often than you would ordinarily." Kurt understood the phenomenon that when people are looking for something, they tend to see them everywhere and likened this to racism (i.e., if one wants to find racism, one will see it).

Others viewed higher education as playing a role in developing and fostering heightened racial sensitivity and a sense of victimization among racial minorities. In the previous chapter, Trevor was highly critical of ethnic-specific campus organizations. In this instance, he took issue with ethnic studies courses: "And, and I think that a lot of the dialogue that you get in, you know, ethnic studies departments is all about this historical narrative that has oppressed people, et cetera. People really internalize that, and then they feel like they're always being oppressed." This belief was contextualized within some tense cross-racial interactions Trevor had on campus. He thought ethnic studies, in part, might be responsible for promoting racial antagonism where, in his view, none previously existed.

Martin took a different approach to this subject. He expressed concern regarding how people "playing the race card" undercut the legitimacy of actual instances of racism: "I fear for minorities that too many people can be opportunistic like that, just like with anything else, the second you can levy agreements, you can, and people that kind of ruin it for other people I kind of suspect." Talking with Martin, he was generally suspect of claims of racism, but in his mind it was People of Color crying wolf who ruined it for the few with legitimate grievances. This belief, like others in the participant narratives, was contextualized within an ideological orientation where race and racism were seen as having minimal contemporary importance. These beliefs then allowed the White guys to frame racial joking as rather innocuous, and therefore if there were a problem, it was primarily due to the sensitivity of People of Color. These three issues—People of Color are "overly sensitive" on race; segregated, White environments; and racist joke telling—became mutually reinforcing structures and ideologies, as I will explore in chapter 8.

Racist Jokes and the College Environments That Enable Them

The issue of racist joking was an unexpected component of these interviews with White guys, but emerged as the most common example of racism they identified, with a very consistent pattern of behavior and rationalization. The White guys tended to tell and hear racial jokes in racially homogenous, White environments where they did not find this problematic. Instead, they tended to believe that People of Color are too sensitive regarding race to find the jokes amusing, thereby justifying the telling of these jokes behind closed doors—a tight, cyclical logic.

The framing of racial sensitivity, in particular, was very interesting. Returning to Kurt's "Slug Bug" analogy, he believed that people who are playing the game tend to be more aware of vehicles on the road than those who are not playing. He inadvertently offered a substantial critique of his own worldview. Whether or not a person is aware of VW vehicles, they still exist on the road. Kurt saw little evidence of racism and did not believe racism was a significant social problem, and therefore in his understanding, racial minorities who talk about racism were seeing something that was not there. An alternative explanation is that racism exists, but Kurt's White immunity allowed him to ignore it. Kurt, like most of the other participants, additionally enacted part of his White immunity to determine what constitutes reality (i.e., that racism does not exist), thereby framing those who see racism as creating a problem where one did not previously exist.

When discussing their perceptions of "minority sensitivity," the White guys I spoke with frequently brought up how much it upset them when People of Color "play the race card." During these conversations, I was reminded of a piece Tim Wise wrote on the subject of the race card (2006). Within the article, Wise detailed the predictable response and persistent racial denial by White people when racial issues arise. He then offered, "The regularity with which whites respond to charges of racism by calling said charges a ploy suggests that the race card is, at best, equivalent to the two of diamonds. In other words, it's not much of a card to play, calling into question why anyone would play it (as if it were really going to get them somewhere)." Wise posed a critically important question the White guys failed to explore: How has "playing the race card" tangibly benefitted Communities of Color? In Wise's assessment, not much. Instead of being an analysis of the behavior of People of Color, the "race card" is actually a demonstration of White denial—a refusal to believe the reality that racism is still a powerful social force. Within this context, the race card is less a problem of People of Color and more one of White people.

Within these discussions, most of the White guys framed racist jokes as harmless. Taken on the surface, this is generally true. One racial joke does not deny a Person of Color admission to a university or subject the individual to racial violence. Rather, the problem lies in the underlying ideologies and attitudes that make the joke funny. Jokes are a performative form of communication that requires a receptive audience (Picca & Feagin, 2007). Thus, racial jokes are funny only if people are laughing, and the salient question becomes, what makes these people laugh? Or returning to Pierre Delacroix's provocative question at the beginning of the chapter, the jokes are "funnier to who and at whose expense?" (Lee, 2000, p. 56). In Jeremy's case, his peers used the n-word and laughed at its use perhaps because of its shock value. But have they ever been the target of racial discrimination? Given the nature of the contemporary White supremacy (Bonilla-Silva, 2006; Omi & Winant, 2015), the answer is no. White people may be subject to a degree of racial bigotry and prejudice, but they are not systematically disadvantaged due to their racial background (Tatum, 1992, 2003). Jeremy's peers played with a term whose true negative meaning they can never experience, and thus they found the shock value funny as opposed to offensive. From Jeremy's narrative, it was clear that the jokes were funny for other White guys like him; however, he never considered asking, "At whose expense?"

This is equally important given the emerging scholarship on racial microaggressions (Sue, 2010; Yosso, Smith, Ceja, & Solórzano, 2010). Racial joking can easily become a microaggression, and this is important in terms of Students of Color in higher education. Sue (2010) further argued that racial microaggressions actually take a greater psychological toll on minorities than does overt racism because they are more prepared to deal with racial assaults that stem from the overt as opposed to the covert. Thus, racial joking is, from an empirical standpoint, not as innocuous as these White guys believed it to be. As they were telling these racist jokes and using the n-word behind closed doors, how did their actions affect Students of Color? Are they not self-contained? Again, the short answer is "no." These *backstage performances* (Picca & Feagin, 2007) are just on the cusp of slipping out into the general public, as demonstrated by the OU Sigma Alpha Epsilon incident (Cabrera, 2015).

As O'Connor (2002) outlined in her insightful *Oppression and Responsibility*, there is much more going on than simply students telling inappropriate jokes. From an environmental perspective, they are able to exist in racially homogenous, White environments where they are immune to criticism from People of Color. It is primarily within these environments and among peers whom they consider to be like-minded (i.e., those who would not "misconstrue" the jokes as racist) that the participants tell racist jokes. These environmental conditions highlight an institutional issue: compositional diversity alone is insufficient to disrupt campus balkanization. WU was approximately 35 percent White, while SWU was 65 percent, yet on both campuses White men were able to self-segregate. Within these White enclaves, both the joke tellers and listeners share responsibility for their respective roles in creating racist social practices. These White guys usually described how one of their friends told a joke, but within O'Connor's (2002) framework, those who are laughing at the racist jokes are also complicit in the reification of White supremacy via the tacit approval of racial joke telling.

Despite the engrained nature of these social practices, there is also possibility. As O'Connor (2002) offered, "It is extremely important for people to have intentions and interpretations of words and actions that are rebellious and undermine the dominant social practices" (p. 74). This requires a great deal of work to reach the point where White male undergraduates will even see racism as a problem (Reason & Evans, 2007). Many are unconsciously embedded within racially homogenous friendship groups where they see few signs of racial tension, which in turn signals that racism is of minimal importance (Cabrera, 2014d; Chesler, Peet, & Sevig, 2003). Only when they see racism as a pertinent issue that advantages White people and marginalizes People of Color can they begin to struggle against it (Reason & Evans, 2007). There is no silver bullet in promoting this development, and it is made increasingly difficult because, as Mills (1997) described, *Whiteness* is an epistemology of ignorance. Therefore, the first step in disrupting these racist social practices becomes disrupting the epistemology of ignorance that allows White males to frame racist actions as innocuous (Reason & Evans, 2007). Within this context, the narratives of these White guys I talked with point to some tensions that can be a starting point for posing the problem (Freire, 2000). If the jokes were as harmless as these White guys claim, why would they need to hide from People of Color to tell them? Why not talk with People of Color about these jokes instead of assuming they are "overly sensitive"?

5

"I Almost Lost My Spot to a Less Qualified Minority"

Imagined versus Real Affirmative Action

There are few places where the myth of "reverse racism" is manifest more than in White people's discussion of affirmative action (Bonilla-Silva, 2006; Cabrera, 2014d; Crosby, 2004). They myth of meritocracy runs deep in American society, and extensively documenting the effects of racism on contemporary inequality (e.g., Brown et al., 2003) has done little to stem this ideological orientation (Guinier, 2015). Taking this one step further, it has been well documented that White people frequently blame affirmative action when they do not earn a position or admission (Bonilla-Silva, 2006; Crosby, 2004). There is a very interesting vein of the social psychology literature that highlights how White people's belief that affirmative action is a quota system maintains their egos, and this trend is particularly pronounced among White men (e.g., Unzueta, Gutiérrez, & Ghavami, 2010; Unzueta, Lowery, & Knowles, 2008). That is, if they are not offered a position, White people frequently believe that affirmative action quotas gave it to the "less deserving" minority and the White people's positive sense of self remains intact. In other words, beliefs about affirmative action frequently become a crutch for White people to use to mask their own shortcomings.

Usually, White people's beliefs about affirmative action follow an arc that is decontextualized from the realities of contemporary systemic racism (e.g.,

Bonilla-Silva, 2006; Cabrera, 2014d; Crosby, 2004). Not surprisingly, the bulk of White men I talked with were against affirmative action, but there was a qualitative difference in their responses based upon which school they attended, and this was where things became really interesting. Those at SWU tended to oppose affirmative action but were not particularly troubled by it. For them, it was more of an abstraction—something they opposed in principle but not something that affected their day-to-day lives. Those at WU tended to be strongly against affirmative action and had a host of personal narratives that explained their opposition. These stories tended to focus on individual examples of a "more qualified" White person being rejected at the expense of a "less qualified" minority applicant. There is some overlap with the racial victimization the participants discussed in chapter 3, but there was a unique issue at play when discussing affirmative action.

Those students at WU tended to feel a lot more strongly against affirmative action and felt racially victimized by it (or "reverse racism"), even though they attended a university that had *not* practiced affirmative action for more than a decade due to a state proposition. In contrast, SWU *did* practice affirmative action, but the students were bordering on ambivalent about their opposition to this program. Strangely, the students at the university that no longer utilized affirmative action protocols felt oppressed by a program that existed only in their imagination. To explore this phenomenon, I offer some of these White guys' rationales about their opposition to affirmative action, specifically highlighting the differences that arose between those attending WU and SWU.

The "Threat" of Affirmative Action for Students at WU

Given the academic selectivity of WU, the White guys I interviewed at this institution were used to be being part of highly competitive admissions processes. This also meant a number of them received rejections and/or were waitlisted. When this occurred they consistently blamed affirmative action, even though it was not practiced at WU. For example, Jonathan was initially waitlisted and he described his immediate thought process: "I mean, I don't remember when I first learned of affirmative action, but when I didn't get accepted to WU and then I saw that these friends of mine did. . . . At least I thought they were friends of mine. . . . It's just frustrating, and even despite my own personal case, just the idea." It was really interesting because Jonathan was truly upset by being waitlisted, but instead of thinking he was not competitive enough, he blamed affirmative action. There was no way for him to know that affirmative action played a role, though he assumed it had. He offered an elaborate explanation of how he felt he was disadvantaged because he was White:

I mean, you have these two individuals, you know, you see them as completely clear from. . . . No race at all, just two people going to school and both working equally hard and trying to get into college, in my opinion the one who works harder or the one who has the greater desire to do it should be the one that has a greater chance of making it into a university. So, I think it should be totally based on academic ability, off of character, off of the attributes of the individual and have nothing to do with their skin because . . . or with their color or whatever because to me that's just not fair. It doesn't . . . like the end doesn't justify the means. You know, you have someone who works really hard and then they miss out because of their color.

Jonathan was very clear that he thought affirmative action not only was unfair in theory, but also discriminated against him as a White man. Jonathan developed a *sincere fiction* (Feagin & O'Brien, 2003) that affirmative action led to him being waitlisted. He had no evidence that affirmative action actually limited his opportunities, but he strongly believed it had.

Jonathan's sincere fiction formation did not begin with his being waitlisted. Rather, his older brother played an instrumental role in fostering the idea that WU continued to practice affirmative action. "I also knew already that WU has like a certain quota of races it tries to fill when it takes in students. I found that out from my brother. . . . It doesn't have to, it's not required, but it tries to obtain certain percentages of different ethnic classes." This combination of his brother's assurance and his own waitlisting helped Jonathan construct a reality that WU practiced not only affirmative action, which was outlawed more than a decade before the interview, but quota-based affirmative action, which was outlawed three decades earlier! I modestly challenged Jonathan on this, stating that affirmative action no longer existed. Instead of changing his view, he doubled down on his opposition to the program and returned to his original point: "I worked really hard and just the idea that maybe I could have been rejected based on my race just doesn't seem right, it doesn't seem fair because it goes against the very fabric of what freedom is."

It was interesting and bordering on bizarre how so many of the White men at WU were extremely opposed to affirmative action, said WU had a quota to fill for Students of Color, and claimed this potentially hurt them as White men. When I dug a little deeper, I discovered their basis for disdain was predicated on a shaky foundation. For example, Ryan described WU as having to fill a quota of Students of Color, and I probed on this issue:

N: Okay. And so then, in, in, in terms of your own personal experience, where do you—where have you been around situations where quotas needed to be filled?

R: Um, I personally haven't.

N: Do you know of people who have?

R: Um, no [laughs] I actually haven't.

This did not cause Ryan to self-reflect. Instead, he was staunchly opposed to affirmative action and thought that WU had a quota system and that it was unfair to White applicants—in particular White male applicants. His sudden awareness of his personal ignorance did nothing to change his viewpoint.

Derek offered a similar view to those of Jonathan and Ryan, but began from his general views on affirmative action and how White people in his experience see the program:

D: I think a lot of White people, especially those applying to colleges, they feel like if they didn't get into those colleges, "Oh, it's because of Affirmative Action. They let in a number of minorities and I would have gotten in normally." They feel like that they deserved it more.

N: Okay. Are their feelings warranted? Are their feelings justified?

D: I mean, obviously they were definitely good enough to get into the school perhaps, but because of affirmative action or certain things, like socioeconomic background, like reviews and everything, they didn't get in.

Derek was an interesting case because he heard a number of White people, especially men, get rejected from school and then blame affirmative action. He framed the issue as one where "obviously they were definitely good enough." Derek's immediate response was to assume the White men complaining about affirmative action were actually qualified for the position and that they were therefore being discriminated against. I explored this a little further and discovered his belief was largely because of his personal history with a university that practiced holistic review instead of affirmative action. He offered,

D: I definitely feel sympathy in regards to. . . . I wasn't accepted to [selective university] and so I remember when I first heard I wasn't accepted, the whole affirmative action thing ran through my head and stuff. . . .

N: Okay. That's interesting because . . . I mean, do you feel that holistic review is . . . represents Affirmative Action?

D: I think it's sort of a different form of Affirmative Action.

We had previously discussed the movement from affirmative action, where race was considered in the admissions process, to one of holistic review, with merit assessed based upon more than just test scores, but not including race. In Derek's understanding, this was a "backdoor form" of affirmative action. Much like the previous narratives, he did not have any experiences with admissions, did not study affirmative action, did not know people who worked in admissions, but he was still convinced that the practice discriminated against him as a White man. In this instance, it was the belief that holistic review was affirmative action in a "different form."

Andy moved the discussion beyond simply affirmative action in college admissions, although that is where he began. He started by undercutting what he thought was the primary rationale for affirmative action: racial discrimination. Andy offered, "I honestly can't imagine a university discriminating against minorities." In his view, this made affirmative action unnecessary; however, he still believed his university practiced it. He then couched his opposition affirmative action in terms of what he thought it does to racial minorities: "From what I've witnessed firsthand or just from what I've heard, just sort of the atmosphere here is that some students come here that are unqualified that they're from different minority groups, and then they have a really tough time adjusting and making it here." In his personal experience and the testimony of his peers, there were a number of unqualified minorities who attended his university and struggled. Andy offered that it would be more beneficial to all people (Whites and People of Color) if these spots went to "more qualified" White people. He directly blamed affirmative action for this trend that he and his friends saw and disregarded the idea that WU no longer practiced affirmative action. Andy then discussed the larger culture among White male undergraduates regarding their views on affirmative action: "Yeah, I've heard undergraduate students applying for an internship and when they don't get it, they say, 'It's because I'm a White male,' you know, and that's definitely making the accusation that affirmative action is why they didn't get in." Andy not only heard but also believed these narratives, and within his peer group there seemed to be a strong culture of racial victimization. That is, when they were selected for college admission or an internship, they earned it based on their own merit. Conversely, when they were rejected, it was due to affirmative action that "unfairly harmed" them as White men. What did not enter the equation was the possibility that they might not be as good as they thought, as meritorious as they thought, and that was the cause of their rejection. It was easier to concoct narratives about imaginary affirmative action programs. The (lack of) evidence these White men offered to substantiate their views that they were being discriminated against due to affirmative action was equally telling. It is worth noting that Andy's peers, in addition to feeling injured because they were White, also felt marginalized as a result of being male.

Creating Credibility: Testimonials and Personal Observations of Affirmative Action

The White male undergraduates I interviewed at WU tended to be very specific about how they formed their views on affirmative action. A number of them found personal testimonies, like the one from Jonathan's brother, particularly compelling when forming their views about affirmative action. George recalled in detail how his dad helped shape his beliefs on affirmative action as a boy. George's dad was a lawyer and frequently told the following story: "[Dad] mentioned—He's also against affirmative action. He mentioned that uh, uh, he said that there were twenty-six students who were let into his class by affirmative action. And I don't really know what that means. That might just mean that there were twenty-six Black students accepted to his class for law school." George admitted he was not entirely clear on the meaning of his father's claim, so I probed a little deeper:

N: How did your dad know they were let in [based on] affirmative action?
G: Uh, I think he just assumed.
N: Okay.
G: Because, I dunno, maybe he was hearing about affirmative action in the admission department, but I'm not sure about that.

George had to reflect a little and began to admit that this story he was telling was not based on the strongest factual foundation. What was interesting was that George was strongly against affirmative action and began offering this narrative to illustrate how he formed his opinion. With a little focused questioning, he started to doubt this foundation of his anti–affirmative action beliefs. As the previous chapters have demonstrated, George strongly believed that being White and male was a social disadvantage, but when we explored the foundations of the views, they began to fall apart.

George's subsequent statements were very telling because he decided to continue on the same vein as before—using his dad's story as an example of why affirmative action is an unfair and unmeritocratic program. He reiterated his dad's assumptions about the twenty-six Black students being "affirmative action admits," then centered minority student attrition as a reason for opposing affirmative action: "Uh, I dunno. Maybe they, they got, I assume- He assumes they were let in because they were Black, they were given, an unfair advantage getting in and then they ended up not being able to do the work, and failed out. And that takes away twenty spots from somebody like me who's trying to go to law school and could do the work. . . . But, but they're still getting preference. And, I mean, when, out of twenty-six guys let in, only four remain. I mean it, it, it's really upsetting and angering to White people." There was a lot going on in George's narrative. He gave a token nod to the idea that maybe his dad did not know what he was talking about. Despite this doubt, he built his beliefs on the following evidence: twenty-two Black students dropped out of his dad's law school class, leaving four. He then jumped to the conclusion that this must have been because affirmative action led to the admission of unqualified students. It was extremely telling the number of logical leaps George was willing to take instead of just admitting that maybe both he and his dad did not know what they were talking about when it came to affirmative action. Instead, he strongly believed that the Black students were "given preferences" and "taking away" spots from people like George who "could do the work."

Roger used a mixture of familial story and personal experience to develop his opposition to affirmative action. Like George, his understanding of affirmative action began with a family member, in this case his grandfather, describing the "evils" of university admissions systems. Unlike George, he did have more of a historical foundation for this belief, beginning with Jews being excluded from higher education via quota systems (Karabel, 2005); however, he then declared that contemporary affirmative action is also a quota system:

> So, I don't like affirmative action, the way the word tends to be used, because it usually. . . . It tends to talk about quota-based affirmative action, which is very disturbing to me. As a Jew, Jews were limited by quotas for years in higher education and it wasn't until about forty years ago when those were lifted in most schools. My grandfather is most proud of where he went to high school because he went to this very prestigious high school that he got on full aid when he was living in New York. During the same time of rampant anti-Semitism, before the Holocaust. And he was very proud of that and after that, largely because of the gentlemen's agreement if you will, and you're certainly familiar with the film and book, he wasn't able to go. He had better grades and scores than many of his classmates who were going to Stanford, Harvard, and Yale, and he got into USC which then was nowhere near as prestigious as it is now.

It has been well documented that quotas kept Jewish people from accessing higher education, in particular elite higher education (Karabel, 2005). Roger's grandfather's narrative is largely rooted in this historical reality.

Roger then linked his grandfather's story to the present to contextualize why he actively opposed affirmative action: "And here I am. But that is something that disturbs me a lot. Quotas bother me a lot, as a form of affirmative action." As I did with George, I probed Roger about his framing of affirmative action as a quota system, and he simply offered that this was what he understood the practice to be, and then he elaborated: "I think quota-based affirmative action is unfair to Whites. I mean the most obvious example is looking at very wealthy, privileged People of Color who have gone to schools like Harvard Westlake or whatever. Other private schools, prep schools, who get to go to the finest institutions in the world on the basis of their color. At the same time, there are so many poor White if you will, redneck, hick, whatever, elsewhere in this country who are not exposed to those opportunities for education and who in a certain sense are being punished by a system that is not interested in them." Roger believed WU practiced quota-based affirmative action and that it was unfair to White people. Part of his rationale came from personal experience at WU, where some affluent Students of Color attended. Ultimately, it was fascinating how he was so strongly against a program at WU that did not actually exist, in particular against a quota system that was outlawed in the 1970s.

There were others who relied on only personal experiences and observations to form their opinions about affirmative action. Hoyt was direct and said that he definitely believed affirmative action was a form of discrimination against White men. The evidence he offered for his opinion was very telling. It also made my head hurt a little. He stated,

> H: I would classify [affirmative action] as giving minorities a not necessarily fair advantage, but certainly a higher chance, which might . . . at attaining employment or higher education . . . which might come at the expense of Whites.
>
> N: And where does that information come from?
>
> H: That is primarily an opinion of mine derived from observation where I see different . . . businesses, primarily small businesses, or franchises that have probably a majority staff of minority workers.
>
> N: Could you give me an example?
>
> H: There is a local Burger King, which appears to be primarily staffed by Latinos. I haven't yet seen, to my knowledge, one White person there. But there may be somewhere I can't see.

Hoyt believed that affirmative action hurt the life chances of White people, but his example was a Burger King that employed only Latinxs. The obliviousness of this statement was mind-blowing. Burger King positions are largely minimum-wage ones, and the concentration of Latinxs in this area is more a function of the minimal opportunities afforded to them. Despite this reality, Hoyt interpreted this situation as one that marginalized White people. He had to be a relatively intelligent person due to his acceptance to the highly competitive WU, but this did not translate into an ability to interpret and understand this social issue. His narrative would be almost comical if it did not have potentially devastating consequences for the People of Color whom Hoyt will be interacting with in the future.

Finally, several participants at WU blamed affirmative action for campus racial unrest. That is, in their personal experiences they saw the campus as a racially tense place and believed affirmative action was the cause. This became part of their basis for opposing the program, as Jeremy explained: "I just want to say . . . I'm sorry, one more thing. About affirmative action, I think the process itself is creating prejudices because of the fact that there is not really affirmative action for Whites. That's my knowledge of the program, and I think because of that, because minorities are the ones that are utilizing affirmative action, it's going to create tension. The program itself is going to create tension, so I think it's just embedded within affirmative action that there's going to be conflict. I just wanted to say that." Jeremy's views are telling in a number of ways. First, he blamed a nonexistent program for fostering prejudice that led to campus tension. Second, even if affirmative action did exist, Jeremy disregarded the idea that campus racial tension may be a type of preexisting condition. In his lived experiences, generally among other White people, Jeremy did not experience a lot of racial tension or discrimination. Within this context, he blamed race-conscious social programming for fostering prejudice instead of seeing it as an antidote to racism.

The White male undergraduates at WU offered detailed, specific examples of their thought processes regarding affirmative action, and they voiced a strong sense of frustration and anger at the program—again, one that *did not* exist. Responses at SWU were dramatically different. Students there tended to oppose affirmative action, and their responses were vague and less passionate.

Affirmative Action, Ambivalence, and Misrepresentation at SWU

Most of the White guys at SWU had not really thought about affirmative action much, which was interesting because SWU did have an affirmative action program at the time of these interviews. They knew the program existed, but did not know a lot about it or how it operated. Within this context, they had views on the program, just not strong ones. Kevin, who was a prime example of this, described affirmative action as follows: "I've had somebody explain it to me that it's whenever you apply for a job, if there's candidates and the majority of the firm is of one race and the candidates are basically equal and one's of that race that the rest of the firm is and the other is not, they would pick the one that is not, so . . . and that might be a misunderstanding. I don't know." Kevin admitted that his description might be a misunderstanding, and that fundamentally he did not know. It was interesting how he learned about affirmative action through personal narrative, like many of the White guys in the previous section, but this story was not told as a racial parable—that affirmative action did or will oppress him. It was more of a description devoid of passion or investment. Kevin was still opposed to the program: "I guess I don't see it as the most unfair or the greatest evil or whatever, but I do . . . I wouldn't have put it in place, so I'm opposed to it, but I guess not that strongly opposed." In this part of the interview, it almost seemed like Kevin was making up his mind regarding his opposition or support of the program on the spot. He began by saying it was not the biggest evil in the world, then paused, regrouped, expressed his opposition to affirmative action, then framed his position as relatively weak.

Jack was similar to Kevin. He opposed affirmative action, but also lumped all race-conscious programming under this umbrella. He actually focused his answer on race-specific scholarships but, like Kevin, did not have a lot of information on the subject and expressed an opposition that was relatively tepid: "It's nothing that I've really researched myself. There's a general idea or education about it throughout high school and whatnot, especially with scholarships and stuff like that. When you're starting to get into college, that's when you really, really see it." Jack became more aware of the program when he entered college, but also admitted that he had not researched it himself. It did not really affect him in a meaningful way—his family was not struggling to support him financially through college and his acceptance to SWU was never in question. Justin offered a similar view from the orientation of being a White male from a relatively affluent family: "I was applying for colleges and stuff like that, I felt kind of . . . not that I ever had to worry about college money or anything like that because I always did very well academically and I got all my scholarships before I even left high school, but I felt that if I were to be a minority student, I felt like I could get more of these types of scholarships. . . . I got a book for college, it was like 5001 Tips for College or something like that . . . and I would flip through the book and I'd see Hispanic Fund, Black Fund, Feminist Fund." A key to Justin's narrative was that he never "had to worry about college money." While he exaggerated the prevalence of race-specific scholarships, as demonstrated in chapter 3, he was neither angry nor frustrated. He opposed race-conscious programming, but not strongly. Like Jack, he (mis)understood affirmative action to be anything race-conscious, did not think about it much, and did not see it as a program that had a meaningful, adverse impact on his life.

Ken's beliefs were slightly different because he was struggling more to pay for college, and therefore seeing race-conscious scholarships piqued his opposition to this mislabeled affirmative action. However, his angst was tepid relative to the responses from students at WU. He elaborated, "I was looking at scholarships offered by SWU and they have scholarships that are directly . . . like the Hispanic Foundation Scholarship, the African American Foundation . . . you know, of that type and they have one of those for every single possible group . . . and the only one that's not specifically mentioned is White men and I can see how that . . . I mean, it angered me a little bit. I was like, 'Well, if they're going to help everyone, why aren't they helping us?' So, kind of either help everyone or don't help anyone." Even in this case, Ken's anger was not nearly as strong as that of the students at WU who were visibly upset by affirmative action—even though it was imaginary. As Ken said, it angered him "a little bit." He was mad but not *that* mad.

Martin was more strongly against affirmative action, but not because he saw it adversely affecting him personally. Rather, it offended his conservative values: "But to answer your question, just because I'm a conservative, just because I oppose something like affirmative action or just because I believe that people use racism . . . or people use the existence of racism inappropriately to justify things that really shouldn't be justified." Martin was very sensitive to people referring to conservative ideas and legislation as racist, and he also believed that liberals used racism to justify programs that in his mind should not exist. In his understanding, it was actually race-conscious programs that were the racist ones: "Well, absolutely. I think, to be honest with you, that affirmative action is inherently racist." Unlike many of the participants at WU, Martin had a relatively nuanced understanding of affirmative action. He discussed how it was initially a quota-based system, but that specific practice was outlawed a few decades earlier, even though the program continued. Interestingly, none of the conversation centered on affirmative action at WU. Instead, it was more about affirmative action in society at large.

Jeff had the strongest opposition to affirmative action of the White men at SWU, but he also came from a slightly different context. He originally was from California and had a personal narrative to share, just as those at WU did; this one centered on his brother and his brother's girlfriend:

> I mean, my brother had a girlfriend in high school who was El Salvadorian, very Hispanic . . . not Hispanic, very Latino and didn't speak much English. My brother tutored her and she got about a 4.1 I think in high school and my brother got about 4.3, and my brother applied to [selective school]. He didn't get in, so that's why he went to [less selective school] and then she got into [the selective school brother initially applied]. For what reasons . . . you know, they applied for the same majors, the same things, the same essays essentially. I think he wrote them for her. And so just why didn't my brother get in, but she did? Well, you have this Latino girl who doesn't speak English and doesn't come from that much money, but then my brother's a White wealthy male from, you know, a suburb of Los Angeles. I don't know. It broke my brother's heart because he wanted to go to [selective school].

It was interesting how Jeff framed his brother's girlfriend as "very Hispanic," meaning she did not speak English well. He then portrayed her as almost dependent on his brother academically, even to the extent that he might have written her college essays. It was a narrative fraught with both racist and sexist overtones, as the "very Hispanic" female could not possibly have gained entrance into a selective university of her own merit. Jeff was primarily concerned with the plight of his brother, a "White wealthy male." Within this context, Jeff was strongly opposed to affirmative action because the rejection from the selective school broke his brother's heart. Again, the interesting part about his narrative was that it fell into the same imagined affirmative action that so many at WU were railing against. The specific school his brother was rejected from also did not practice affirmative action. Thus, the pain his brother felt was absolutely real. Affirmative action keeping him out, however, was not.

Imagined Affirmative Action: What Is Going on Here?

The narratives of the White guys in this chapter are both fascinating and frustrating because of the massive disconnect between perception and reality. Those at WU, where affirmative action was not practiced, felt threatened by a nonexistent program, relying on what Mills (1997) referred to as an "invented delusional world" (p. 18) to justify their beliefs. They developed their views through a combination of interpersonal narratives as well as personal observations, but when challenged by the fact that affirmative action no longer existed at WU, they stubbornly refused to believe it. They were steadfast in their views that WU practiced affirmative action and that it could potentially harm them as White men. Their feelings are doubly fascinating because they had already gained admission to WU—their place at the institution was not threatened.

Conversely, those at SWU tended to be ambivalent about affirmative action. They did not like the program, but were not wholeheartedly against it. Most acknowledged they did not know much about the program, and it was almost as if they were forming their opinions about affirmative action as they spoke with me. This stood in stark contrast to the WU students who were retelling stories and views they had held for years. The major exceptions were Martin and Jeff. For Martin, affirmative action was an affront to his conservative values. While he thought about affirmative action more than most, he was not very strongly opposed. Jeff, on the other hand, saw the painful process his brother experienced being rejected by a selective university. His narrative was interesting on multiple levels. First, he used the *sincere fiction* (Feagin & O'Brien, 2003) that many of the WU students relied upon—that affirmative action was responsible for keeping White people out even though it was no longer practiced. Second, his narrative was rooted strongly in his White and male immunity. That is, as a self-described "rich White guy from Los Angeles," he did not have to see the pain experienced by many qualified minority students who were also rejected. Instead, he centered his brother's pain and was even able to elevate it as unique and a cause of outrage.

So what is going on here? White narratives of "reverse racism" are very common in the scholarly literature (e.g., Bonilla-Silva, 2006; Cabrera, 2014d; Chesler, Peet, & Sevig, 2003) and are extremely easy to find in popular culture. Frequently, affirmative action is at the center (or at least part) of these discussions. Rarely, however, are the views on affirmative action among White people, especially White men, so varied. One part of this puzzle might be the institutional contexts. WU is an academically competitive institution, while SWU is almost an open-access university, as approximately 80 percent of students who apply gain admission. SWU also costs substantially less than WU. These two stressors, academic competition and finances, might be the causes of this differentiation. That is, the students at WU were constantly pushing themselves academically, while many at SWU coasted through high school, taking required classes and earning a 3.3 GPA. It also helped that the strong majority of those at SWU were comfortably members of the middle or upper-middle classes. Thus, being in competition for admission or scholarships was generally not on the minds of the SWU White guys I talked with.

Central to these narratives is the perceived threat the White guys I talked with felt. In one of the classic sociological statements on race, Blumer (1958) argued that racial prejudice is a form of group positioning. Bobo and Tuan (2006) further developed this concept when analyzing a dispute between White people in Minnesota and Native people trying to exercise their treaty rights (e.g., spearfishing). The more the Natives pushed for what was their inalienable right, the stronger White people expressed their opposition and verbalized racism. Returning to the narratives in these interviews, it was easy for most at SWU to not form opinions about affirmative action on their campus because it largely did not affect them personally. Their sense of group positioning was not threatened. Conversely, those at WU were so threatened by affirmative action that they concocted stories about a program infringing on their fundamental freedoms that did not even exist. This is the power of the White imagination (Morrison, 1992) as well as White racial emotions (Cabrera, 2014b; Matias, 2016). The factual absence of affirmative action was not relevant to the students at WU.

One additional component of this group positioning is the issue of ego maintenance, as explored in chapter 2. That is, some scholars argue that a lot of racial views stem from White people, in particular White men, wanting to maintain a positive sense of self (Unzueta et al., 2010; Unzueta, & Lowery, 2008; Unzueta et al., 2008). For example, a number of White men I interviewed framed affirmative action as a quota system, even though this type of affirmative action was outlawed decades before the interviews occurred. Unzueta et al. (2008) specifically demonstrated that the more White men viewed affirmative action as a quota, the more their beliefs preserved their self-esteem. That is, if they earned a position, they did so of their own merit. If they were rejected, it was because an "undeserving" minority took their position due to a quota system. Either way, the White men did not have to consider their own relative merit in the situation. Rather than thinking they were not qualified or competitive, they were able to blame imagined affirmative action.

Please do not misinterpret these findings to say that students at WU were bad and those at SWU were good. They all tended to be strongly rooted in a color-blind view of U.S. race relations (see chapter 2), and it is likely that the SWU White men, if challenged, would react in kind. It would be really interesting to follow up with them as they enter an incredibly competitive workforce to see to what degree this speculation actually comes true. Regardless, the findings from this chapter send a troubling message. That is, the White men at WU were generally oblivious to the realities of race, and this contextualized their beliefs about affirmative action. Their views were almost always framed as something being wrong with the program or with those in society who advocate being race-conscious. Noticeably absent from their narratives was their own individual responsibility as White members of a racist society. I was reminded of a quotation from James Baldwin's *The Fire Next Time*: "Therefore, a vast amount of the energy that goes into what we call the Negro problem is produced by the white man's profound desire not to be judged by those who are not white, not to be seen as he is, and at the same time a vast amount of the white anguish is rooted in the white man's equally profound need to be seen as he is, to be released from the tyranny of his mirror" (Baldwin, 1963, p. 109). In many respects, the White men at WU wanted to be released from the "tyranny of their own mirrors" and construct a fictional world where they could be the real victims of racism via affirmative action. This is troubling because it is difficult to determine what can be done with this analysis. To borrow from Bush (2011), where are the *cracks in the wall of Whiteness*? While the narratives do not offer much along these lines, I think there are two key points that White men need to continually hear from the administration, professors, student affairs professionals, and their peers. First, if you were rejected from a position, it was probably because you were not good enough and had nothing to do with affirmative action. Second, due to White immunity (and male immunity), you are at the greatest systemic advantage of anyone on the campus, so give "reverse racism" a rest. Focus on real instead of imagined problems. The first point is especially important in contexts like WU, where affirmative action is not practiced. Left to their own devices, the racial imaginations of these White men are going to run wild, and the more they feel threatened, the greater the perceived anti-White racism becomes. Or, to borrow from the hip-hop group the Geto Boys, *their mind's playing tricks on them* (Jordan, King, Dennis, & GTA, 1991).

6

"They'd Never Allow a
White Student Union"

The Racial Politics of Campus
Space and Racial Arrested
Development

Questions of race frequently center people and social structures, but what about physical space? George Lipsitz's (2011) *How Racism Takes Place* both addresses this issue and is a frequently misunderstood title. Many interpret it to mean a description of how racism is manifest. Instead, it is a searing analysis of how systemic racism confers ownership (*takes*) of space (*place*) to White people. This issue has gained a great deal of contemporary attention as issues of gentrification, especially in the San Francisco Bay Area, are highlighting the displacement of low-income Communities of Color to make room for largely White "tech bros" (McElroy, 2018).

Critical philosopher Shannon Sullivan (2006) developed the concept of *ontological expansiveness* to describe one central facet of this intersection of race and space. In her theorizing, Sullivan argued that a core component of Whiteness is that White people act as though all space (literal and figurative) should be open and accessible to them. This is frequently rooted in a color-blind view of the world (Bonilla-Silva, 2006). Derek, one of the White guys I interviewed, was very passionate about this issue: "I think it's because I personally don't . . . like race is not really an issue in the sense that it's like it doesn't matter what race you are, you can attain anything, you can do whatever you want, you can marry whoever you want." Derek believed that people in the United States can do anything, attain anything, and even marry anyone, and race does not play a role. This is a very common yet profoundly naïve comment. Race and racism inform almost every facet of contemporary life, inequitably structuring access, opportunity, and success in favor of White people (Bonilla-Silva, 2001, 2006; Brown et al., 2003; Omi & Winant, 2015). What is interesting when diving into these narratives of open access to all physical and cultural space is that they almost always, from the perspective of the White guys I talked with, involved White people feeling excluded. That is, they almost never discussed the ways that People of Color or Students of Color are excluded from space (Ross, 2015). Rather, the subtext of "all people" should have access to space frequently and implicitly meant "White people." Ultimately, these discussions centered the intersection of race and space even though the White guys I talked with were not explicitly asked about this issue.

Understanding Space as Raced

At the beginning of the interviews, I asked the White guys to offer a definition of racism while also giving a contemporary example. I had to add the modifier "contemporary" because I kept getting some version of the response Lance offered: "Slavery and all the aftermath of that would be an example of historical racism." While obvious, examples like this do little to explain how these White guys understand how racism contextualizes their experiences here and now. After working beyond this initial hiccup, the examples of racism they gave frequently centered the intersection of race and space.

The White guys tended to racialize regions of the country, whether this was intentional or not. Specifically, they tended to think of places outside their hometowns as being racist or having racial issues, in particular the South. Concurrently, they tended to *not* think of areas close to themselves as being racist. For example, Ryan offered the following:

N: Okay, can you give an example more contemporarily?
R: Uh, of racism?
N: Yeah.
R: That still occurs? Like the KKK that's still around, but that's somewhere in the South. I don't know.

Ryan struggled to name a specific example of contemporary racism, but he thought the KKK still existed. To the extent that it still existed, it was primarily in the South. He elaborated further: "I live in California and California's such a diverse state that … I mean … I'm sure there's people here that could be similar, you know, associate with the KKK. But I mean, in my experience, I've never met anyone." Ryan held a very narrow view of what constituted racism, and this included manifestations like cross-burnings and lynchings. He was very clear, however, that racism was not part of the fabric of "diverse" California. Instead, it was a problem elsewhere, like in the South.

This was fascinating because he did not see race playing a role in his hometown while in grade school, even though (or maybe because) it was overwhelmingly White. However, this dynamic changed as more People of Color moved into his home neighborhood, which Ryan described: "And so . . . um . . . the more ghetto people if you wanna say, are moving into the suburbs. And um, that's basically what's happened to my neighborhood." Both the attention that Ryan gave this issue and the lack of attention he gave his previously vanilla suburb were telling on a number of levels. First, his comments highlighted how he did not consider it a problem when his suburban existence had a large percentage of White people and Whiteness was the norm. Second, when people engaged in what Bourgois (2003) referred to as a *violation of American apartheid*, Ryan experienced "a racial issue." That is, there were unspoken rules of racial separation in the contemporary U.S. context, but they became visible only when people violated those norms. In this instance, it was when People of Color came into the suburbs. When it was largely White people in a White environment, he saw no issue.

Jay also came from a suburban community, but he did not experience any of the demographic shifts Ryan described. Instead, his hometown was strongly White, and for Jay that also meant there were no racial issues. That is, racial tension was a problem for other communities, just not his: "Well, I actually. . . . My high school was probably 95 percent White or Caucasian, so race was just not anything that was ever talked out, was not anything that was ever brought up, just because there was just a lack of ethnic, or lack of ethnicity or lack of racial groups at my school, so it was one of those things where it was out of side, out of mind." Jay believed the relative social tranquility of his hometown as meaning that there was not an issue of racism there. This is a very common way of framing racial issues and reminded me of Lewis' (2003) *Race in the Schoolyard*. At the school Lewis studied where White people were in the supermajority, she continually heard them say that race was not an issue in this area. That was a problem in more "diverse" areas, overlooking the idea that segregation does not simply happen by accident.

Trevor implicitly understood the intersection of race and space. He and his high school friend would go to the movies together, and there was frequently a discussion of which theater to go to. Race played an interesting role in these decisions: "And I have a White friend there who um, didn't want to go to the movie theatre there because he had an experience. . . . The movie theatre was heavily, you know, mostly Black people who went to this theatre. And he has this experience where these, you know, Black people were being really loud, and like talking through the movie. And he was like, 'Let's go to [other side of town].' Which is the White place where there won't be talking." Trevor was very explicit in the way he and his friends understood these spaces as racialized. One side of town was the Black side, the other was White. In the Black side of town, they, as White people, experienced some degree of social discomfort. These discussions about the intersection of race and space were not limited to their precollege experiences, as they also played out when the White guys offered their narratives of university life.

Race and University Campus Space

Much like perceptions of society in general, the White guys I spoke with implicitly understood campus-based spaces to also have racial dimensions. Much like the narratives in chapter 2, Mark saw the housed Greek system as being White dominated. Unlike the narratives in chapter 2, Mark was moderately critical of this issue: "Um, and especially when you think a big part of the social scene comes through uh, the Greek system. And the Greek system is very, very segregated. Like there's no Black people in, uh, in our fraternity. Um, it's kind of, it perpetuates the uh, a kind of a self-segregation model, you know?" Now, Mark did not think that any tangible steps needed to be taken to racially integrate the housed Greek system at his university, but he did see it as a form of White self-segregation. Within this paradigm, it was not coincidental that his fraternity had no Black people and Whiteness was the cultural norm. Again, Mark was not so troubled by this form of campus-based racial exclusion that he thought reform was necessary. Rather, this was an observation he made about his campus and the intersection of race and space.

Also telling was when the unspoken rules governing these spaces were violated. For example, Trevor described being at parties on campus with mostly White people in attendance. He described the social dynamic changing dramatically when Black people showed up:

T: Certainly, I've been, I've been to parties, for instance, where a bunch of Black people walk in.

N: Mhm.

T: And, you know, they're dressed differently. They're dressed like, you know, in African American fashion. Which is different.

N: What do you mean by different? Like what, er—or them specifically, what did they—

T: Them specifically, okay. Like, bigger pants, you know? Saggy, baseball hats, big polo shirts, you know, it's just tons of like, students dress like that. But there was definitely this question, are these people violent?

Trevor's description was interesting on a number of levels. Although many students on campus dressed in "African American fashion," especially White students, only when Black people showed up in a White space dressed like this did it become a problem for him and his friends. Trevor was then very open about his apprehension, and many of his friends shared this feeling. He elaborated, "Immediately, because they were Black, we said, er, people thought, you know, there's this immediate thought in your mind, 'Oh, you know, these um— these, these people don't belong here.'" The lack of belonging stemmed from them being Black in an ostensibly White space, which led to White social unease. Trevor then described that the Black people at the party would be closely scrutinized until it was proven that they were students. Essentially, they were guilty until proven innocent due to White fear.

Bernard was very explicit about the dividing lines on campus in terms of the physical geography: "Well, I'd say there's . . . sort of the White half of the university and then there's the Black half of the university, and then . . . well, the Hispanic and Asian populations aren't large enough to sustain." Bernard was clear that there was a strong division between the Black and White halves of campus and that people did not mix across these lines. It was more telling that Bernard framed the White and Black sections as "halves" considering that during his undergraduate years the Black population composed about 4 percent of the student population. Despite the questionable accuracy of Bernard's statement regarding the demographic profile of his campus, he still felt that it was heavily segregated and that certain areas were culturally owned by different segments of the population.

Lance was particularly critical of Students of Color on campus whom he saw as taking over different space in his college environment. He was direct about his condemnation of the practice: "I think they're horribly wrong to engage in this sort of race-based self-segregation." Lance never held White students accountable for campus self-segregation. It was only when Students of Color did it that he saw it as a problem. He elaborated his reasoning: "Just grouping together on the basis of race, this so called self-segregation, right? I mean that's a force of racism even though they're not really discriminating against anyone else. The point is that they're forming associations with other people on the basis of their race or if they think of themselves. Even, forget about their actions with other people. Just thinking about yourself, like, as your 'core identity' as like being part of some race. I mean, that's a racist attitude or view, so that would be, you know, these instances of racism." Lance viewed anything race-conscious as a form of racism, consistent with his Objectivist beliefs. Therefore, when Students of Color had groups centered around their racial/ethnic identity, Lance found this to be a form of racism. This also meant that if student groups had a White-dominant population but did not have "White" in their name, they were not being racist. He specifically discussed the Russian club may have a majority White membership, but that was not an example of racism because they were grouping based upon an intellectual interest. Groups like MEChA and the Black Student Union, by contrast, were in his view gathering based upon race.[1] Lance then continued that he thought a lot of campus unrest came from the spaces where Students of Color in race/ethnic-specific campus organizations congregated: "Yeah, I think that the racial minorities who clamor the most about racism on campus are the most guilty of self-segregation and racism itself.... You know, they're the ones that are kind of, you know, grouping themselves together in these racial groups and saying, 'We the victims.' The Blacks or you know the Latinos or the Asian American Pacific Island, you fill in the, you know, blank classification. Um, Middle East groups, you know they race groups or anyway. This is clanism. So, I think that's the most prevalent racism on campus." Again, Lance did not criticize spaces where White people congregated as being a form of campus-based racism. Instead, he thought these groups were the most culpable, as he offered this was the "most prevalent" form of racism on his campus. Within these environments, Lance saw the strongest vestiges of campus-based racism he could identify. The tension regarding cultural ownership over campus space quickly led many of the White guys to claim that they as White men were being excluded from fully participating in university life.

Campus Space and "White Male Exclusion"

As demonstrated in chapters 3 and 5, narratives of "reverse racism" were very strong among the White guys. Not surprisingly, as they gained an awareness that space was raced, this also tended to trigger a feeling of "reverse racism." Please be clear that there were some White guys I spoke with who acknowledged that some areas on campus, in particular the Greek system, were ostensibly White. These areas did not lead them to claim that racism was at play. It was primarily when space was racially normed in favor of minoritized students that the White guys felt excluded or marginalized. Returning to the example of the Greek system, Bernard was very direct:

Q: Do you consider a Black fraternity to be a racist organization?
A: Yeah, if they're not allowing different races in or they're ... I mean, they're allowing it unofficially, but not practically allowing.... Well, I suppose you could argue that any type of club or organization that specifically limits itself to a certain race, like if you had a Black fraternity or an Hispanic fraternity or what have you, then you could argue that that's racism.

This was really interesting because most thought that the traditional Greek system was dominated by White people, but for Bernard minority fraternities were the ones that were racially exclusive in their membership. That is, when White people congregate together, it is happenstance. When minoritized students do it, it is an example of "racism" or "exclusion" against White people.

Minority-focused Greek organizations were not the only ways that the White guys saw space being "taken over" by Students of Color. Many expressed tension and social discomfort when the campus space was no longer White. Hoyt spoke of campus-based groups that have a specific racial/ethnic focus: "I've observed a high number of minority-focused groups on campus that I would have to judge to be exclusive to members of those ethnic groups and so they do, in my opinion, do a lot of self-segregation, and therefore not mixing as much with Whites. . . . And because of that, I think that, Whites tend to feel like they don't want to mix with them, so they tend not to feel quite as welcoming." Hoyt directly linked the issue of "self-segregation" to minority student groups on campus, and then blamed this phenomenon for causing White people to not feel welcome in certain spaces. Again, and noticeably absent from Hoyt's understanding, was that White racism might play a role in this dynamic. Instead, he believed it was squarely the fault of Students of Color for fracturing the campus environment. This was consistent with Hoyt's beliefs about "affirmative action at Burger King" marginalizing White men.

Kurt was an interesting case. He still blamed Students of Color for creating space-based division across campus as he succinctly explained, "It seems like they do definitely segregate." Kurt then explored what it would mean for him to enter non-White campus space: "I mean, personally it would probably be hard for me to approach a group. Not because of how I view them, but just because how they might view me." What was interesting about his narrative was that he did not frame the issue entirely in terms of Students of Color being "standoffish." Rather, he was honest about his nervousness in how they might perceive him as a White man entering this space. Unfortunately, that moment of reflection was quickly overshadowed by a return to the framing of the issue where Students of Color self-segregate, and that, in his understanding, was the center of the problem.

Andy was very frustrated by people on his campus who gathered by their racial/ethnic background. Actually, and as a point of clarification, he was frustrated when minoritized students grouped together. Consistent with the other White guys in this chapter, he rarely saw a problem when White people grouped together. Andy began by outlining what he saw as the line of demarcation he, as a White man, could not cross: "Student groups on campus have such diverse interests that their one commonality is their race that it's hard for someone else to sort of enter." Andy moved beyond this line a few times, and his narrative quickly turned into one of "reverse racism": "When I try to interact sometimes with these groups, I'm the one who's subject to racism because it's almost like they're either assuming that I'm going to be the racist or they're just . . . and I'm saying 'they' in the most general sense, just people that form a cluster . . . sort of, I don't know, maybe feel threatened by me possibly as a White male, but with that being said, there are often times where I'm the only White guy in a group and perfectly comfortable." It was interesting because Andy was one of the few White guys who actually did have some substantive interactions across race/ethnicity on campus. Within these, he did find himself as the only White guy in social circles, but also felt that there was a social unease by racial minorities with him in the group. He speculated that it might be due to them thinking he was going to be racist, or some undefined threat that he as a White man posed. Andy did not know what that threat might be due to his White immunity, but he also said White people generally felt uncomfortable when they entered these spaces: "I think that there's a great degree to which there is an ethnocentrism of these groups and to which other people are not welcome. I have friends who have been . . . who have gone to different other student groups and tried to fit in but felt very uncomfortable as everybody was looking at them as they were the only non-Chicano/Chicana person in the room or the only person that wasn't of color." This was fascinating because Andy was direct, placing blame on Students of Color in general, and Chicana/os in particular, for being "ethnocentric" and "unwelcoming." When I probed a little deeper, I discovered that Andy's friends who went into these Chicana/o spaces were White, as I expected. That is, when he said "my friends," he meant "my White friends." He did not initially offer this in his narrative, falling into the trend of leaving White as an unmarked social identity while identifying all others (Sue, 2010). Andy's White friends were extremely uncomfortable being the only White people in a campus environment; however, it never occurred to Andy that this might be the way that many Chicanx students on campus regularly feel given the dismal number of these students on campus. Rather, Andy had a great deal of empathy for White students experiencing this and little for Students of Color. In addition to the physical environment, the intersection of race and space also involved issues of curricular and linguistic space.

Multicultural Curriculum and Disrupting White Cultural Norms in Classroom Space

The White guys, as demonstrated in chapter 2, were strongly oriented in a color-blind worldview. They tended to deny the relevance or power of contemporary racism, and Bonilla-Silva (2006) argues that this ideology is actually a form of racism because of how entrenched White advantage is in society. Most of the White guys had unremarkable narratives about race in their classrooms. For example, Ryan said, "Um, well, I'm an econ student, so a lot of stuff they don't really talk about the race of the person." Most were comfortable in their classes as long as there were no explicit discussions of race and racism in these spaces.

However, when the norm of color-blindness was disrupted in classrooms and curricula, the responses were very telling. For example, Jonathan took a Chicano literature course, and while he found the content interesting, he felt that it was too oriented toward analyses of race and racism. He was not entirely comfortable with this: "After taking this class, from everything I was taught and from everything we discussed, I honestly felt I could just write in my bluebook, 'White people are evil,' and I would get an A. That was a sincere feeling. It literally felt like that, just . . . I mean, I was the only White person in class . . . I mean, there were obviously clusters, but just the sentiment that came out was basically, you know, I'd just write, 'White people are evil,' and I'd be guaranteed an A, that's the way it felt." To Jonathan, ideology trumped analysis. That is, the way to succeed in the Chicano literature class was to toe the line that "White people are evil." Now, Jonathan did not actually complete his test booklet with such a basic answer, so I probed as to why he felt that way. He elaborated,

> The whole class was about how terrible the United States was and the discrimination against Hispanics, which some parts of it are absolutely true, but it's almost like they try to pin it on people nowadays, you know, the faults of people in the past on people who have no idea of what happened, don't even have the ability to know history when they're born. But they're White, so they're painted to be these monsters, and it's just every lecture as we moved through history from the conquest of Central America to the present. You have . . . I mean, you have just White people are terrible. And some of the things they did, like for example California, you have the divestment of the ranchero owners and by the White people moving and. . . . Yeah, the laws were basically made to be in favor of what the White people were doing and disfavor of what any other race was doing.

Jonathan did not dispute the factual accuracy of the history he was learning. What he objected to was that he and White people like him were in some way complicit for this history, and this became another example of Yes, but. . . . Yes horrible things have been done to Latinx people, but it is not my fault. It was really interesting because a factually accurate history, in Jonathan's framing, painted White people as "monsters." In classroom space where racism was ignored, he was comfortable; where racism was engaged, he was uncomfortable.

Dwight had a similar reaction to a curriculum that engaged issues of race, although he did not feel as strongly as Jonathan. He began by talking very generally about being aggravated when issues of racism arose on campus in general. I tried to more specifically identify the source of his angst, and Dwight was very clear that it happened in classroom space.

N: Okay. Why do you say you get aggravated? First of all, who brings up issues
of race and . . . ?

D: It happens in classrooms all the time.

N: Okay, like in classes here or classes that you're teaching.

D: Yeah, race. . . . Because I'm a literature. . . . So, when we . . . you know, we'll
read something by Toni Morrison and race will get brought up and
inevitably we get to racism here, racism on campus. . . . It just seems like
we're beating a dead horse.

Dwight, like Jonathan, had difficulty in classroom space where issues of race
were engaged. It was really interesting that he would be flippant about reading
something by Toni Morrison considering she is a Nobel laureate. That issue
aside, Dwight was not only uncomfortable with race being part of the classroom environment, but doubly uneasy when those discussions were linked to
contemporary society. He was generally skeptical that race was an important
societal issue, so when the color-blindness of classroom space was disrupted,
he saw it as "beating a dead horse."

Lance spoke more generally about these issues, expressing disdain at liberal
professors in the academy who "made everything about race." Again, Lance's
framing was really interesting because he did not think that racism was an
important societal issue beyond a few bad actors. He elaborated on how he
thought that these contests over space take place in academia: "Yeah, you now,
there's an example of Whites being racist against themselves. This is sort of
just their ingrained. . . . You know having to view everything in terms of race
and racism. I think it's a very predominate view in academia. You know trying
to [whispers] make everything about race. The pinnacle of that will be when
we have, you know, the Chicano Math Department." Lance generally dismissed racism as a system or structure of society, and placed all onus on individual actors as either racist or not. He postulated that, if multicultural higher
education was taken to its logical conclusion, there would eventually could be a
Chicano Math Department. These examples of race-conscious classroom space
led these White guys to feel uneasy and sometimes upset. They generally did not
want to engage with issues of racism as a system of oppression, and definitely did
not feel they had any responsibility for it. They also felt a great deal of unease
when campus space was no longer color-blind, and this corresponded to more
feelings of "reverse discrimination" or "White exclusion." Not as frequently discussed, the White guys also explored the intersection of race and language.

Race and Linguistic Space

The intersection of race and language became another strong line of demarcation regarding race and space. In particular, when minoritized populations spoke

languages other than English, this was another marker of space and perceived division that these White guys discussed. Devin was particularly critical of what he perceived to be Latinx students "self-segregating," and language played a central role in his unease: "You know, we're outside of class, they tend to . . . seem to want to speak in Spanish, to speak Spanish with each other, and that just I think sort of contributed to it, that we felt that they weren't necessarily approachable, that they weren't interested in approaching us and so on and so forth." For Devin, it was not just that there was physical separation between White and Latinx students on campus. Rather, their speaking Spanish signaled to him and a number of his White friends that Latinx students were not "approachable." That was really interesting because the Latinx students were obviously not talking to Devin or his friends while they were speaking Spanish. Yet, the message that sent to this group of White men was one of exclusion.

George felt the same way about Asian Americans on his campus. He not only was critical of Asian Americans clustering by race, but also felt uneasy when they were speaking non-English languages within their friendship groups: "I mean, I don't think there's problems with race on campus, but people do feel very separated. Like people think, I mean, there are barriers when interacting with people. I mean, the fact that there's groups of ten, fifteen Asian people all speaking Chinese to each other." It is interesting that George not only located issues of campus self-segregation among Asian Americans, but also included language barriers as part of this discussion. He never mentioned that White people bear responsibility for the separation of races on campus, what Duster (1991) refers to as *campus balkanization*. Rather, it was the fault of Asian Americans, in particular those who decided to speak Chinese within their peer groups. George did not describe how he knew it was Chinese that his peers were speaking instead of, for example, Korean or Japanese. His primary concern, like that of Devin, was that speaking non-English languages created campus space where he felt he was not welcome.

Moving in a slightly different direction, but maintaining a focus on language, a few White guys discussed the public use of the n-word. While most of their n-word usage occurred behind closed doors (for obvious reasons), it sometimes did slip into public discussions. This was one way that the White guys engaged in ontological expansiveness (Sullivan, 2006). The reason this represents ontological expansiveness is that in order to use the n-word, the White guys and their friends had to act as if its use is open and accessible to all people regardless of the historical context. Ken offered the following:

> [Political correctness] takes away from expression to where it puts up a barrier between different race groups to where they can't openly communicate with each other. Example, I actually saw a couple of kids get in a fight because of the use of the word "nigger," and in retrospect, the use of the word "cracker." And it

was basically a group of Black kids were hanging out and they were using the n-word frequently amongst themselves and they'd call different White guys walking by, they'd just go, "Hey, look at this cracker over here, blah, blah, blah," so on and so forth. One guy turned around and said something to them on that effect. They go, "Hey, how come you can call me cracker, but I can't call you nigger?" and frivolities ensued.

Ken did not specify whether the Black kids were using the n-word with the soft "a" ending (frequently a term of comradery) or the hard "r" (one of the most historically racist terms in the country). It was likely the soft "a," as it is hard to imagine a group of Black guys using the other form in public. The true offense, according Ken, however, came when one of the Black kids used the word "cracker," which a White guy then thought gave him license to call the Black guys the n-word with the hard "r." During his telling of the event, Ken had a lot of sympathy for the White guy in this story because he thought the n-word and "cracker" were equivalent. Also, as the Black guys were using the n-word, he thought that it made sense for anyone to use it. Ken did not consider the history of violence and dehumanization against Black people that was linked to the use of the n-word (Kendi, 2016). Rather, he simply thought that if one person could use it, everyone should be able to. He then made light of the subsequent physical altercation by framing it as "frivolities."

The intersection of race and space, whether physical, curricular, or linguistic, took many forms in the narratives of the White guys. There were, however, four elaborated narratives that provided an interesting depth to the issue of race and space while also addressing some of those from chapters 2 through 5. Specifically, Trevor, Roger, Matt, and Andy offered individual stories that illuminated specific contours of how they as White men navigated and felt entitled to space—both literal and cultural. All of the tales demonstrated how the relationship between race and space was deeply rooted in color-blindness and White immunity. Ultimately, the stronger the White guys' level of racial entitlement, the stronger their perceptions of "reverse racism."

"I'm Just Trying to Understand": Racial Entitlement, Space, and Trevor's Story

One White guy I interviewed provided a particularly interesting and telling narrative that hit upon a number of issues regarding race, space, and White entitlement. Trevor was a reporter for the student newspaper and wanted to explore the history of the Chicano Moratorium, which meant interviewing a number of people within the Chicanx community—both off and on campus.[2] He began with his rationale for undertaking this project:

Um, and this was really important uh, during the time of the Chicano Moratorium. Chicano rights thing, 'cause the area is heavily Chicano. I don't know if it's heavily Chicano, but I know it's heavily Hispanic and heavily Latino. . . . Um, and you know, I—I basically wanted to investigate this issue a little further. I wanted to talk with people and write an op-ed on it because I thought it was interesting . . . I wanna learn about other cultures, and I want to share my culture with them and learn about them. And I think that's what our ideal, multicultural society should be about.

This opening is very telling on a number of levels. First, Trevor felt entitled to tell this story in an op-ed. That is, he was not simply doing research on the Chicano Moratorium for his own personal knowledge. Rather, his research was part of a journalism assignment, and he felt that it was perfectly acceptable for him as a White man to tell the story, without his racial identity playing a role. Second, Trevor framed his research as a mutual exchange of cultures, with his actions being a manifestation of the "ideals" of a "multicultural society." This is important because he encountered a lot of resistance on campus while researching the piece, and the exchange of information tended to be one sided.

Trevor's research did not start on campus, however, as he interviewed people in East LA and found many willing to share their stories. To complete the interviews for his piece, he thought, "Finally, I wanted the perspective of the Chicano rights groups on campus." This was where the situation became messy. He continued, "So, I did two things. One was I went to the MEChA office, and tried to talk to them. Um, and first of all, they were *totally* unwilling to talk to me. Um, you know, they were like, 'The, the [student paper] misrepresents us,' and I understand those biases they have. But, um, a lot it I felt, was because I was White." Again, Trevor's framing of the issue is very interesting. The MEChistas were apprehensive about having him in their space because the student newspaper had a history of misrepresenting the beliefs and actions of the group. Instead of seeing this as a legitimate point of view, Trevor was dismissive ("I understand those biases they have"). When he was not welcomed into their space, he turned it into a case of "reverse racism." That is, he felt they would not talk with them because he was White, overlooking the entitlement and dismissiveness he displayed while researching his article.

As the MEChA office was a dead end for Trevor, he went to the Chicano studies library. He did not have a specific person with whom he wanted to speak, but rather thought it would be a space where people would have opinions on the Chicano Moratorium. Trevor offered: "I really wanted to talk to a, like, you know a person who identifies as Chicano and is an activist on campus. So, you know there was a guy sitting at the computer um, who very clearly looked, you know, Latino, and was wearing a shirt with a you, Chicano Power fist on it. So, I thought, well, this is pretty safe to assume this guy's, you know, knows what he's doing. Uh, and so I asked him, and he was *really*, really like, hesitant in like speaking to me. Very guarded." As a White man, Trevor entered an ostensibly Chicano space, made a number of broad assumptions about a stranger in this space, approached this person, and then was confused as to why the individual was "hesitant." Trevor felt that he did not do anything wrong and never took the time to think about his positionality as a White man in this space. Instead, he thought all space should be open to him in a textbook example of ontological expansiveness (Sullivan, 2006).

Trevor continued to describe the specifics of his experience: "I started talking to him for a while. And, anyway, I heard about what he said, but was very unwilling to speak, and you know, he actually didn't know a lot about the issue. Um, but then I started delving into you know, what do you think about race? Do you think it's important? What is Chicanismo? Like, you know, all these things. And, eventually, um, he said, you know, 'I'm hesitant about talking to you because you're White.'" There was a lot going on in this brief part of Trevor's narrative. He noted the stranger did not want to speak with him, but he still pressed with deep and frequently personal questions about ethnic identity and Chicanismo. In his understanding, he was engaging in the "ideals of multiculturalism" by talking across race and ethnicity. In reality, he was engaging in a form of White entitlement and then was shocked when the stranger stated that his hesitation stemmed, in part, from Trevor being White. In Trevor's understanding, if this student and the Chicanx community wanted to create an inclusive, multicultural campus, it was this student's responsibility to talk with him. Seeing that Trevor was not leaving the student alone, a librarian intervened: "The librarian asked me, 'Oh, do Brown people interest you?' To which I responded, sort of sarcastically, 'Yes, but not as much as Africans.' Uh [laughs], I—I also use humor to talk about this stuff 'cause it's, you know, important that we don't take ourselves too seriously." He entered a Chicanx campus space, profiled a student as a "typical Chicano activist," approached this student whom he did not know, asked him unsolicited questions while the student was studying, and when Trevor met resistance he made racial jokes. Trevor also knew the student newspaper was frequently criticized for misrepresenting the campus Chicanx community, but this did not matter to him. He felt it was Chicanx student's responsibility to educate him, and he thought his fellow student and the librarian took themselves too seriously. He had no idea how much his White entitlement informed people's resistance to him, and rather than self-interrogate, Trevor framed the librarian and student as the problem. Trevor further downplayed the significance of his racial joking to the librarian as he explained, "We all made like joking generalizations about each other, but it didn't structure inequality within our neighborhoods. So, like it wasn't a big deal."

Eventually, Trevor left the library with no interview and a lot of frustration. He elaborated: "I mean, 'cause he judged me. He says, 'Your White privilege, blah, blah, blah.' And like yes, you could say, on average White people have higher incomes. . . . But other than that, I don't think he really knew a lot about me, and it was actually, he did judge me. He said the skin color of your race, there's something bad about that. There's something inherently annoying to me." The lack of self-awareness in this situation was astounding, and please keep in mind this is his own recollection of the events that transpired. Trevor described an instance where he openly admitted to stereotyping, White entitlement, harassment, and publicly telling a racial joke, yet he also thought of himself as the victim. He was openly dismissive that his racial background should be considered in these interactions ("blah, blah, blah"), when it clearly played a central role. He never once considered that maybe people in the Chicanx community were warranted in their reservations regarding White people coming into their space, and ironically, the racism of Trevor's narrative demonstrated why their apprehension was justified. There was no "exchange of cultures" as Trevor professed in the beginning of his story. Rather, he was extracting information from a community, expected it to be readily available, and when he was met with resistance, turned himself into the target of "reverse racism." As he concluded, Trevor offered, "And [racial/ethnic campus groups] don't stop for a second and say, 'Wait, I might wanna forget about this for just a second, and just be a person, and say "hi" next time to the person on the bus next to me.' You know?" For Trevor, it was the responsibility of the librarian, MEChistas, and the stranger to give him the benefit of the doubt. It was *their* "biases" that he identified as the core problem. In his understanding, he did nothing wrong and it was these isolationist Students of Color who were fracturing the campus community. He wanted them to "forget" the racist incidents in the past and treat him like an individual, and Trevor did not think he needed to change his approach. Similar to Trevor, Roger had a story rooted in a contested racial space. In this instance, it centered on the university's student government, where he was part of a group that won several campus-wide elections against a slate of Students of Color.

"Minorities Took Over the Student Council, So We Took It Back": The Example of Roger

Roger was very involved on campus and was concurrently frustrated by what he saw as a community fractured along racial/ethnic lines. Like Trevor, it was very telling where he placed blame for this phenomenon. He began by offering, "I think race relations on campus are poor at WU largely because while there is a diverse view within the student population, there isn't very good integration of that diverse population." Roger then offered his explanation as to why the community was so divided:

It is absolutely the case that minorities self-segregate. If it wasn't there wouldn't be a number of clubs that identify solely by ethnic background. There wouldn't be a MEChA. There wouldn't be an African Student Union. There wouldn't be an Asian Pacific Coalition, a Samhan, a Filipino, a Vietnamese Student Union, and a this and a that and the other thing. Even within the queer community at WU the queer community or the queer alliance is a number of ethnic queer organizations that come together. Mishpacha is the Jewish queer organization. There's Blaq with a "q." There's *La Familia*, which is the Latino/Latina. There's Mahu, which is the API, Asian/Pacific Islander queer organization on campus. So, there are. . . . There's this massive self-segregation.

It was telling not only whom Roger mentioned in this impressive list, but also whom he left out. Specifically, he never mentioned groups that have predominantly White populations as being responsible for campus self-segregation. Instead, he thought that blame fell squarely on Students of Color. Roger was very direct on that point: "I don't know of a White Student Association." It was from this orientation that Roger described his involvement in his university's student government.

Roger began by saying, "I'm also part of [slate's name], which is one of two major parties in student government. It's the party that is the less ethnocentric of the two parties." This frame was telling because he did not see his largely White group as being "ethnocentric." It was, in his understanding, the group of Students of Color who gained control of the student government about a decade earlier were the ones being ethnocentric. Roger offered a historical perspective: "One of the interesting phenomena that's occurred here and this is one of the reasons that I'm so involved in the student government is about the same time that Prop 209 was introduced a number of student organizations on campus got together and created the first student government political parties at this university.[3] It used to not be so political. It used to be that not really anyone wanted to do it and a few people had a popularity contest. And it was kind of heavily Greek dominated by like the fraternity/sorority system." This was a fascinating intersection of race and space. For Roger, student government was not political when it was "dominated" by Greek members who were also heavily White and affluent. He never expressed any discomfort at White people owning this space, but he was uncomfortable when a slate of Students of Color were elected and tried to use these positions to address the waning campus diversity that was the result of Prop 209.

Roger continued with his history of student government at his institution. He claimed he was somewhat appreciative of the slate's initial efforts, but was extremely critical of the group's contemporary ones:

But what happened was there was this group that came together of different student organizations that kind of overthrew the student government. They won every seat in I think the mid-nineties. And they continued for over ten years controlling every seat, and in that time, they did a lot of great things especially in the beginning. Reforming things and creating new outreach and retention programs but then over time they became more corrupt and selfish and created office, gave themselves the office space and took office space away from other student organizations and limited funding to only student organizations that were within this elite clique if you will.

Again, it was revealing how Roger lodged his criticism. He framed the Student of Color in the student government as an "elite clique" that was "corrupt and selfish." At the same time, he was uncritical of student government when it was dominated by White people associated with the Greek system. Roger believed the Students of Color slate used the system to exclusively serve their interests, and he saw this as limiting the space available to other student groups. When White Greek students did the same thing, Roger believed they were engaging in a nonpolitical popularity contest.

From this context, Roger and several others ran in the student government elections to challenge the "dominance" of Students of Color. Returning to his previous statements, Roger felt he was part of the less "ethno-centric" slate of candidates: "And I was part of a group of students that came together to oppose that and last year for the first year ever they didn't have the majority and somewhat else did and we had a majority. Which was a coup and one of the things that we were very involved in was opening up funding so every student group for funding and opening up other resources and right now we are working on opening up offices." I am still not sure why he specifically referred to winning a student body election with a military metaphor, but it does seem telling how important he felt his mission was. He was particularly interested in opening up space for Dance Marathon, a charitable event that raises money for children living with AIDS but also one dominated by Greek life. It was then very interesting that Roger offered the following critique of his Peers of Color in student government leadership positions: "But I think that often times student leaders have a lot more to work for in advocacy for their explicit communities than trying to build some sort of relationship with the other." Roger saw the Students of Color in student government as acting out of self-interest. When he and his colleagues took over control of student government and reopened space to the White Greek community, he did not see this as advocacy for a specific community. It was just "opening up space."

Once Roger's group gained power, they did exactly as they said they would. They reopened access to space and resources for student groups not directly associated with Students of Color, and this necessarily meant fewer resources available for WU diversification efforts. Roger and his colleagues focused on Darfur Action and thought that maybe people dedicated to the dwindling diversity numbers at WU would be happy switching issues because it was an issue in Africa: "And I could see, I mean especially because we tried to do a lot of outreach to African American students on campus. Most of those students were much more interested in the diversity crisis at WU and the fact that admissions numbers for their community were so low and not as interested in helping out with the genocide happening in what I would think of as their ancestral homeland. . . . There's a certain distrust they have of you just because you're White. And that makes working together that much more difficult." What he missed in this assessment was the numbers at WU were dropping for *African Americans*, not *Africans*, but Roger did not see much difference because the genocide that was occurring was in the "ancestral homeland" of African Americans. Roger and his slate took resources away from their organizing efforts and then framed himself as the victim of unwarranted "distrust." He concluded by saying that it was their distrust, not his actions, that made working together difficult. A group of White people took over a space and redistributed its resources to other ostensibly White groups, and Roger still could not understand why Students of Color distrusted him and his colleagues.

Roger felt that he was just engaging in politics as usual and failed to understand the resentment of dedicated people having resources stripped away from them. He simply thought it was a reallocation of space and resources that was more "equitable." Roger, by his own admission, was central in wresting control from the slate of Students of Color in his university's student government, but he still felt the attacks on him and his character were unwarranted: "There is a certain demonization that occurs largely within the student government kind of elections mentality. It's an us versus them thing. And so, it's easy to demonize the other rather than talk to them. That's something that's very frustrating to me. And lots of time I feel uncomfortable with People of Color because I feel like their attacking me." Roger very quickly turned his aggression in terms of taking control of student government into Students of Color "attacking" him. He even openly admitted to not feeling comfortable with People of Color, but never once considered that he might bear some responsibility for this dynamic. Instead, it was Students of Color who were being hostile toward him, and he offered the following as a solution to the problem— although he made this suggestion specific to his interactions with the Muslim community on campus: "Having like dialogue programs. And then that happened and all of a sudden like everything stopped and it was an us versus them thing. And I feel that the Muslim community made it that more than our community because our community tends to be much more interested in dialogue than theirs does." Roger could not understand the unease of the Muslim students, instead saying that he was interested in reaching across the aisle while they were not. That was a consistent theme throughout my time talking with Roger. He thought of himself as fair and open-minded, so campus racial tensions were the fault of others. He held no personal responsibility. While there were a number of similarities between Roger and Trevor engaging raced space, Matt and Andy took a slightly different approach. They described their personal histories of being White guys appropriating and critiquing Black culture—more of a figurative space.

Everything but the Burden: Matt and Andy as White Experts on Hip-Hop and Black Culture

Greg Tate (2003) offered a simple yet profound thesis in his edited volume *Everything but the Burden*, where he and his contributors explored White people adopting Black cultural styles. They can adapt their dress, style, language, and music, to be aligned to a Black aesthetic, but they will never have to face the persistent racism Black people regularly experience. Essentially, White people will never have to suffer the ill effects of being Black (*White immunity*; Cabrera, 2017) while thinking and acting as if it is acceptable to appropriate Black culture (*ontological expansiveness*; Sullivan, 2006). By "appropriation," I mean those not of a specific ethnicity adopting the cultural symbols of said minoritized group—usually in very stereotypical and racist ways (Keene, 2015). There were some among the White guys I talked with who discussed appropriating cultural styles, especially from hip-hop, which they ostensibly associated with Black people. Please be clear that *I am not* making the argument that hip-hop is equated with Black people. Rather, I am reporting how the White guys tended to engage hip-hop and its association with Black culture. Matt specifically began by describing the way that he and his White friends decided to dress and act in their suburban enclave: "Maybe that for a lot of my life, my childhood, I really identified with African Americans. I love rap. I liked rap . . . I was one of . . . like a lot of the kids around my neighborhood. . . . For some reason, I don't know why around my neighborhood in [hometown] . . . in [hometown] there's a lot of White kids trying to act like Black kids." While I did not name Matt's hometown, a little context is necessary. It is over 80 percent White, and the median household income is more than $17,000 above the state average. That is, he came from a strongly White and affluent community, where Black folk represented less than 5 percent of the population. Thus, it is interesting that he and his friends were so drawn to hip-hop because they lived in a social environment largely devoid of Black people.

Despite not having many Black people in his hometown, or maybe because of it, both Matt and his friends fetishized hip-hop—in particular commercially successful artists. I make this distinction because neither Matt nor the other

White guys who spoke of hip-hop ever referenced more "conscious" rappers like Blackalicious, KRS-One, Eric B. & Rakim, or Dead Prez. Rather, they viewed hip-hop as those artists who were more mainstream. In particular, Matt discussed how he and his friends were drawn to White rapper Eminem:

> M: No, I don't really know why. I mean, I started listening to rap music at a young age and . . .
>
> N: When did you start listening to it?
>
> M: I think Eminem was probably the first rapper ever, and that was around . . . I was in sixth grade. My best friend was the first kid to start listening to him and he buzzed his hair and bleached it and he was one of the first kids in the school to bleach his hair. He was like my best friend, and I don't know why, I don't know why I started acting like that, but I mean. . . . Yeah, I don't know.

Matt and his friends' entry into hip-hop culture began with a White rapper, Eminem. This is interesting because there were many other commercially successful rappers when Eminem burst on the scene, including DMX, Nas, Puff Daddy, Ja Rule, Jay-Z, and Dr. Dre. However, Matt and his friends were drawn to the White rapper. Additionally, the exposure to this White hip-hop artist led them to emulate Eminem's style of short bleached hair. It was not enough for Matt and his friends to listen to Eminem, but they adopted his style along the way.

Strangely, adopting Eminem's style became a segue for Matt and his friends to begin appropriating Black culture. Matt explained that while in high school he would act in an extremely stereotypical fashion vis-à-vis Blackness and hip-hop: "For a long time in high school, I wore chains all the time, tried to . . . I listened to rap all the time so I'd always buy the Nike shoes they'd rap about and stuff like that. I'd buy anything that they'd rap about and trying . . . I'd try to act like . . . In high school, I think I tried to act like the teachers were racist against me like, 'Why are you trying to hold me down?'" This part of Matt's narrative was the most telling. He openly admitted to emulating anything he associated with Black or hip-hop culture such as Nikes and chains. Then, as part of his performance of Blackness, he took on the view of racial oppression (i.e., "Why are you trying to hold me down?"). The problem with this formulation is that real anti-Black oppression continues to exist (Bonilla-Silva, 2006; Omi & Winant, 2015). For Matt and his friends, it was part of the game of "putting on Blackness"—a type of modern-day minstrel show. He eventually told me that he didn't really believe racism was that important contemporarily (see previous chapters), and part of that assessment stemmed from his ability to "play" with this very serious issue. Matt used to critique his high school teachers for being "anti-Black," but he admitted that this was part of a game he was playing. Once the game became boring, he moved on to a different style. Matt believed that racism was not an important issue contemporarily, and a large part of that stemmed from his ability to play with it while in high school, adopting *everything but the burden* of being Black (Tate, 2003).

There were others who talked about hip-hop from the perspective of being a White guy, and they also tended to be very stereotypical in their (mis)under-standings of what constitutes hip-hop and implicitly Black culture. Andy was similar to Martin in chapter 3. Instead of emulating hip-hop culture, he was highly critical of it: "You know, the African American rap scene, sort of talk-ing down on women and calling them ho's and whores is a good thing and I find students sort of, you know, 'Where's my bitch,' and all that kind of shit. It's like I don't really think people would be doing this if they weren't emulat-ing what they see the stars doing. And I feel like that's sort of one of the big-gest issues of race, is the different racial groups in Hollywood definitely spawn different racial actions just in the everyday scene, and when I see people sort of blindly emulating these actions." It was really telling that Andy framed this overt example of misogyny ("Where's my bitch") as both emblematic of Black culture and "one of the biggest issues of race." Implicitly this meant that con temporary issues of race had nothing to do with White people. Rather, it was projected onto this narrow view that equated Black hip-hop culture with being inherently misogynistic. Andy held a general disdain for what he considered hip-hop clothing style as well: "I don't know, it's ignorant. I haven't really ques-tioned people very much about, 'Why are you exactly wearing a do-rag, a shirt down to your ankles and you're cursing at your girlfriend like a good thing and does she actually like that?'" Andy equated Black and hip-hop cultures with being *ignorant*. Additionally, the question he posed was merely rhetorical. He frequently thought about this question, but later admitted that he did not have much interpersonal contact with Black people, so it is not clear how he could have actually asked it.

It was really interesting how Andy shifted from his critique of commercial hip-hop to a general and relatively uninformed view of what constituted Black culture. He was very critical of Black people "not questioning" why they act the way that "*they* do." Fittingly, Andy avoided posing these questions to him-self and other White people appropriating these styles of dress and speech. Instead, he was centrally focused on Black communities:

And so, I feel like just in general—society in general—you know, people don't really question what they do as much as maybe they should. This is definitely a case when it comes to racism, and people sort of do stuff that their parents did or their society did. A lot of minorities grow up in neighborhoods where other minorities. . . . You know, you had a question on the [questionnaire] about would I feel offended if an African American was living next door. You know, just sort of looking at that, I feel like people are brought up a certain way and they just sort of do things and people don't always question what they're doing and that's definitely apparent when it comes to racial issues.

Andy did not come right out and say he would be uncomfortable if a Black person lived next door to him; however, he did express a strong disdain for his narrow view of what constituted Black culture. That is, he created a straw person by offering an openly misogynistic and ignorant view of essential Black culture, feeding age-old stereotypes of Blackness and Black masculinity (Allen, 1997; Sulé, 2016). He then offered this as evidence of why he was justified in his discomfort around Black people. Thus, an imagined version of Black culture led to his aversion to real Black people. Existing in ostensibly White environments not only corresponded to expressions of racism, but also provided an interesting context for personal growth. This was common, as the bulk of the White guys described their racial identity and racial awareness development as either minimal or regressive.

Racial Arrested Development and Racial Regression in Higher Education

In addition to space being racialized, this context also affected the development of these White guys. There were two key ways that they described the evolution of their views on race/racism during their undergraduate years. I detailed one in chapter 3: they became more keenly aware of "reverse racism." The other dominant form of development was simply that "nothing changed." There were some who became more racially aware and moved toward allyship, and I will detail their experiences in chapter 7. Across both institutions, however, the most common description of personal development was some version of "none" or "minimal." While this is not the most dramatic component of this book, it is one of the most important because these White guys professed profoundly racist beliefs, as demonstrated in the previous chapters. To the extent that their college campuses leave them in this state of racial arrested development, their lack of growth is also telling in terms of the role that higher education plays in reproducing the existing racial paradigm.

"I Haven't Changed": Whiteness and Racial Arrested Development in College

Time at university can be one of great development—both cognitive and social (Pascarella & Terenzini, 2005). Within this paradigm, many have theorized what White racial identity development looks like (e.g., Helms, 1990). Cabrera et al. (2016) argued that a campus environment that centers racial comfort will likely leave White students in a state of *racial arrested development*. While

Cabrera et al. (2016) offered a theoretical argument, the interviews I conducted tended to corroborate this idea. That is, despite the numerous developmental opportunities on college campuses, the bulk of the White guys I spoke with said they did not change much during their undergraduate years in terms of their views on race. This was consistent across both institutions as well as years in college. For example, Adam offered,

> N: Okay. How have your view changed on race since coming to campus?
> A: Um, I don't know if it's changed all that much.
> N: Okay.
> A: I don't know . . . I'm more informed, I suppose.

Adam's response was very common. The strong majority of these White guys, when they reflected on their college experiences, thought little had changed in their racial views.

Dwight offered more details into his thinking. He began by saying that if he was interviewed on the same subject while in high school, "I would have answered things the same as I did today." This was interesting because he subsequently said that in college, he was exposed to a greater diversity of people and thought relative to his high school environment. "I mean, it doesn't inherently change your views if your observations tend to coincide with your previously established views. . . . I guess I haven't really made a change one way or the other. I mean, I'm still pretty much the same as I was back then as far as I view race or racial issues." This was interesting because exposure to racial difference, in the empirical literature, usually leads to personal change—in particular, adopting more egalitarian social views (e.g., Bowman, 2011). In this instance, exposure to diversity did not produce tangible change.

There were some who more directly declared that their experiences in college did not affect their views on race in any way. Both Hoyt and Keith were very sure, very firm, and very succinct in their responses.

Not at all. (Hoyt)

They haven't. (Keith)

While these were not typical responses in terms of length, a substantial number of White guys were very forceful on this point: their views on race did not change at all during their undergraduate years. Their reasons for a lack of change were equally succinct, and they offered no substantive reasons.

When Roger described the ways he changed during his time at WU, he was one of the White guys who actually claimed he changed a lot as a function of being a university student. He did not think he was uncomfortable with People of Color prior to college, but he also thought that his undergraduate years made him more comfortable interacting across difference: "So, they've changed in a lot of ways. I think that there are certain times where I feel like I can go around it and feel comfortable with everybody and there are other times where, especially when I first came here. When I first came to college, I was really excited to meet so many people from diverse backgrounds. Especially the people on my floor. And being exposed to them." This statement is really interesting when juxtaposed against the bulk of Roger's interview. He spent a great deal of time explicitly blaming Students of Color for fracturing the campus community, taking over the student government, and not being willing to work with him as a White man. This begs larger questions: Was Roger talking about only one segment of the Student of Color population? That is, was he referring to Students of Color who agreed with his views, and that is what he based his comfort on? These are important questions because Roger's statement stands in stark contrast to the content and tone of the rest of his interview.

Jeremy explained his lack of growth during his undergraduate years. He was only comfortable being as color-blind as possible, and his rationale for this was telling:

> I don't like [being racially cognizant] because I honestly never even used to think about and it just . . . I think that if you're truly not thinking about it, about something like that, it's not going to have an effect on anything you do involving the subject, and that could be a good or a bad thing. Like if you're trying to be a racial activist in supporting diversity in whatever you do, it could be a good thing, but for me, that's the field I'm going to or anything and I feel like just being a person and interacting with people it'd be much better not to even notice things like that and I do more now.

Jeremy did not see race as affecting him as a White man, so he preferred not to think about it. He thought that being racially aware was for "racial activists," but not like people such as himself. That is, race was not *his* issue but someone else's. In addition to these views that "I haven't changed much," some of the White guys claimed that they became more open-minded and racially accepting as a result of being in college, but these descriptions did not always hold up to scrutiny.

I've Become More "Open-Minded"

Some of the participants described feeling that their university experiences led them to be more "open-minded" or "tolerant" regarding issues of race. This was interesting when juxtaposed against their earlier comments because, given the racist nature of them, how racist must they have been entering their freshman year for their self-assessment to be true? Kevin gave a fairly standard answer: "I've probably become more accepting. Not that I was incredibly racist or anything like that, or not accepting, intolerant, anything like that beforehand, but definitely . . . I mean, I come from an area that's like 90 to 95 percent White, so to have friends that aren't. . . . It's not like a completely new thing, but it's still . . . I mean, it's helped me kind of just become more tolerant I guess." What being more "tolerant" or more "accepting" meant was not very clearly defined. Kevin simply felt that he had been exposed to more diversity as a result of being in college, and that made him more accepting of these cultural differences as a result.

Kurt was an interesting example because in his description of his personal growth he directly contradicted himself. Kurt quickly offered an assessment similar to Kevin's: "I think I've definitely become more open, I guess. I mean, I think with higher education you become more open to racial equality and you aren't so ignorant about things." For Kurt, being racist and being ignorant were negative attributes, and he thought that he had grown to be more "open" about issues of race as an undergraduate. Kurt said he thought about race very rarely, and believed minorities read too much into issues of racism. From this context, I probed to see if he could point to any specific changes he experienced or anything that might have led to these changes. After some reflection, Kurt offered, "I don't have anything specific that has changed my viewpoint." That is, he was more open and less ignorant on issues of race; however, nothing had really contributed to these changes. Returning to other sections of his interview, he tended to be very color-blind in his worldview and skeptical of minority claims of racism, and it was unclear how he actually grew and developed.

Nick was one of the more self-reflective of the White guys I spoke with. Being a self-identified progressive liberal, he struggled to answer my question and ultimately offered: "That's the last thing a liberal-thinking person wants to admit, not changing that much, but I . . . I feel like almost on that I'd have to get back to you on because to me there's really nothing that tangible that I think I really changed on." Nick admitted that he was feeling pressure to say that he grew as a result of being an undergraduate, but he could not point to anything specifically. He continued to explore and reflect, and then he arrived at the following conclusion: "Maybe I [became more] cognizant of those issues for a while, but I can't really say any major or even minor change." While many of the previous White guys were not really concerned by their lack of personal growth, this did trouble Nick. He had never been asked to reflect on this dynamic before, and he struggled with this realization. Beyond this, however, there were a number of White guys who became more aware of "reverse racism" as a result of their undergraduate experiences.

"Reverse Racism": Racially Regressive White Guy Development

In chapters 3 and 5, the White guys discussed a number of the ways that they felt that "reverse racism" was the norm on college campuses specifically and in contemporary U.S. society in general. Thus, it is not surprising that many described their undergraduate years as a time when they became increasingly sensitized to this issue. For example, Ryan both had minimal cross-racial interactions and saw minimal changes in his views on race since entering college. He did see one development however: "Um, actually I have become more aware of racism against White people in general, and that's what I've come to see more." Ryan was racially insulated within the fraternity system, and in this environment he developed an increased sense of ethnic victimization consistent with the findings of Sidanius, Van Laar, Levin, and Sinclair (2004). Ryan was clear about how he viewed and experienced his personal development.

Lance described the general process of his intellectual growth during his undergraduate years. Being an Objectivist, he was constantly engaging in debate that he thought honed his capacity for rational thought. Lance offered, "And most of it just, you know comes from late night arguing in the dorms, or you know, I mean I guess now, you know, ever since starting LOGIC, discussions within LOGIC.[4] Discussions like this morning with my roommate." From this description, Lance reflected on his undergraduate years and offered the following: "I've refined [my views on race] a great deal in terms of refining my ideas about racism's origin and its relation to other forms of collectivism. Its relationship to discrimination more generally. What basis upon which one should discriminate in what context. Things along those lines. So yeah, no fundamental shift, but certainly a refinement and sort of more sophistication in terms of understanding about it." In his analyses, as previously illustrated, Lance believed the greatest source of campus-based racism stemmed from racial/ethnic groups at his university. He viewed anything race-conscious as a form of racism, collectivism, or clannish behavior, all of which he saw as the antithesis of individual freedom and rational thought. While Lance came into college with this orientation, he became more acutely aware of these issues through experience and debate, which led him to a few conclusions: First, White people were the frequent, if not predominant, targets of contemporary racism. Second, the best way to get beyond racism is to stop being racially aware. Third, it is everyone's individual right to discriminate on any basis they wish, and it is improper for the university or government to interfere in anyway. Ultimately, Lance's studies and experience reinforced all of these regressive views on race and racism. While he attributed this growth to his increasing development of his rational capabilities, I cannot ignore that this occurred primarily in the presence of other White students.

Race, Space, and Development

While the bulk of the White guys thought of racism as an interpersonal phenomenon, their narratives in this chapter made a strong link between race and
space. They tended to think of some space, such as the Deep South, as racist.
While they acknowledged that some campus-based spaces such as the housed
Greek system had a disproportionately high number of White people, they were
reticent to claim that these spaces were raced. Instead, when Students of Color
clustered and disrupted the normativity of Whiteness in space, the White guys
became uncomfortable. Non-White space extended beyond the physical, as they
also tended to have difficulties when curriculum was non-White and when
Students of Color spoke languages other than English. They also tended to
experience discomfort when people "broke the racial rules" of a space. That is,
when People of Color entered a White space or White people entered a
minority space, conflict frequently ensued. However, the White guys I talked
with did not treat these two phenomena equally. Rather, they tended to be
oriented in *ontological expansiveness* (Sullivan, 2006), whereby they thought
that all space (literal and figurative) should be open to them as White people.
When there was resistance to this expectation (e.g., Roger and Trevor), they
blamed Students of Color for "excluding Whites."

This became a tight, cyclical logic that concurrently justified White guys'
frequent existence in ostensibly White space, while concurrently turning themselves into imagined racial victims when they tried to enter or take control of
non-White space. Within this context, it is not surprising that the White guys
experienced few developments in their racial selves during their undergraduate years. This is interesting given how White racial identity development is
currently theorized and empirically explored. Cabrera and Holliday (2017)
offered this overview of how scholars understand White people progressing in
their racial identity development: "[White people] (1) tend to begin their
development in a state of relative racial ignorance, (2) are taken out of this
ignorance via contact with the racial other, and (3) can progressively move
toward a healthy racial identity that is racially cognizant, self-assured, without
hatred of the racial other" (p. 2). The foundational text in White racial identity
development is the work of Helms (1990), who described White people progressing from racially ignorant and generally racist through several stages, ending
in an anti-racist stage. This is consistent with a great deal of the racial justice ally
work in higher education where allyship is framed as the most developed racial
stage for White people (Cabrera, 2012).

How does this theorizing relate to *racial arrested development* (Cabrera et al.,
2016)? How does it account for people who regress and become more racist in
their racial identity development? The short answer is that there is insufficient
theorizing at the intersection of White racial identity development theory and

higher education to explain this issue. Sidanius et al. (2004) empirically demonstrated that White undergraduates who exist in primarily White living/learning environments are more likely to develop a sense that they are targets of "reverse racism." Regardless, this is an area that needs to be more deeply explored because it appears that the more that Whiteness was the physical, cultural, and social norm in the lived environments of the White guys, the more likely they were to think of themselves as the targets of "reverse racism" when this cultural norm was disrupted.

These White guys had a fundamental tension within their narratives across chapters 2 through 6. They tended to believe that race did not matter that much in terms of structuring inequality or interpersonal relationships (chapter 2); however, they also tended to feel most comfortable in the presence of other White people and in particular other White men (chapters 2, 4, and 6). If race truly did not matter, why were they so drawn to racially homogenous spaces—or what some scholars refer to as homophily (e.g., McPherson, Smith-Lovin, & Cook, 2001)? It seems like these professions of race "not mattering" were more aspirational. The White guys wanted race to not matter, but their experiences told them otherwise (see chapters 2, 5, and 6). However, when they were in space where their White immunity (Cabrera, 2017) insulated them from having to even think about race, they were able to delude themselves into thinking that race was no longer an issue. Essentially, the dominant message they were receiving from their White learning/living environments was that racism was not a pressing social issue. This led to them feeling entitled to racial social comfort, and when that comfort was disrupted, they were insistent on returning to the state where race was no longer an issue—even if this was what Mills (1997) refers to as an "invented delusional world" (p. 18).

So, the pressing question becomes, what can be done to disrupt this invented delusional world? Part of the solution might lie in the issue of agitation. This term frequently has a negative connotation, but W. E. B. Du Bois turned the term on its head: "Agitation is a necessary evil to tell of the ills of the suffering. Without it many a nation has been lulled into a false security and preened itself with virtues it did not possess" (1971, p. 4). In Du Bois's understanding, agitation can have a productive function if it alerts people to social suffering, and that is precisely what institutions of higher education need to proactively be doing.

This poses an additional problem when analyzing the ecology of the college campus because as Cabrera et al. (2016) demonstrated, social comfort is prioritized in ecological analyses. This is a problem because in order for people to grow, they need to experience a certain degree of cognitive dissonance: "people generally strive for cognitive consistency, and moments of inconsistency produce moments of disequilibrium that need to be addressed so that consonance (i.e. agreement) can return" (Cabrera et al., 2016, p. 129). As applied to racism in higher education, "Multicultural education can function as a form of cognitive dissonance for White students. Instead of awakening White students to the realities of oppression and White privilege, they frequently deal with their dissonance by portraying themselves as the true victims of racism" (Cabrera et al., 2016, p. 129). That is, cognitive dissonance can lead to racial growth, but White students frequently turn it into a moment of racial regression. Instead of being awakened to the realities of racism, they use these moments to increase their own sense of racial victimization.

Essentially, I argue from this perspective that we need to shift this paradigm and be comfortable with institutions of higher education functioning as forms of cognitive dissonance for White students. Yes, there will be a lot of pushback via White fragility (DiAngelo, 2011) and avoidance via White agility (chapter 2); however, the end result of prioritizing White social comfort is either racial arrested development (Cabrera et al., 2016) or racial regression (Cabrera, 2014d; Cabrera & Holliday, 2017). This task is made even more difficult within contemporary institutions of higher education because students are increasingly treated as customers instead of students (Singleton-Jackson, Jackson, & Reinhardt, 2010). Therefore, they frequently feel entitled to avoid discomfort, and this poses a challenge to university leadership. How willing are university chancellors, presidents, and provosts to tell their incoming classes that they will experience a great deal of racial discomfort during their undergraduate years? Some might ask, "Why would anyone pay to feel uncomfortable?" I offer this reframe: people pay to experience pain all the time through personal trainers as long as growth accompanies that pain. Racial cognitive dissonance will produce pain and potential growth for White people if they actually deal with rather than avoiding it.

Therein lies the problem when the subject becomes the intersection of Whiteness and masculinity. Disruption of Whiteness can create dissonance, which is an opportunity for growth; however, to realize this potential requires White guys to understand and explore their emotional responses to these situations. If emotional illiteracy (Kindlon & Thompson, 2000) is a central facet of dominant forms of masculinity, this can become an important barrier to racial growth. Emotions are a form of cognition and are critically important to the maintenance of White supremacy (Matias, 2016). The narratives of "reverse racism" outlined throughout the previous chapters are an indication of how powerful the combination of White male racial emotions and imagination can be. These White guys frequently had feelings that something was wrong, but instead of asking what was wrong with them individually, they invested their energy maintaining the sincere fiction of "reverse racism." An important missing component was a self-awareness of their racial-emotional reactions to situations. Instead, the White guys tended to frame these emotions as facts ("it *is* reverse racism" vs. "I *feel* discriminated against"), again falling into a trap of hegemonic masculinity where men are supposed to be rational and emotionally unexpressive (Connell, 2005; Edwards & Jones, 2009; Laker & Davis, 2011).

The potential of racial dissonance is demonstrated in the work of racial justice allyship development (e.g., Broido, 2000; Cabrera, 2012; Reason, Millar, & Scales, 2005; Warren, 2010). That is, there is potential for anti-racist growth among White male undergraduates. Even though they are in the minority, they are an important subsection of this population. Being White in a racialized society means having to engage with, instead of avoid, issues of racism. As Joe Feagin argued, "There are two types of white Americans: racists and recovering racists" (Maynard, 2004). The next chapter highlights how some White men in college have become and are negotiating what it means to be a *recovering racist*.

7

"Because It's the Right Thing to Do"

Racial Awakening and (Some)
Allyship Development

The previous five chapters have highlighted cause for concern. If college-educated White men tend to be more racially progressive than non-college-educated ones, what do these narratives have to say about the state of contemporary White supremacy and the role of higher education in maintaining it? Instead of dwelling on this question, I instead offer the narratives of the White guys in this chapter who actually engaged the process of *working through Whiteness* (Cabrera, 2012). Their examples more clearly demonstrate where, to borrow from Bush (2011), the *cracks in the walls of Whiteness* are. They are in the minority among White guys I talked with, but that also makes their personal narratives so important.

There is a constant debate surrounding terminology: What do you call a White guy who challenges racism? Anti-racist? Ally? Racial justice collaborator? To be honest and a little blunt, I do not care. It is probably a better idea to call him Steve or whatever his first name may be. I will dive into the traps of anti-racist identity sometimes stifling anti-racist action later in the chapter. Until then, I will instead focus these White guys' actions, racial environments, experiences, and ideologies that begin disrupting the normality of Whiteness. This is a difficult undertaking because the empirical scholarship on the subject is severely lacking. As Warren (2010) observed, "White studies of white racism could fill a small library, the studies of white anti-racism, if you will, could fit in a small bookshelf" (p. xi). In other words, the subject of White people challenging racism is wide open in terms of scholarship and scholarly debates.

I want to be very clear on one point. While the White guys I interviewed for this chapter were actually engaging issues of race and Whiteness, very few of them could actually be considered allies (or whatever term is appropriate) because their anti-racist actions were few and far between. Regardless, the White guys who are the subject of this chapter demonstrated a stronger willingness to engage issues of racism than did those highlighted in the previous chapters. They were able to identify racism in society *and* within themselves, had a number of experiences that opened their eyes to the realities of historical and contemporary racism, and sometimes explored ways to challenge racism through tangible actions.

A lot of their development was contextualized within substantially more diverse living/learning environments than the White guys in the previous chapters. While these White guys still tended to exist in environments where they were in the majority, a large proportion reported coming from neighborhoods and high schools where Whites were *not* a clear majority (see Appendix B). Additionally, their friendship groups and dating lives included substantially more People of Color than those White guys in chapters 2 through 6. This poses a chicken-and-egg conundrum. Did these White guys exist in more racially diverse learning/living environments, which led to their more advanced understandings and engagement with race? Or did they have a better understanding of racism than the White guys in the previous chapters, which led them to pursue greater racial diversity in their interpersonal relationships? It is likely both of these working in conjunction with each other instead of an either/or dichotomy.

While those working through Whiteness had increased interactions across race relative to those in chapters 2 through 6, this did not preclude some of them from existing in either racially homogenous environments or at least those where they were in the clear majority. Additionally, almost half of these White guys thought about race only once per week. This was noticeably more consideration of the subject than the White guys in chapters 2 through 6 offered, but substantially less than many Students of Color, for whom it is an omnipresent reality (Feagin, Vera, & Imani, 1996; Yosso et al., 2010). This set the context for beginning the process of Whiteness disruption, but a number of factors played into this process, helping these White guys become more racially cognizant.

Disrupting Epistemologies of Ignorance

Reason and Evans (2007) argued that one of the biggest barriers to developing racial justice allies is White people working from color-blindness to color-cognizance. Color-blindness is so structurally embedded in contemporary society (Bonilla-Silva, 2006) that it is not surprising that the bulk of these narratives involved this issue in particular. Therefore, these narratives were both frustrating and promising. They were frustrating because this subsample of the White guys I spoke with were the most racially progressive, and yet their personal developments tended not to approach any form of allyship. They are promising because these White guys did begin the process of understanding themselves as being White in a racialized society and the accompanying social immunities. Therefore, I outline the primary focus of their narratives—the multiple avenues for overcoming color-blindness. While I offer several factors, please understand that they did not exist in insolation. Rather, these White guys I spoke with tended to experience multiple areas concurrently, including *listening to non-Whites, multicultural education and humanizing pedagogy, non–racial minority experiences,* and *being biracial but White-identified.*

Listening to and Personally Connecting with Non-Whites

I really struggled with this section because I faced the following tension. On the one hand, cross-racial friendships tended to be a really important means for this group of White guys to begin understanding and engaging issues of race. On the other, Larry, one of the White guys I spoke to for this chapter, succinctly offered, "I don't think it's Latino or Black people's responsibility to educate White people about how it is. The burden shouldn't be on them." I tend to agree with Larry's blunt assessment. This is particularly important given that not all cross-racial interactions lead to greater racial understanding, as the previous chapters demonstrated. Within this context, I am not as concerned *that* cross-racial interactions led to greater racial consciousness, but rather I want to examine *how* cross-racial interactions fostered this outcome. In particular, I am interested in the different ways that the White guys featured in this chapter approached these situations and interactions. Essentially, I want to focus on both the impact of these examples, but also how the White guys I talked with for this chapter approached them differently than those in the previous five chapters. Benji was a prime example of this. He began by saying, "Actually, this is more of a new development. Since I've come to WU, I've had this dialogue with members of different communities and that sort of thing and it's really something that I've kind of come to realize, like it's something that I have never thought about, race on a daily basis, but then talking with a friend of mine who's a Black female who says she has to deal with it all the time. It's something that she constantly has to deal with, has really kind of opened my eyes." Benji was clear that this was a new development in his life. In high school, he admitted that he did not think about race that much because, as a White man, he did not have to engage as part of his White immunity. However, this dialogue with a Black female friend helped "open his eyes." I asked Benji why he would believe his friend's reality when it was so different from his own, and this was especially important given the narratives in the previous chapters where White men tended to be skeptical of minority claims of racism. He said it started with their friendship, and then the dialogue about racism emerged. That is, there was a relationship in place, and then he started hearing about her racial reality. In addition, it was not a one-time discussion. Rather, it was a reoccurring dialogue over an extended period of time. Hearing about the discrimination that his friend continually experienced led Benji to the following conclusion: "I suppose as a White person, you don't really think about it on a day-to-day basis, like race or that sort of thing. So, when a minority would say, 'I have this issue,' and then Whites dismiss it, it's just because they have different perspectives and because the White person doesn't have to necessarily think how their race plays into a specific situation." Benji understood that White people were frequently skeptical when minorities made claims of racism. Instead, he directly linked this skepticism to White immunity because White people like himself did not *have to* think about race if they did not want to because they were not the targets of racism.

Larry was relatively unique among this group of White guys. During his pre-college years, he lived in a predominantly Black environment. This did not happen by accident. Larry explained that his parents were extremely committed to public schools and racial integration:

> My parents sort of started leading this crusade of White students back in the Oakland public schools. You know, me and all my cousins went there and they started talking to their White friends, this idea like, "No, let's bring everybody back to the public school system," and how there was still this mentality. . . . Some White parents were like, "No, private school because I can afford to do it and it's a safety issue," and all these things. Even people that talked all high about stuff like public education, but then when the time came, it was a little bit different.

Larry described his parents' actions as a "crusade," but one that acknowledged that they were in privileged social positions because of White flight and their socioeconomic status. This meant that Larry grew up in an environment where he was an intentional minority, learning from racial difference, but with a family-engrained social justice orientation.

Interestingly, one of the ways that Larry learned about race was through cross-racial fighting. It was a relatively common occurrence for Larry to get into physical altercations with people from his neighborhood. It was not so much the fights that were illuminating to him but others' reactions to the fights—in particular law enforcement:

I would say on a personal level, just having been involved in fights and what-not . . . like one time I got jumped because of whatever and the police came and took a report from me rather than first assuming that I was at fault because the people that jumped me were Black. Or another time when I got in a big fight it was me and a couple of my other White friends got in a fight with these Vietnamese dudes and the police were automatically like, "Oh, what happened to. . . ." It was very much like we were clearly the victims and even if it were or wasn't true, there's been so many other. . . . You know, witnessing fights where there's two Black dudes going at it or a Latino dude and a Black dude and it's like both are handled like they did something wrong.

In this way, Larry became keenly aware of his White immunity throughout his time in Oakland public schools. Fighting was a fairly common activity in his neighborhood and among his peers; however, when the police were involved there was an assumption that the People of Color were at fault. Larry was more frequently seen by law enforcement as the victim instead of a perpetrator or aggressor in the fights.

Beyond the fights, Larry also thought that his home environment greatly influenced his worldview. In particular, Oakland was not just an incredibly diverse area but also one that had a strong rooting in social activism.

> L: I think they changed mostly based upon the types of people I've been around.
> N: What do you mean by that?
> L: Going to Oakland public schools, I was exposed to a particular subset, like a particular type of person. You know, it was like an Oakland culture that was had across races. There was some variance, but it was a little violent, a little rebellious, but there was also a little of the conscious side of things that filtered down from sort of the activist culture.

It was not only that Larry lived in this racially progressive area of the country, but he also believed he was insulated. While there was a lot of racial conflict in his home environment, there were few people who ascribed to color-blindness, and he also described it as a bubble from what he labeled "aggressive conserva-tivism." He struggled with that at WU, as he explained: "I mean, fuck the [student conservative paper]. There was nothing like that in Oakland. The White students I went to high school with, they may have been a little bit scared and intimidated, but they were all very liberal." It was really jarring for Larry to come to college and hear his peers openly think, for example, that racial inequality stems from Black people being lazy.

In addition, Larry met Black students on campus who grew up in majority-White environments and who did not associate with the Black community on campus. These students also tended to shy away from activism or community organizing, which for Larry were ways of life. He explained, "Down here I meet Black people that are raised in all-White environments and they're not trying to identify at all with other Black people on campus and things like that, so I would say as far as types of Black people, one, I feel like I got down here and I was like, 'Whoa, this is kind of strange.' So that kind of challenged me to think of things in less of a racial lens and more in a like-minded lens." These interactions pushed Larry because he began to understand more heterogeneity within the Black community. His experiences in Oakland led him to conflate racial activism with the Black community, and many Black students at WU disrupted that notion. Overall, the combination of high school and college experiences helped Larry gain an understanding of the way racism operates while also challenging him to not essentialize groups. Larry, however, was not typical of any of these White guys. Instead, even the more racially progressive White guys talked about cross-racial interactions, but their personal developments were not of the depth Larry experienced.

For example, Derek described his personal growth during college, in particular having a lot of exposure to Asian Americans in his living/learning environment. While Derek was definitely more racially aware and engaged than the White guys featured in chapters 2 through 6, he did not have as thorough an understanding of racism as many of the White guys in this chapter. His description of cross-racial interactions while in college offers some insight into his process of beginning to understand and appreciate cultural difference, but this did not mean he became aware of social hierarchies and oppression. He offered,

> Like coming here to college, it's definitely . . . it's so I guess exciting in the sense that I get to see people interact in different . . . like with their parents in different ways. For example, they'll call up and they're speaking Mandarin Chinese or something . . . like my roommate, he's constantly on the phone with his girlfriend in Korean and everything, so I hear Korean every day. Every day, I hear Korean, and that's just something I don't get at home, and I think that's really cool personally. I think just being exposed to the different cultures and different races and everything, I think that's really cool.

From Derek's racially sheltered upbringing, this was a dramatic development for him personally. Being constantly exposed to different cultures helped Derek expand his horizons, but it did little to help him understand how racism inequitably structures society. Later, he described these experiences leaving him more open to hearing about systemic racism, but these environments by themselves did not lead Derek to better understand racial oppression. Rather, they served as a foundation for deeper engagement at a later point in time.

Frequently, there was overlap between developments that occurred through interpersonal contact and those in the classroom. Josh was a bit of an outlier in a very interesting way. He was a White guy who was also an African American studies major, and I will discuss his academic development in the next section. Regardless, he discussed an interesting cycle where the personal and the academic became mutually reinforcing areas for continually learning more and more about racism: "Well I was, I transferred from [institution], and um, I was in the, I started attending Black Student Union meetings there. Um, this girl in my African American history class was the vice president, and um, she had mentioned it to me once, and she said that I should come." From this brief interaction, he became a full member of the Black Student Union, and this also translated into a number of tangible, anti-racist actions in conjunction with this student group. Again, it was not that the interaction with the vice president of the Black Student Union was socially transformative by itself. Rather, his interpersonal relationship with her and his academic studies led to this opportunity for more anti-racist engagement and action, as I will detail in a subsequent section. Regardless, the classroom was also a strong site for disrupting *epistemologies of ignorance* (Mills, 1997), but this involved more than simply adding a few People of Color to the curriculum as these White guys' narratives demonstrate.

Multicultural Education and Humanizing Pedagogy

Many of these White guys discussed course content, in particular college classes, influencing their increased understandings of contemporary racism. However, their narratives moved well beyond simply "I learned this fact." While statistics and historical narratives can be important, they were insufficient by themselves to open the eyes of these White guys, as there tended to be a human story behind the social science analyses. This was incredibly important because, as Leonardo (2005) argued, "Countering with scientific evidence an ideological mindset that criminalizes people of color becomes an exercise in futility because it does not even touch the crux of the problem, one based upon fear and loathing" (p. 402). Within this context, Jay described his experience taking an African American studies course. It was a strange environment for him because the instructor was the only Black person in the class: "It's funny because the only African American person in the entire class is the teacher, but we bring up such deeper issues that I would never really talk about. So every week, I'm reminded that there are injustices or there is racism going on that I might be blind to, but just because I'm blind to them doesn't necessarily mean that they don't exist." It was really important for Jay to be in this environment because he came to realize that being White, and thus not being a racial target, he was systematically unaware of a lot of racism. Rather, it was his White immunity (Cabrera, 2017) that allowed him to be insulated from this social reality. Strangely, he learned that while the class, his peers, and the instructor helped him begin understanding issues of race, he continued to have massive blind spots on the subject. That is, he became awakened to his own ignorance.

Jay and I more deeply explored the role of this particular class in his personal development. There was one assignment, involving interviewing a Black professional about her or his experiences with workplace racism, that helped opened his racial eyes:

> I've learned through my interview with an African American professional woman last week and my class is that racism, from what I gather, is an ongoing everyday thing and it's something that they don't. . . . And by they, I mean African Americans . . . don't need to necessarily need to search for, it's just always there, at least that's what I've been told. Personally, that's never really happened to me because I've never really been the minority somewhere, so I wouldn't know firsthand how that would feel, but I gather and I what I tend to believe is that it's . . . certain incidents occur on a daily basis that remind them that they are African American. Whereas, I'm not usually reminded that I'm White.

Jay learned about the discrimination that Black people face through both this class and the specific assignment, but they also made him reflect on his personal experiences. In his everyday life, Jay was rarely reminded that he was White, whereas his Black interviewee said she was consistently reminded of her race. The interview further opened Jay's eyes in terms of racial discrimination, in particular because he was hearing about firsthand human experiences:

> [The interviewee] always felt that she had to overcome. . . . You know, give 110 percent at all times and otherwise she would be labeled as the Black girl or the African American girl who was falling behind when she necessarily. . . . So, she was adamant about the fact that she felt that she had to overcome these unfair situations that were going on in the classroom and it continued on in her professional life where she was passed up for a promotion. She had worked for the company for seven years and had come to work every day, worked really hard, and was a self-proclaimed "damn good worker." And she explained that racial stereotypes actually worked against her in that the promotion was given to an Asian woman who was on vacation or on sabbatical at all times and did mediocre work at best.

Again, it was not only that this Black woman's experience was strongly different from Jay's, but the assignment also made him consider how immune he was to this type of discriminatory action: "I think that the interview, that definitely opened my eyes to a lot of things that I wasn't aware of necessarily or didn't like to think about or just kind of liked to turn a blind eye to." This was a critically important first step for Jay as he described his views in high school as aspiring to color-blindness, ignoring issues of race, and also being skeptical when people in the mass media thought that racism played a factor in an issue. This class and interview did not completely change his views, but he was more open to understanding how racism structures contemporary society and was more willing to explore the need for race-conscious social policies.

Josh's experience mirrored Jay's in that he learned not only from course content on race/racism but also a strong humanizing pedagogy that accompanied the material. Josh openly admitted that in his suburban high school environment he had minimal contact with People of Color. From that orientation, he (mis)understood racial inequality to be a function of minorities, in particular Black people, being lazy. His courses provided salient challenges to this perspective. In particular, he discussed a history class that particularly resonated with him:

And the way that he would affirm the, the dignity of people who we might think were lesser because of maybe they lived in uh, um, substandard conditions. Or that they were, you know, I thought for . . . "Oh, they're, they're lazy. They don't have personal responsibility." . . . And um, [the professor] helped, he helped me rethink my assessment of that as far as well, you know, are people, I don't know. Are Black people lazy? Well, you know, if you go, and if you look in neighborhoods that are, that are underdeveloped, there's a definite, there's a relationship between self-responsibility and the kind of development. But also, when we're talking about how, how really powerful the uh, you know government policy is. You know, just as ghettos are state-sanctioned, suburbs are as well. And I just, I started looking at uh, rethin—rethinking the way that I, I saw certain ethnic groups.

Josh began actually thinking about the people in these substandard living conditions and empathizing with them, but also seeing his privileged suburban existence stemming from the same social policies. Keep in mind, he did not pity or sympathize with them. He was very clear on that point. Rather, his professor helped him understand the human dignity of people living in *barrios* and ghettos across the United States, which, to use Josh's words, began to foster a sense of "linked fate" with these communities. That is, it is easy to blame poor people for being poor or People of Color for the discrimination they face, as if their condition has nothing to do with yours. Josh instead began to conceptualize his role in the world. Josh started to view a number of his social advantages as directly related to the marginalized status of People of Color, rather than his advancement being independent of them. For him, this helped foster a sense of social responsibility that I will elaborate on in a subsequent section.

There were some White guys for whom learning historical and contemporary facts about racism was compelling, but the information needed to be linked to *systemic issues* that marginalized People of Color. Jason remembered one particularly enlightening moment from a class that was part of a consistent "flow of information":

> I think that it's mainly a general flow of information, but there are a few details that really did stand out to me. One of my classes, "Social Inequality," that was last semester and it had one particular detail that really did stick with me as I was reading, "In 1860 African Americans owned 0.5 percent of American's total wealth. As of 1960, African Americans owned 1 percent of Americas total wealth." I mean, arguably since things are a little bit better, racism is becoming more and more of a socially stigmatic thing . . . that hopefully if the percentage has gone up somewhat since then, but still when you've got roughly a fifth of the population with 100th of the wealth . . . it just seems perhaps there's something unfair going on.

The beginning part of Jason's statement was particularly telling. While this may have been his "ah-ha" moment, it occurred as part of his classes that centered racial inequality in the content. It was a moment that solidified his understanding amid *consistent* engagement with the issue. In addition, linking statistics to systemic reality showed Jason that there was something structurally wrong in society that both disadvantaged People of Color and advantaged him as a White person.

Alex also talked about the importance of consistent engagement. He took a yearlong sequence on interracial dynamics, which he described as critically important in developing his understanding of how racism operates. For him, it was the intentional sequencing of the class as the content linked the history of colonialism to contemporary realities:

> A: Actually, what drew me to it is I'm taking . . . or this year I've been taking a class, a yearlong class on interracial dynamics, and just sort of that whole social science aspect really kind of drew me in.
>
> N: What is this class on interracial dynamics?
>
> A: First quarter is, was sort of just like the history of race and colonialism, slavery, things like that. Second quarter, more the social implications and the implications of today. I mean, we looked at the Watts riots, the LA riots, civic rights movements, stuff like that, and this quarter it's a seminar, so we're just . . . my seminar is about . . . it's called the "White Flight in Los

Angeles after World War II." It's sort of how World War II shaped race relations in LA today. It's really interesting. It's really actually opened my eyes to a lot of things that I like.

N: Okay, in what respect has it opened your eyes?

A: Just the way . . . looking at race not as much from a minority viewpoint, but as sort of looking at what's behind race, like the unspoken White majority and things like that.

Alex was honest that he did not have a lot of friends of color from whom he could learn, so this class was critically important to helping him understand what racism is. It was a difficult experience for him because, as he said, "I don't see myself as racist." He instead linked this history and contemporary realities to a structure of oppression that marginalized People of Color. Much like with Jason, it was central to Alex's development that he was engaging with these ideas over an extended period and also that the racial facts were more than abstractions. Instead, they were directly linked to contemporary realities, offering a new lens through which Alex was able to explore and understand society.

Max made an interesting point about racism that he learned in class. Most of the White guys discussed "lightbulbs going off" or "ah-ha" moments that really helped them understand the nature of contemporary racism. Max also had an "ah-ha" moment, but like Jay, it meant realizing what he did *not* know: "[Classes brought] out all these issues was what really kind of made the light bulb go on, but I still have a lot to learn." He took several classes and saw many lectures on campus that helped him explore different facets of racism, and the consistency of engagement echoed the narratives of both Jason and Alex. What was unique about Max was his central lesson continued to be how much he did not know. This was a stark contrast to the White guys who were the center of chapters 2 through 6. They not only were generally ignorant on racial issues but insisted they did know. By contrast, Max learned important information on racism, but he also came to understand that he had a number of glaring holes in his knowledge base. Essentially, he began to know what he did not know, and that became his new epistemic orientation.

Benji was more philosophical on the importance of higher education institutions engaging racism and how they are ideal environments for this kind of learning: "The more educated we are, the better able we are to understand these issues and to intelligently grapple with them. I think that universities offer a place where people can explore these ideas in a safe setting, and so it's really important I guess that universities maintain that role and I guess are kind of the . . . act as the center of exploring these ideas and helping introduce them into the community and just as a society, making sure that we move forward on issues of race." In stark contrast to the White guys featured in chapters 2 through 6 who frequently considered White men to be racial victims of multicultural higher education, Benji saw his university as an important space for the exchange of ideas on race and racism. It was personal for him because he saw this as a place of great personal growth via both classes and cross-racial friendships. He believed that universities bore social responsibility in challenging racism and that they also offered uniquely safe spaces to work on these issues. In addition to course content, another way that this group of the White guys disrupted epistemologies of ignorance (Mills, 1997) was through being a non–racial minority.

Non-Racial-Minority Experiences

Many of the White guys in this chapter discussed being a non–racial minority, and this helped them be more open to learning about systemic racism. In terms of defining majority/minority, I rely on Baldwin's (1984) conception that is more than simply one side having more numbers: "The only useful definition of the word 'majority' does not refer to numbers, and it does not refer to power. It refers to influence" (p. 109). I do take some issue with Baldwin's distinction between power and influence; that is, in my understanding influence is a manifestation of power (Lukes, 2007). Despite this semantic issue, Baldwin's point is clear—that the definition of minority means having less systemic influence than the majority. In a contemporary context, this means that the majority is defined by Whiteness, heterosexuality, masculinity, Christianity, and ability, among many other -isms in society (Evans, Forney, Guido, Patton, & Renn, 2010).

While, for example, being gay in a heterosexist society does not lead one to understand the nature of racism, many of the White guys I spoke with in this chapter discussed how being a sexual minority left them open to understanding issues of racism. Please understand, it would be asinine to claim that there are no issues of racism within the LGBTQ community (Han, 2008). Rather, there was a strong trend among these White guys linking their experiences as sexual minorities to being more willing to understand race, as Chris highlighted: "Well, I guess if you haven't experienced being in a minority group, you wouldn't have an opinion that matches that minority group. So, even though I'm not a racial ethnic minority, I'm a minority in terms of being gay and sexual preference. So, I can identify with these different racial groups. So, that's how I . . . that's where my understanding comes from. Maybe if I were straight and White, I would probably have a different opinion." Chris knew firsthand the experience of being gay in a heterosexist society, and from this he knew that "it seems like there's more disadvantages just being gay." He was able to make a connection from that positionality as a gay man to understand that People of Color have similar experiences relative to White people like himself. Chris, however, also understood that people of the majority group could and should be part of struggles that did not adversely affect them directly. He began by describing his involvement with a gay/bisexual fraternity: "I belong to [fraternity name], which is a national fraternity primarily with gay men. But we welcome what we call progressive men, so men who would identify as gay or bisexual or straight, but they would have to be comfortable around gay or bisexual men." Even though Chris's fraternity was overwhelmingly made up of gay and bisexual men, straight men could participate but had to meet some conditions.

Chris then drew a comparison between this dynamic and the relationship between White people and systemic racism. That is, as a White man he could, and should, be involved in the larger struggle against racism. Chris did not go so far as to claim that he truly understood racial issues, but instead he called for greater understanding and engagement across marginalized communities: "I think that both gay people in general need to understand race matters and people that are minorities need to understand gay matters because there's a lot that we all have in common and that.... You know, a lot of things are.... Well, some people say that White rich people dominate a lot of things and it's partially true, but I would say that if we can team together and actually make some kind of political difference, it might be definitely a good thing and progress can be made." Chris's statement has a great deal of nuance. He offered a vision People of Color and the LGBTQ community coming together to challenge the existing power structures, but in his understanding, this meant both communities working through their engrained racism and homophobia. What was troubling about this statement was that it meant Chris's gay community was largely White, which he openly admitted. Regardless, Chris still used his experiences as an openly gay man to begin to understand issues of race and disrupting the *epistemology of ignorance* (Mills, 1997).

These minority experiences also occurred when the White guys in this chapter practiced non-Christian religions. Half of David's family was Palestinian, and he identified as Muslim. He was born in Russia, was visibly White, and this created a difficult situation for him. In a post-9/11 world, he was keenly aware of Islamophobia, and he could have chosen to keep his religious beliefs to himself to avoid social persecution. He knew that phenotypically he could assimilate into society, but he chose a different route. Instead, he joined the Muslim Student Association, which sometimes led to difficult interpersonal situations: "You know, if [non-Muslims] learn I'm from the Muslim Student Association or they learn I'm Palestinian they're like you know, on edge." It was a relatively constant process for David as people rarely assumed from his physical appearance that he was either Muslim or Palestinian. He discussed a number of stereotypes he had to navigate as a result (e.g., Muslim equals terrorist), and David offered, "Well, you know, there's just certain things people assume about you and there's even the, a lot of visibly when they realize you're from some racial or religious minority, like even for myself." David did not consider himself a racial minority, but he did see the situations as analogous. That is, anti–People of Color racism had many similar features to anti-Muslim Islamophobia. He did not go so far as to claim he truly understood racism because he was still learning about the issue. Instead, David's experiences as a religious minority helped him to be more open to engaging issues of race.

Alex and Zeke were both Jewish and thus religious minorities who had to navigate a number of stereotypes as a result. For example, Alex offered, "Well, I'm Jewish, so Jews are good with money, stuff like that." Zeke had many similar experiences, and he said he learned to see and engage issues of anti-Semitism from his father: "You know, I'm going to take a different angle from that, which is . . . I think my father is a . . . he sees that. . . . Yeah, he's very sensitive to that and he thinks people see him as Jewish and he's hypersensitive to what they say and says, 'Oh, they're saying that because I'm Jewish,' and I think some of that has spilled over to me." From this perspective, however, Zeke understood that many People of Color are sensitized to issues of racism in ways that he could not be as a White man: "I would say that if you're a White person, you're looking at the world through, okay, a White person's eyes." To Zeke, that meant not being the target of racism in the way that many People of Color experience on a regular basis. His experiences with anti-Semitism did not make him an expert on racism but increased his sensitivity to racial issues.

Jason was a relatively unique case because he was both bisexual and one of the few White people at a predominantly Latinx high school. In high school, he was a self-described loner and was constantly getting beat up by Mexican American kids. He was convinced that the reason he stood out was because he was White in a predominantly Mexican American environment, but what was remarkable to me in his narrative was that he never framed himself as a racial victim—standing in stark contrast to the White guys in the previous chapters. Strangely, he said it increased his sensitivity toward other issues of oppression: "I think I got sensitized to race when I was in the minority. . . . I feel sometimes that I'm much more aware of race than I might have been if I had grown up in say Minnesota." I wanted to explore this in more depth because it would have been very understandable for Jason to be angry:

J: Of course, I felt like, "Fuck you. You guys beat up on me, so I don't want to have anything to do with you." But on the other side, it also increases the sensitivity to what it could be like to be in a minority position.

N: It's almost like . . . you almost have a paradoxical response to what. . . .

J: You could almost say that it sensitizes you to racial issues, but the treatment that sensitizes you makes you negative towards them.

Jason did not want anyone to experience that kind of treatment. This did not make Jason understand systemic oppression, but he did get a sense of mistreatment that can occur when one does not have the power of numbers.

Additionally, Jason was openly bisexual. It bothered him hearing slurs like "that's so gay," and he was sometimes guarded about to whom he divulged his sexual orientation. Like other White guys in this section, being a sexual minority further helped Jason understand what it meant to be socially marginalized. However, Jason also saw society changing, and there were times when he felt he could use his bisexuality to his advantage. For example, the "don't ask, don't tell" policy was still in place when he was a senior in high school, and he recalled, "Okay, my parents were both Navy espionage agents and so they had a kid, the kid was having good grades, they really wanted me in the military. I really did not want to go, so it was very convenient being able to, 'Hi, we're looking for Jason.' 'Who is this?' 'Oh, yeah, this is the Navy.' 'I'm bisexual.' 'Oh, well, then have a nice day,' click." Beyond this, however, Jason felt his multiple minority experiences allowed him to be open to better understanding racism: "Yeah, and so it's only because of my experiences as a minority simultaneously with college that have finally allowed me I think to get a better picture of everything." Jason was clear on this point: the combination of personal minority experiences and his college experiences (classes in particular) made him begin to understand racism. The final method that the White guys in this chapter used to begin opening their eyes to the realities of racism was unexpected: being White-identified but also biracial.

Biracial but White-Identified

There was a curious issue that arose in this work. I explicitly told people I wanted to talk with White male undergraduates, and there was a small but visible group in this sample who were biracial but White-identified. I did not anticipate these guys would participate in my study, but they all considered themselves White because they were treated as White—or could pass as White whenever they wanted. Additionally, they were not strongly connected to their ethnic heritage. Coming from mixed-race families, these White guys developed their racial awareness from a very early age, as they did not have the luxury of ignoring race. In addition, it was much more difficult to vilify and demonize the racial other, as many in the previous chapters did, because this "other" was represented by people within their own families.

Among this subsection of the White guys I spoke with, one was part Japanese and White, and three others were a mix of Mexican/Latino/Hispanic and White. I grappled with whether or not I should use these interviews and eventually decided to include them for the following reasons. They primarily self-identified as White, were phenotypically White, and said that other people almost exclusively viewed them as White. With this ability to pass, they were not racially targeted and their social experiences tended to mirror those of Whites.

They had different means of negotiating their biracial background, but through this process, being racially aware was part of their lived familial existence. Jacob was very conscious that people viewed him as White: "Most people are surprised. I mean, for the most part, because of my appearance and diction and surname, they tend to just think, 'Oh, he's got some sort of White heritage, whatever,' and then when they find out I'm half Hispanic, they're a little . . . they're taken a little aback." Jacob was both Latinx and White, although people tended to perceive him as White. Even with this mixed racial background, he did not feel very connected to his family's Mexican culture. His Latinx grandparents pushed for cultural assimilation, and consequently Jacob did not speak Spanish: "I mean, the most exposure I ever got to like even the language would be like my grandparents fighting in Spanish and that was about it. . . . So, it was like I picked up all the curse words and not a lot else." This did not mean Jacob disavowed his Latinx familial heritage. Rather, it was a constant negotiation for him to understand exactly what this meant to him. This was promoted by his grandparents' cultural assimilation where they lost a number of their Mexican traditions in the process:

> J: I suppose [my grandparents] were sort of the Cosby brand of Latino.
> N: What do you mean by that?
> J: They were a little on the white-bread side comparatively, but you know, it was a little strange. So, I suppose in terms of identity, I don't really gravitate towards either side. I'm just sort of here.

Jacob found himself in a type of racial limbo, not really being drawn to either side of his family's racial heritage. Regardless, being biracial meant to Jacob that he had a lot of interactions with Latinx people because they were part of his family.

Greg had a similar experience being a light-skinned Latino who people almost always thought was White. Of the four biracial but White-identified guys, however, Greg had the strongest connection to his familial culture. He began by describing how he was generally perceived as White, but he and his older sister together worked through their biracial heritage: "Me and my sister joke like we're half-breeds. I mean, our mother was born in Mexico and our father was born in Italy, so I think Chicano is very . . . I mean, is one that I don't go around saying I'm Chicano. I just say I'm a Mexicano, I just say Mexicano, and I'm one of those where you look White." Greg identified more strongly with his Mexican heritage than Jacob, and this is due, in part, to the fact that his mother came from Mexico whereas Jacob's grandparents were the cultural gatekeepers of the family and they were trying to assimilate. However, Greg admitted that the different sides of the family were frequently at odds with each other as his White side frequently disliked Mexicans and his Mexican side frequently disliked the White: "And you'll be around people growing up and talk shit about Mexicanos because it's something you grew up with. And then on the other hand, I haven't spent as much time with our family, but I'm told from my sister I'm very close with that what's interesting is on the other side of our family. . . . I mean, because we look White, people are like . . . making fun of us kids." More dramatically than Jacob, Greg found himself in a type of racial limbo between the two cultures; not entirely accepted by either. Regardless, this meant that from a very young age, he had to work through his racial background being very racially cognizant. While this did produce a lot of confusion as a child, it meant that as an adult he was better able to navigate multicultural environments.

Benji's experience was more similar to Jacob's. His biracial background came from his mother who was half Japanese, but Benji primarily identified as White: "I just . . . I don't look very Japanese. Like Japanese is not a very big part of my culture or anything." Benji did not speak Japanese, but one cultural tradition persisted: "On New Year's [my family] used to get together with my great-grandmother who was alive and do this traditional . . . have the certain [Japanese] foods that you'd eat." His grandmother no longer spoke Japanese, and slowly Japanese culture was leaving the family. Regardless, Benji, like Jacob and Greg, had early and extensive exposure to non-White people, and this helped him work through his own racial background starting the process of becoming more racially aware.

Jay was even further removed from his mixed-race background. As he stated, "I am Caucasian. My mom, on the other hand, is Italian, Mexican, and Portuguese. So, I have little bit of mixed blood in me, but I always identify myself as Caucasian." Jay did not have as much confusion about his racial/ethnic ground as the previous three participants because being biracial meant very little to his social identity. It was a part of his mother's identity, but he exclusively saw himself as White. His mother did not transmit any Mexican cultural traditions to him, and she did not speak Spanish in the house while he was a child. Regardless, his mother never hid her mixed racial background, and thus, he became aware of racial difference at a very young age. His process was not as pronounced as those of Jacob, Greg, or Benji, as his familial culture was even less a part of his upbringing. While the White guys in this section were not targeted based on their biracial backgrounds, their identity left them open to understanding and engaging issues of race when they arose. Regardless of the method for disrupting epistemologies of ignorance described above (or combination thereof), the White guys highlighted in this chapter were markedly different from those in the previous chapters in three key ways: (1) they could actually identify instances of racism in contemporary society, (2) they saw themselves as either complicit in or responsible for issues of racism, and (3) they frequently took tangible actions to challenge and disrupt racism.

Eyes Wide Open: Seeing Race and Understanding Racism

The White guys in this chapter tended to have very nuanced definitions and examples of racism. Many in the previous chapters had extremely simplistic and antiquated ones, and those parts of their interviews were borderline boring or repetitive. Therefore, I omitted these discussions from the earlier chapters in this book, but readers are more than welcome to explore what they said (see Cabrera, 2014d). Returning to the White guys in this chapter, David both gave a definition of racism but also explained why it is so difficult for White people to understand it: "It's systematic. It's kind of structured that way. And, you know a lot of times in a lot of cases it is White male privilege and you know in education a lot and in hiring and stuff like that. It's hard to break through that. . . . And as a White person, you know, you've never known any other system. You've never known any other situation. So, it's really hard to see what benefits you're getting in this society. What privileges you're getting without even knowing. Without even realizing it or being able to confront it." David learned a lot about White privilege in college, but again his experiences as an American Muslim post-9/11 made him sensitive to the idea that beneficiaries of oppressive systems do not necessarily understand how the system advantages them because it is a normal way of existing. David then gave an example of racism that stemmed from his involvement in his fraternity. In contrast to the fraternity-based narratives in previous chapters, David offered the following: "I don't want to air the house dirty laundry, the dirty laundry of my house, but there's you know, I find the racism there problematic. People, you know, for some they're just joking, some really mean it. I don't even know, I don't you know, don't accept it right away and its, I find it very problematic. You know there's, even in our house, there's you know a conscious effort to recruit, you know, Whites and Asians for GPA boosting. You know. Its sick." David witnessed firsthand the mechanisms by which Black, Latinx, and Native American students were excluded from participation. It began with the racist stereotype that they would have low GPAs. It then moved to targeted recruitment of only White and Asian members. David was very prompt to label this a racist practice, although it was troubling that he did little to stop or even disrupt it, simply bearing witness.

Jacob offered an example from the mass media that he thought was an instance of racism. NYPD officers killed an unarmed Black man, Sean Bell, after his bachelor party in a hail of fifty bullets (Borger, 2006). Jacob thought this incident was a clear-cut example of racism:

J: Well, I suppose the biggest deal recently would be the acquittal of those officers in that shooting in New York.

N: Okay, and pretend that I don't know anything. What happened in that situation?

J: From what I know, there was this guy who's basically out with his friends whooping it up before he got hitched and he's at a strip club. Apparently, he was coming out and he got into some kind of altercation with police officers who thought he was armed and they shot at him more fifty times.

N: Okay, and so then why was it a racist event? Or were you talking about the acquittal or the actual event or both as being racist?

J: Both.

N: Okay, so explain the shot. . . . Explain the homicide and then the acquittal.

J: Well, the event itself, you would have to wonder, well, would a White guy coming out of the same club be shot at fifty times in the exact same circumstances?

This example really resonated with Jacob because he has been in similar situations, and nothing like this had ever happened to him or his White friends. His analysis was really interesting because he never tried to see what was in the officers' hearts to determine if their hatred or fear of Black people led to this incident. Rather, he focused on White immunity (Cabrera, 2017) and asked a provocative question: when was the last time a similarly situated White person was killed by the police?

These examples were contextualized within a much more complicated and systemic understanding of the nature of racism—beyond simply "hatred of the racial other" or "belief in the superiority of one race over another." Larry, like David, gave a strong definition: "Racism to me is institutionalized discrimination based upon aesthetic differences that we have sort of conjured into social relevance. I think the key part of it is that it's institutionalized because a lot of people will talk about reverse racism and things like that and not that People of Color can't be discriminatory or bigoted because that's definitely true. But I think when there's a power structure behind your particular discriminatory belief . . . I think that's what constitutes racism." Within these five short lines, Larry described racism as a systemic reality where social significance is attached to arbitrary characteristics. He then linked these beliefs to a power structure and explicitly debunked the notion of "reverse racism." Larry then offered a number of examples of discriminatory lending practices, NIMBYism, and equating safety with White suburban segregation.

While few White guys in this chapter had as nuanced an understanding of the nature of racism as Larry, most framed it as a systemic reality informed by power dynamics that continually re-created racial inequality. From these contexts, there were several examples of racism that the White guys in this chapter offered. Greg, for example, thought the use of the term "illegal" in reference to immigration was racist: "If you just call someone illegal, you completely take out humanity, you completely take out human agency, and you're just talking about a thing." He saw this term as dehumanizing, and he also did not find it coincidental that it was lodged against Latinx people in general and Mexicanos like his mother in particular. Greg read between the racial lines and thought that when people used "illegal," it tended to be against Brown-skinned folk because he never heard someone talk about "illegal Canadians." This, according to Greg, was both racist and dehumanizing.

There was one incident that a number of the White guys in this chapter discussed as an example of campus-based racism. It was extremely telling not only that they continually highlighted this issue, but also how their peers at WU in the previous chapters never mentioned it. This was not a story that garnered headlines, but it did spread through word of mouth and social media—although it never went viral. Larry provided the greatest detail on the incident:

> The president of the African Student Union (ASU) was on campus, it was in the evening, and was unloading some boxes after an ASU event. I think Amiri Baraka was here speaking. And so, after that we all went home or whatever, but then he was unloading some stuff and CSO (campus security officers) came up on him like, "What are you doing?" Other CSOs came and surrounding him, he's like, "I'm just putting stuff away. . . ." He had his wife and daughter in the car and he drives off campus and he's immediately pulled over by the police and there was an assumption that he was stealing stuff from the student union, that he was. . . . And if that was anybody else, that would have never happened. They cuffed him, he's like, "Please, my daughter. . . ." You know, they cuffed him and only after he said, "I'm the head of ASU," and then, "Oh, we don't want to be affiliated with doing this." But if I was there unloading stuff, they wouldn't have said shit to me.

To summarize, a Black student was cleaning up after a campus event, loading supplies into his car. The CSOs assumed he was stealing, pulled him over, and handcuffed him in front of his child. For Larry, this was a clear-cut example of racism because as a White man he would never be questioned or detained for this behavior. While the narratives in this section highlight the White guys' abilities to see and critique systemic racism, they were also willing to examine their own complicity in its perpetuation (Applebaum, 2010).

Pointing the (Racial) Finger Within and Self-Reflection

An additional way the White guys I spoke with for this chapter can be distinguished from those in the previous ones was that they were willing to examine

instances when they were personally racist while also owning their White priv-
ilege/immunity. It is one thing to criticize the racism of others, but it is an
entirely different level of commitment and analysis to look within one's self and
find complicity with racism (Applebaum, 2010). For example, a number of the
White guys in previous chapters spent a lot of time explaining why the student
groups to which they belonged were not racist—or how race-conscious student groups were either divisive or racist. In contrast, many of the White guys
in this chapter were willing to lodge constructive criticisms against their own
campus-based organizations. For example, Benji was extremely active in the
campus Democrats and offered, "Like with organizations on campus, a lot of
them are affiliated with a certain group or something, like Samahang Filipino
is Filipino groups or the African Student Union is African groups, and then
there's the campus Democrats, which is not a very diverse organization. So,
that's kind of what got my mind thinking about it, like why are the Democrats
a White liberal organization? What are we doing that is not attracting this
broader . . . a more diverse and more representative group of who Democrats
are in the community?" This was a fascinating way of framing the issue. Benji
was committed to the campus Democrats as his primary form of involvement
during his undergraduate years. He loved the group and his friends in the group
and cherished the many opportunities his participation allowed him in terms
of engaging the political process. However, his group was not above criticism.
Benji observed that the organization did not have a lot of racial/ethnic diversity, and he placed blame for that on the organization itself instead of seeing it
as a Student of Color issue. We explored this further:

N: So, then it's an interesting perspective because you seem to be pointing the
    finger inside, saying, "What are we doing that's not attracting them?" as
    opposed to saying, "What's wrong with them not coming to us?" Is there
    any particular reason why you would take that perspective?
B: Well, I mean, because what can I do to change how they act? You know, I
    can make deliberate steps within my organizations and who I affiliate with
    to start this dialogue and to move towards more diversity.

Benji saw that he had influence within his group, and he wanted to do something from that orientation. He valued diversity and thought that beginning
this dialogue started with the campus Democrats. That did not mean it would
be an easy task, but if his group was to live up to what he saw as one of their
core values, they needed to change their modus operandi. Their previous methods did not work.

Jason was very clear about the systemic nature of racism marginalizing
People of Color and offered some interesting discussions about being White
and social responsibility. He also dived into the psychology of Whiteness and

the effects it has had on him and other White people as they navigated racial issues:

> J: I consider it the right thing to do because I recognize that I have privilege and most White people do, and I think we're unaggressively blind toward it. I think the reason why when anyone points out that White people have privilege it upsets us is because the privileged person in any relationship really doesn't notice that privilege, even on a micro-structural level between two people. I don't think that White people realize how much we just get for being White and it's only. . . . Affirmative action is the right thing to do because it's fair.
>
> N: And do you think overall that affirmative action is unfair to White people?
>
> J: If I stole your pen and then you took it back, I might call you unfair, but I really don't think in the long run it was unfair at all.

Jason was clear in his thinking: Racial inequality stemmed both a history of racial oppression coupled with contemporary, systemic racism. This created an environment where he and White people like him continually struggled to see the realities of this oppressive system because they were immune to its adverse impacts (Cabrera, 2017). However, Jason continually reminded himself that the system favored him and other White people like him, and this guided how he saw issues of fairness.

Alex saw racism as a systemic reality from which he and other White people benefitted at the expense of People of Color. From that perspective, he felt that he and other White people needed to take greater responsibility for the issue: "I believe that the nature of race relations and racial hostility today is a White problem or a majority problem, if you want to call it White." He later clarified that he was not saying People of Color should wait for White people to become involved in anti-racism. Rather, it was his belief that White people like himself, as beneficiaries of this system, held a unique and pressing responsibility on issues of race. Devin also played off this theme of racial responsibility:

> I think . . . I mean, I think it's a difficult thing . . . I mean, it's something that I as a White person have struggled with quite a bit actually. . . . When you accept the history and you say that people have done what they've done and people have been discriminated against say by our group, by WASPs or whatever you want to call us. . . . You know, there's a phenomenon that has been studied in social psychology called collective guilt and I definitely have experienced my share of that and if you accept the history and face it, then you kind of have to . . . you have to feel like, "Oh, my gosh, look at the stuff we've done to these people," that to some extent we continue to do.

As Devin became more and more aware of the realities of racism both historically and contemporarily, his knee-jerk response was to retreat. He did not want to be privy to this reality as it made him very uncomfortable, but he pushed himself to sit with this discomfort—to explore its roots and his personal social context that helped him stay ignorant to this reality for so long.

Larry was incredibly introspective in terms of constantly negotiating race and racism from the position of being a White man. He gave me a detailed account of his personal history, in particular how he navigated community work in predominantly Black parts of Oakland and his racial identity development:

> I think is interesting is, as a White person, growing up in Oakland, being here as a part of the Black community, there's this validation of, "Oh, that's my nigga," or whatever, saying that to me or, "Larry, whatever, you're Black anyway. Shut up." And sort of . . . that in a way is sort of like a rite of passage like, "You're cool, don't worry about it," but . . . and for a long time I'm like, "Yeah, okay, cool," and even occasionally, like at high school, the n-word would slip out of my mouth and not in a discriminatory way, but just to my Black friends and they would never say anything.

Larry realized he became too comfortable, especially with the use of the n-word, and needed to reappraise his thinking being more aware of his positionality as a White man doing community work in Black neighborhoods. The big issue for him became owning his Whiteness, especially because a number of his friends and colleagues began to say that due to his grassroots commitment, Larry was Black. He offered instead, "In Oakland it was, but it's just fascinating to me and I started being like, 'I'm not Black, I'm White,' Like, 'No, whatever, you're Black.' And I was like, 'No, because if I conform to that, you can still in your mind think that Black people are cool and White people aren't and the only reason that you are is because you're not really White,' and that doesn't help us progress anywhere as far as race politics." Larry did not like being associated with racial privilege or White immunity, but that was the reality of the situation. He acknowledged that it felt good to have the validation of his Black friends saying, "That's my nigga," but he also understood that it made him step out of his lane and start using the word himself—something he did not think White people should do. Larry did like Black community activists telling him he was "down," but he concurrently felt it was necessary for him to own his Whiteness and the social privileges and responsibilities associated with it.

Greg was more philosophical on the intersection of Whiteness and personal responsibility, and his thinking began with the following questions: (1) What is my role in perpetuating systemic racism? and (2) What can I do to disrupt it? That is, he began with himself in the critical analysis and explained why:

> I'd say something that I think is a foundational base in any sort of problem one is trying to get over in society. I think recognize it in yourself. I mean, I think that we're all racist. . . . Especially if you're somehow connected in any way, I think that you need to recognize the problem in yourself first before you can even presume to change. . . . To participate in changing it and I think that that's like . . . I think it's very common, that it's one to get over and recognize that we're all racist. Like that's a relevant moral position from which to begin. I mean, certainly not end.

I was fascinated by Greg's narrative, but I was also a little concerned that he might be pulling an *Avenue Q*, where "everybody's a little bit racist."[1] I asked Greg to clarify what he meant, and he said he was referring to White people specifically. From this perspective, Greg believed the system of contemporary U.S. racism was one that necessarily benefitted White people, and therefore a relevant moral position for him was to understand his own personal responsibility within the situation. For Greg, this type of critical social analysis was not an end in and of itself. Rather, it was a means to the end of informed, antiracist action.

Critique into Practice: White Guys and Racial Justice Actions

To critique White supremacy without challenging it is a form of racial navelgazing. It may make people feel good, but in the absence of actions, there is no social transformation. This connection to action is why Dr. Robin DiAngelo rejected the identity of *racial justice ally* because, "I am a white woman whose academic, professional, and personal commitment is for people of color to decide if, in any given moment, I am behaving in anti-racist ways" ("Multicultural, Social Justice Educator," 2015). DiAngelo believed it was incumbent upon her to take anti-racist actions, and it is up to Communities of Color to determine if she is their ally or not. Similarly, Josh was a really interesting case because he demonstrated the most growth and took some of the most visible anti-racist actions, but was not concerned with being labeled "an ally." It was just work he did. A little context, however, is necessary. As he came from a suburban high school and White, Christian, conservative upbringing, college was a time for deep exploration into issues of race. However, the foundation of his moral compass was forged prior to his undergraduate years: "Another part of it was coming from the Christian background. You know, okay, well, they, the moral issues. Well, I even started to complicate those. And then, as far as the social policy, I thought well, um, it seems like the, the most Christian [laughs] political philosophies would *not* be something that was individualistic, isolated, etc., etc. So, did, and you know, reading people like Martin Luther King, Malcolm X, and others who, ended up adopting somewhat of a socialist, um, worldview at the end of their lives." Josh believed that Christianity was inherently a collectivist moral philosophy, and he really struggled with the direction that many Christian leaders were taking the church. When he started reading more about radical leaders like Dr. King and Malcolm X, he began seeing his moral philosophy aligning with social policy and activism.

As Josh learned more about racism from class and interpersonal interactions, he felt compelled to take action. That is, it was insufficient to critique racial inequality if he did nothing about it. As a starting point, Josh joined the African Student Union (ASU), and it took a while for him to figure out his role as a White man in a largely Black student organization. He showed up consistently, and then his number was called: "Uh, well last quarter they had the admissions crisis rally. Uh, I spoke somewhat on behalf of ASU to the regents. Um, in the formal um, presentation part I guess, where they came here." Josh spoke on behalf of ASU because as a collective they thought the regents would be more receptive to a White person presenting about the declining enrollment of Black undergraduates. Josh was aware that there were many problematic issues in this strategy. In the end, they collectively decided they would try to use Josh's White privilege to push for racial equity. His involvement with ASU extended well beyond this singular event, as he was consistently at meetings, working with the group, and constantly asked how his Whiteness could be leveraged to benefit the collective. Frequently, as he later admitted, that meant being quiet in this Black space and listening instead of offering answers.

Larry did not have any high-profile examples like Josh, but he was also consistently involved in community-based organizations dedicated to racial justice. He began this involvement in high school, and Larry admitted part of his *initial* motivation was selfish: "I had these sort of identity issues to where I was . . . I did feel this need to sort of validate myself as the White person and being different from the other White people that I'd be at school with." That is, Larry saw a lot of his White peers segregating themselves from his Black peers in high school and not caring about issues of racism. Larry wanted to prove he was not "one of those White people." However, after a couple of years of consistent involvement, especially in a program called TryUMF (Try and Uplift My Folks), where he and his cousin were the only White members, Larry had an epiphany: "And then my junior year of high school, I felt like I was validating myself to people that didn't really deserve that validation. Based on the fact that I was White, I always felt on the defensive a little bit when really nobody was really questioning me, but it was just an insecurity I have. So, once I sort of just got that confidence I was like, 'I'm confident in my ability, what I bring to the table, who I am and whatever.'" This was extremely important for Larry because once he came to this realization, he could truly focus on the work. He could do it for the purpose of community uplift instead of personal validation. Larry openly admitted his initial reasons for being involved were selfish, but it evolved into a way of being. During his undergraduate years, he became a site coordinator for a university-based program. Through this involvement, he was constantly organizing trainings, tutoring students, and peer advising, all under the guise of offering "socially relevant education" as a means of promoting social justice.

Despite his commitment to the community, Larry was continually aware of his privileged social position as a White man doing this work. Part of this stemmed from his experiences with many other White people in Communities of Color seeing themselves as "saviors" of poor Black and Brown kids: "I don't think anybody wants to be a problem. I think there's this whole concept of White guilt. You know, like the whole White population in the nonprofit industry and all this to where in an effort to sort of assuage that guilt it's like, 'Well, I serve these communities. You can no longer say this and that about me.'" Larry was fiercely critical of people like this, but he also understood where these emotions came from because he had to negotiate them himself. Larry struggled with how often White middle-class people would begin doing this work, and then a few months later they would be gone. While he critiqued this behavior, he also understood the potential for him to become like this: "And regardless of how much I feel like I dedicate myself to these things, I guess I can choose not to and I'll be okay. I can say, 'Fuck it,' and I'll be good and I think that that sort of strikes a chord of why White people or even like progressive left-leaning White people annoy the shit out of some People of Color because it's like, 'Yeah, you're down today, but what about tomorrow?'" Larry understood he constantly had to ask himself this question because he always had the ability to leave the community whenever he desired. He wanted to do the good work and for the right reasons. He needed to continually be aware of his social positioning as White and try to use his social privileges at the service of dismantling systemic racism. This required offering a social critique, being engaged through tangible actions, and avoiding the temptation to run when it became difficult.

There were some White guys in this chapter who challenged interpersonal racism among other White people. A great deal of racism occurs behind closed doors among other White people (Picca & Feagin, 2007), and so those who have access to these spaces are not only privileged but also responsible for doing something. This is not to say challenging interpersonal racism is a substitute for changing social institutions and structures. Rather, it is one component of the overall strategy. Jason gave a very detailed example of what this can look like, the consequences of these actions, while offering a strong justification for why it is so necessary: "Well, only a couple of days ago, my grandfather sent an email [to the family] that said, 'Michelle Obama, her graduate thesis was *How to Kill Whities, Volume I.*'" Jason was both startled by this email forward because he thought it was factually inaccurate and probably his grandfather being racist. He did a mini-investigation on both CNN and Snopes to conduct some fact-checking. He discovered, "Surprisingly enough, *Kill Whities, Volume I*, was not on the New York Times Best Seller List, I went back to my grandfather and said, 'That email you sent me is wrong.'" Jason's email response seemed pretty innocuous, but there were repercussions.

I continued the conversation with Jason and had him explain in more detail how his grandfather in particular and his family as a whole responded to this incident. He continued, "My grandfather said I was an out of touch little kid and the rest of the family just kind of silently ostracized me." I did not know what Jason meant to be "silently ostracized," so he explained. Jason was very close with his family and while away at college, he would call home regularly to maintain contact, in particular with his siblings: "I mean, call home once a week, check on how my siblings and such are doing, and I called, they were very curt, they said they were busy, and I have a pretty extended family and we all do keep in touch. So, at first, I just thought I was hearing some bad schedules, but then as it became more and more consistent. I finally realized that I'm in the racial doghouse for daring to defend a Black person." Jason later elaborated that it was not only that he criticized a racist practice, but also that he challenged the patriarch of his family. He was open and honest that the response emotionally hurt him as he temporarily lost contact with his family, especially given how close they usually were. Also, it was a relatively minor action in the large scheme of racism, so I probed as to Jason's motivation for his actions:

N: So, the question for me becomes, why did you do it?

J: Because it was fair.

N: Okay, but what makes it fair and why is it necessary to promote fairness? Let me put it this way. Growing up all the time, you're on the playground, Mom and Dad say, "Grow up kid, life's not fair."

J: Life is what we make of it and if I want life to be fair, then the thing I have to do first and foremost is be fair to everyone I can around me. If life isn't fair, well, you know who's in charge of your life? You, and if you start making your life fair in the areas that you can influence fair, maybe life in general will get a little bit more fair once enough people do it.

This central frame of fairness and "doing what's right" cut across a lot of the interviews for this chapter. Please keep in mind that I am not saying that Jason's personal sacrifice in anyway compares to the constant and persistent examples of racial oppression People of Color regularly experience. For example, receiving the silent treatment from family does not compare to the threat to physical safety racially profiling creates. Rather, I am saying it is necessary for White people beginning to engage in this type of action to be prepared for the predictable backlash they will experience for being what Ignatiev (1997) refers to as a *race traitor*. It is action that has consequences, but is also part of a moral way forward—that which is required of those who have been given so many systemic advantages due to the color of their skin. Despite the numerous ways that this subsection of the White guys I spoke with challenged racism, I do not want to portray them as idealized, anti-racist White guys. Instead, they continued to struggle with racial issues in their daily lives, and therefore working through Whiteness (Cabrera, 2012) required consistent engagement.

The White Racial Self: Still Work to Be Done (Constantly)

I really struggle with the term "ally" for a number of reasons. At the 2014 American College Personnel Association national meeting, Professor Robert Reason asked the provocative question, "When did ally become an identity and not a description of action?" (Cabrera, Franklin, & Watson, 2017, p. 100). This was very similar to the critique DiAngelo offered as I previously described. When anti-racist ally is treated as an identity, as Reason so amply observed, it can have a number of unintended negative consequences. It can divide White people into "good Whites" (i.e., anti-racists) and "bad Whites" (i.e., racists). The problem is that being in a racist society, one is never entirely racist or anti-racist. As I have previously argued, "If becoming a racial justice ally is an end met, then students who become allies can stop working on their racial selves" (Cabrera, 2012, p. 397). Forgive the bad pun, but the racist/anti-racist social identity dichotomy makes it a black-and-white issue, and I think it is more productive to play in shades of gray. For example, Feagin and O'Brien (2003) argue that being a recovering racist is much like being a recovering alcoholic: overcoming previous habits, forming new ones, and being aware of the potential to relapse. Within this understanding, I conclude with several examples of how the White guys I spoke with for this chapter continue to struggle with issues of race in their everyday lives. For example, Devin fell into the same trap as many of the White guys in chapter 4, telling and finding racist jokes funny. He began by offering some context: "At the same time, I've just grown up in my family with my brothers, with a lot of my friends, really valuing humor in general and again, humor relating to sort of potentially taboo issues, including toilet humor, sexual humor, and then sort of moving to maybe the big ideological bomb of racial humor." Joking, especially about taboo subjects, was part of Devin's upbringing, and he enjoyed how these types of jokes can make people feel uncomfortable. Devin and his family liked pushing the limits of social acceptability and offered, "I enjoy [jokes], I guess maybe just to the extent that they violate taboos or whatever. You know, I've always thought racism was a funny idea or there's just something inherently funny about it." Devin elaborated, "To me there's just always been sort of an appeal to it, an attraction to it. It's funny to categorize all the people in the world and sort of treat them in an abstract way as if they were all just lame caricatures or . . . you know, somehow, it's just amusing and I enjoy material that presents it that way." Devin did eventually acknowledge that racism did cause harm: "I mean, racism can have like very . . . it does have very negative consequences." However, a strong vein that ran through our discussion was his focus on the humor of racism. By doing so, Devin negated the pain that racism causes on a daily basis. He was, however, torn between lessons in college about the insidious effects of racism versus the familial tradition where no subject was taboo and always a source of comedic material.

Max also had some strong tensions between his professed values and some of his actions. He believed that racism was a social evil, that he as a White person benefitted from it, and he wanted to be an agent of social change promoting equity. However, he also described the following reaction he had to interacting with Black people:

> Well, I think when I'm on the bus and I see a young Black male and he's got his shorts lowered and his T-shirt on and his hat backwards and whatever, dressing typical whatever urban style or. . . . First, I have a little bit of apprehension. I think he's going to attack me and stuff and I'm already scared in a way or I'll just have apprehension like, "Oh, this guy's obviously out to rob someone or do drugs or whatever," and the list goes on, and the second thing is I also think this individual probably doesn't . . . I mean, this is what I just assume . . . I assume this individual doesn't realize how he's hurting himself.

Max describes a relatively common occurrence of riding the bus and is open and honest about his apprehension when he sees a young Black man in "urban" style. He thinks that the young man is a threat and is open about the fear running through his head. Instead of owning his fear, however, he sees it as a problem with the young Black man and not himself. In a very patronizing way, he thinks that the young Black man is living up to the stereotypes of people like him, and therefore he needs to change. It was not Max's responsibility to own his apprehension and work through this unconscious racism.

Jay continually struggled with his lack of knowledge on racial issues. He felt that racism was still a pertinent social issue, a systemic reality, but he was so racially insulated that he struggled to identify it. His ignorance stemmed from a very basic issue: "Being White in America? I never actually thought about this question just because . . . I mean, it's just not something that you think about. I mean, here in America, being a White male, you kind of feel that you are of the majority, so as long as you're part of the majority, you can kind of blend in and you can stand out if you want to stand out." That is, a huge part of Jay's White and male immunity meant he never really had to think about or consider issues of racism. While he may have been in a similar state of racial ignorance relative to the White guys in the previous chapters, Jay was markedly different as he acknowledged that his structured ignorance was part of a larger social conditioning. He continued, "You're taught to just not . . . not bring up just because it doesn't necessarily affect you."

What was interesting is that Jay linked his racial ignorance to him being White. For example, he explained, "I don't know if I've necessarily seen evidence of racism on campus or it may be that I'm just . . . I turn blind eye to it or I just tend not to notice it because most of that racism isn't geared towards me." Jay was markedly different than the White guys in the previous chapters in that he did not see racism in his everyday life, but he did not interpret that to mean it was nonexistent. Rather, he saw his lack of exposure to him being a White man who was not the target of racism. This lack of exposure, however, also meant Jay struggled to understand the nature of racism, which meant he continued to exist in a state of racial ignorance (Mills, 1997). The big difference in this instance was that he knew that he did not know.

Zeke was very aware that People of Color received systemically disparate treatment in society; however, part of his solution was a little lacking. "I think there are double standards and some people do treat African American people and Latino people differently. I try to be more positive towards African people . . . African American people and Latino people because I know they sometimes have harder times of it in our society, so I try to hold open the doors, I try to smile more, and then kind of . . . I guess maybe it's a reverse discrimination where I try to make up for what history has done to them." Zeke smiled more and held open doors for Black and Latinx people, but what does this accomplish? How does this improve material conditions for People of Color? It was a slightly heavy-handed method of channeling his racial critique. His heart was in the right place, but his praxis needed some work.

Josh, by contrast, was more self-aware than Zeke, and thus he was also more upfront about the struggles he was having. He began by understanding how socially programmed he has been during his life:

J: Reactions, yeah, I mean. It's, it's, it's difficult to recondition yourself when you think about how conditioned you are. Um, and so that's a constant process that I go through. It's kind of to recondition myself.

N: Mhm.

J: Um, and that maybe there's a tendency on my part, and maybe others, to um, romanticize certain ethnic groups maybe as having all the answers.

N: Mhm.

J: Yeah, um, but uh, I think tha—that we've all been subject to. . . . We're all as Amiri Baraka describes, "trying to survive America."

Josh was one of the most racially aware White guys I spoke with, but he also understood that even he was not above a number of racist traps. In response to learning about racism, there is a tendency especially among White liberals to idealize and romanticize the experiences of People of Color (Trepagnier, 2006). Josh saw this tendency in himself, and realized it was a part of his "conditioning" that he was constantly struggling against.

Larry also grappled with being White and trying to be socially responsible, but in a much different way than many of the other White guys in this chapter. As I previously explored, Larry grew up in Oakland, where his parents were strong advocates of public education. Within this context, Larry described the consistent fight that he and his partner had about their hypothetical children:

> We actually need to stand at the mirror and evaluate as White people what do we really believe in to the point that we will actually do it and me and my girlfriend have this argument all the time because I'm like, "Regardless, my kids are going to all public schools," and she went to all public schools too, she's like, "But you still can't just say that, you have to evaluate the conditions of things. You can't make your child a social experiment." That's true too. So how can we as White people really confront how we feel beyond the rhetoric, beyond the identifying points of, "Yes, I believe in Civil Rights. Yes, this. . . ." Will you really go live in that neighborhood like you said? Will you really let so-and-so live next door and not feel weird about it?

Larry struggled with this issue because it was where the Whiteness rubber hit the racial road. Because he was a student at a prestigious university, his kids likely would not have to go to public school. Would Larry intentionally enroll his kids in racially diverse schools, or would he exercise the social advantages Whiteness afforded him and flee to the suburban, Whiter schools? There was no answer readily available, especially since he and his partner were not even married yet. Regardless, it is this kind of tension that led me to argue, "Working through Whiteness is not an end met, but a continual process engaged" (Cabrera, 2012, p. 397).

White Male Racial Responsibility and Continual Racial Work

The narratives of the White guys in this chapter were both promising and frustrating. They were promising in the sense that they demonstrated a number of ways that White people in general, and White men in particular, could engage in anti-racism. They were frustrating because so much time, energy, and effort were dedicated to the first step in this process: disrupting epistemologies of ignorance (Mills, 1997) and helping these White guys begin to understand the realities of contemporary racism. There was no silver bullet available, and in many respects these developments relied upon a combination of cross-racial living/learning environments; classroom content, especially that which centered a humanizing pedagogy; being a non–racial minority; and being a White-identified biracial person. The commonality across these areas is a strong human connection to the lessons. It was not simply knowing a Black person; more important was having a deep connection with people across race and hearing their lived experiences of racism. It was not simply learning compelling statistics about racial inequality, but additionally, having instructors who were able to put a human face on the numbers. Essentially, each of these fostered a greater sense of racial empathy by the White guys in this chapter, and they tended to exist in conjunction with each other as opposed to in isolation.

I specifically use *empathy* instead of *sympathy* because the latter involves a patronizing view of the target of racism (i.e., "You poor thing!"). The former involves a sense of connection with people harmed by racism. I have no patience for sympathy. Instead, I prefer empathy as a pathway to understanding and establishing what Josh referred to as a *linked fate* with people across racial lines—seeing one's individual experience directly tied to all others in society, especially those whom Bell (1992) refers to as "faces at the bottom of the well." This focus on empathy is critically important because Feagin (2010) theoretically argued that racial emotions are central to the perpetuation of racial inequality: "Over time, white racist thought and action also involves a massive breakdown of positive emotions such as empathy, the human capacity to experience the feelings of members of an outgroup unlike your own" (p. 110). It is not that People of Color are lazy, but rather the same opportunity structure that has favored White people has concurrently disadvantaged them. Awakening to this reality requires White people to develop racial empathy and a human connection across racial lines.

From this orientation, the White guys in this chapter were able to define and identify what constituted racism, even seeing it within themselves. Their critiques of racism did not end there, as they tended to translate their understandings of racism into anti-racist actions. The action component was extremely important because, as Peet (2006) demonstrated, social justice critique without an outlet can be counterproductive and lead to nihilism.

While I appreciated the numerous anti-racist efforts of the White guys in this chapter, I do not want to romanticize their experiences. Within this context, I found it incredibly important to have the "Still Work to be Done" section to illustrate that even racially progressive White people can still fall into racist traps. Jay Smooth addressed this issue when he gave his TEDx talk and wondered why, when the subject is race, "if you're not batting one thousand, then you're striking out every time."[2] That is, we have a discursive way in contemporary U.S. society where we frame people in a binary: either you *are* or you *are not* racist. This does not offer opportunities for growth or development, and I appreciated how honest these White guys were about their continued difficulties as they tried to develop anti-racist praxis. They also demonstrated that they never got to a point where they could "stop thinking about racism." Rather, race was an omnipresent structure of oppression that required constant struggle, and the moment White people forget this reality is the same moment they again become complicit in the system.

Ultimately, these narratives are about the potential for those in the racial majority to be part of creating a racially more just, more equitable future. While revisiting their narratives for this chapter, I was again reminded of some words from James Baldwin (1961): "Yet, it is only when a man is able without bitterness or self-pity, to surrender a dream he long cherished or a privilege he has long possessed that he is set free—he has set himself free—for higher dreams, for greater privileges" (p. 100). In this case, the White guys I talked with for this chapter began to surrender the dreams, privileges, and false promises Whiteness afforded them. Instead, they were in the process of creating "higher dreams"—the dreams of an antioppressive future that, according to Freire (2000), is the epitome of human potential.

8

Conclusion

White Guys on Campus,
What Is to Be Done?

So, what does this extensive journey into the heart of Whiteness in higher education mean? What can we collectively glean from it? As I tackle this challenge, there is an additional layer I need to consider. Apple (1998) offered a strong word of caution for people conducting Whiteness research. He forcefully argued that while it is important to critique systemic racial oppression, one must not recenter Whiteness in the process. Within this context, I will be blunt. I am not particularly interested in the narratives of White men in and of themselves. I am not interested in their racialized awakenings or racial foreclosures as related to their *individual* identity development. Instead, I am concerned about White men because their racial ignorance (Mills, 1997) and their racial arrested development (Cabrera, Watson, & Franklin, 2016) become a foundation for the marginalization of Students of Color on college campuses and society at large. That is, I worry about White guys on campus because of how their actions affect other Students of Color and the contemporary color line. To *work through their Whiteness* (Cabrera, 2012), many White guys will have to grow and develop as people; however, I see this as an added benefit of this work as opposed to the central purpose—the (personal development) cherry on top of the (anti-racist) sundae, if you will.

I understand that many White men feel angst because they are unaware of the ways they are systemically advantaged in society and feel that they are blamed for all of society's ills (e.g., Greer, 2017). However, given their elevated social position, I am as concerned with their trepidation as I am with the Notorious B.I.G.'s proclamation, "Mo Money Mo Problems" (Wallace, Combs, Jordan, & Betha, 1997). Biggie's is a problem I think many of us would love to have. By the same token, the social advantages and immunities White men experience are ones that many a Person of Color, woman, or transgender individual would like to experience. I still engage because I will not be dismissive, but I also do not want White men to become the stars of this racial show.

Herein lies the second difficulty I have with this work as I straddle the generally divergent worlds of higher education and Critical Race scholarship. The former struggles with being too confined within institutions of higher education, and insufficiently paying attention to the larger, oppressive social forces that contextualize this work, especially systemic racism (Harper, 2012). Conversely, the latter is frequently inadequate regarding specific suggestions about what to do with seething critiques of White supremacy. For example, I have a great deal of respect for Bonilla-Silva's (2006) *Racism Without Racists*, but I have been struggling for more than a decade about how to apply this important text. Bonilla-Silva's conclusion is that a multicultural coalition centering People of Color and featuring a number of college students could usher in the modern Civil Rights Movement. How? As a critical scholar of race and higher education, I wanted more direction, but I also wanted to avoid the pitfalls of being overly prescriptive. These are the tensions I battle as I tie this work together; exploring a number of the lessons gleaned from extensive conversations with White guys about race. I begin with the White racial self and move outward to the institutions and society that (mis)educates them on issues of race and reifies White supremacy (Bonilla-Silva, 2006; Feagin, 2010).

White Male Racial Reality and Emotions
-or-
The Delicate Nature of The White Male Ego

Colloquially, I hear that women are more emotional than men. While not empirically true, it is a dominant myth about men that leads to them developing an unaffected "man face" (Edwards & Jones, 2009). This also leads to a situation of *emotional illiteracy* where men experience emotions but are so focused on suppressing and regulating their expression that they are essentially unaware of their feelings and how they are driving behaviors (Kindlon & Thompson, 2000). While the intersection of Whiteness and emotionality is severely undertheorized and explored (Matias, 2016), a great deal of White views on race are informed by a desire to maintain a positive sense of self—in particular for White men (Unzueta, Lowery, & Knowles, 2008). Within this context, it is not surprising the White guys I talked with were extremely sensitive on issues of race.

They felt stifled and sometimes oppressed by "political correctness," racial/ethnic-focused campus organizations, race-conscious social policies, diversity curricula, and campus space where Whiteness was not the norm, and the White guys at WU particularly felt discriminated against by an affirmative action program that *did not exist*. Then, without a hint of irony, these same White guys said they felt racial minorities were overly sensitive on race. This was interesting because none of the White guys I spoke with thought they personally were being sensitive. They implicitly rejected that they were emotionally reacting to a situation, instead strongly believing in an *invented delusional world* (Mills, 1997) where White men are the "true" victims of contemporary campus-based multiculturalism. It is in this way that, as Carroll (2011) argued, "white masculinity makes its own appeal to injury" (p. 6). Instead of understanding their individual roles perpetuating systemic racial inequality, it was easier for these White guys to turn themselves into imagined racial victims. James Baldwin (1961) provided a fascinating analysis on this peculiar psychology of trying to maintain a positive sense of self while contributing to a societal problem: "This collision between one's image of oneself and what one actually is, is always very painful and there are two things you can do about it. You can meet the collision head-on and try and become what you really are or you can retreat and try to remain what you thought you were, which is a fantasy, in which you will certainly perish" (p. 126). Baldwin acknowledged the pain that comes with these types of awakenings, but also issued a dire warning. Those White men who wish to remain in the fantasy world where systemic racism is not a problem and they individually do not bear any responsibility will "certainly perish."

The bulk of the White guys I talked with consistently believed in the myth of "reverse racism." In fact, many of them thought, much like the people in Norton and Sommers's (2011) research, that anti-White racism was prevalent than anti–People of Color. Even if they did not make this assessment directly, they spent substantially more time in their interviews describing "reverse racism" than actual instances or structures of White supremacy. Many visible signs of campus inclusion such as racial/ethnic campus organizations or diversity in the curriculum were reframed by many of the White guys I spoke with as oppressing or discriminating against them for being White. They tended to locate issues of racism among racial/ethnic minorities on campus, particularly blaming them for campus racial segregation. It was rarely seen as a problem when White people congregated together, but when minorities did, they were seen as "fracturing the campus community."

Most of the White guys I spoke with were also against virtually any form of race-conscious social policies. It makes sense that, given the rising cost of tuition, they tended to feel stressed about financing their education. In some respects, race-conscious scholarships became a way to direct their economic angst, but their fears were projected onto relatively tiny programs. Allow me to we return to actual statistics on the matter. First, White people actually receive a disproportionately high percentage of private scholarships relative to their share of the population. That is, White people are still at an advantage for scholarships—an approximate 40 percent advantage—even when including those that are race-conscious (Kantrowitz, 2011). Second, race/ethnic-specific private scholarships compose approximately 4 percent of those available (Kantrowitz, 2011). Therefore, the view that, "If I was a minority, I would have a free ride to college," has no basis in reality. Thus, the White guys I spoke with were not being harmed by race-conscious scholarships, but they thought and acted as though they were.

Again, it is troubling because many of the White guys I spoke with really believed that if they were Black or Latinx, their economic troubles and anxiety would disappear. This belief, of course, overlooks the massive number of ways that racism marginalizes People of Color, leading to significant discrepancies in wealth, health, and education along the color line that favor White people (Brown et al., 2003; Oliver & Shapiro, 2006). That is, most of the White guys I spoke with relied on an ahistorical analysis, as if no legacy of racism or contemporary manifestation of White supremacy informed their current conditions.

This discourse of "reverse racism" was particularly salient when discussing issues of affirmative action, but I was surprised at how bifurcated by campus the White guys' responses were. At WU, the White guys I spoke with tended to be very angry about affirmative action, frequently feeling oppressed by a program that did not exist. While most of the White guys at SWU were against affirmative action, they were borderline ambivalent, even though their university practiced it. The White guys at WU did make a ton of personal investments of time and energy, developing themselves to be academically competitive for admissions. However, they also developed a sense of White entitlement vis-à-vis college admissions.

I am very intentional using the term "White entitlement" when discussing affirmative action for this reason. When was the last time you heard of an academically competitive racial minority from an impoverished community be rejected by Harvard, then publicly claim, "I lost my spot to a less deserving White person—probably a legacy admit"? Compare this to the predictable sob stories every admissions cycle where White students are on the news complaining that affirmative action kept them from "pursuing their dreams" at an elite institution. This discourse is so common and accepted that it was recently heard twice by the Supreme Court when Abigail Fisher claimed she was rejected by UT Austin because of their affirmative action policies, even though she was not academically competitive (Brodin, 2014). That is the epitome of White entitlement, and a number of the White guys—in particular at WU—articulated some version of this narrative.

It was telling not only *that* the White guys in chapters 2 through 6 felt oppressed by race-conscious policies, but also *how* they expressed their opposition and frustration. When they talked about an invented issue like "reverse racism," their voices tended to become more intense and louder, and they frequently spewed profanity. The underlying irony was that these White guys tended to see People of Color as overly sensitive on issues of race when in fact they were the ones being emotionally uncomfortable and sometimes angry about issues of race. It was even more ironic considering that some of the racial issues they discussed (e.g., affirmative action at WU) did not exist in reality, only in their heads.

From a sociopolitical standpoint, it makes sense that these White guys felt oppressed by political correctness in particular. While the precise origins of being political correctness are still under debate, the term is more of a weapon of right-wing activists as opposed to an actual demand from progressive educators, scholars, and students (Chang, 2014; Feldstein, 1997; Wilson, 1995). As Chang (2014) argued, "Calling someone else PC (politically correct) meant never having to apologize for being a racist. It was a phrase with as much power to end a conversation as the 'racist'; the restorationist's trump card" (p. 120). Thus, there has been a consistent messaging by right-wing activists framing political correctness as "McCarthyesque," stifling free speech on college campuses (Spero, 2017). Additionally, some liberals like Bill Maher have recently taken up this call as well (Ernst, 2015).

Within this context of persistent messaging about the "evils" of political correctness, it is not surprising that many of the White guys I spoke with both felt oppressed by it but could not actually identify instances where their freedom of expression was restricted. This again was a testament to the power of the White male imagination at constructing and believing in a social fiction (Mills, 1997; Morrison, 1992). Herein lies the analytical, practitioner, and activist conundrum of engaging White guys on the subject of race. What can be done about this? How much time and energy are needed to help White men understand the realities of racism? To what extent is their participation necessary to advance anti-racist goals? I will explore these possibilities in more detail in subsequent sections.

Interestingly, many of the White guys I spoke with engaged in a type of identity politics, generally associated with women, LGBTQ folk, and People of Color (Chang, 2014; Lipsitz, 2006). In the wake of the election of the Forty-Fifth, liberal comedian Bill Maher blamed Hillary's loss on a too-narrow focus on identity politics (Mazza, 2017). My discussions with White guys, by contrast, demonstrated that White men were also engaging in identity politics, but because of their entrenched social advantages, they do not have to hold a "White Male Lives Matter" sign to support their group position. While this does happen, a more common form is to continually proclaim that White men are the true victims of multiculturalism (i.e., "reverse racism") while attacking anything in society that is race-conscious (e.g., social policy, curriculum, or space). Who benefits from this? White men, of course, without having to overtly name the identities they are supporting through these politics. To put it a different way, when People of Color and minorities push for social policies that can uplift their communities, it is seen as "playing identity politics." When White men advance their social position by claiming an imagined victim status, it is simply called "politics." While I focused a great deal on these White men and their narratives on race, they existed within university environments that helped them stay in a state of racial arrested development (Cabrera et al., 2016).

Institutions of Higher Education: Ecologies of Whiteness?

There is a central tension in higher education. Colleges and universities were formed to offer a space to cultivate some of the greatest examples of human potential, especially through scientific inquiry (Bowen, 1977; Gutmann, 1999; Kerr, 1995). They also serve as social sorting mechanisms, disproportionately allocating their social benefits to those already advantaged by society (Carnevale & Strohl, 2013). Within this context, these White guys tended to exist in university environments where Whiteness was normal or hegemonic. When there were challenges to this normality (e.g., racial/ethnic student group organizing or modest diversification of the curriculum), many of the White guys I spoke with returned to their White racial (usually male) enclaves. This retreat usually occurred when they did not want to engage issues of race and racism.

Institutionally, policies and approaches to diversity are frequently informed by a reticence to proactively denounce systemic racism, in part so as not to offend the delicate sensibilities of White men. At my home institution, the central administration continually uses buzzwords like "our diverse student populations," but avoids mentioning "racism" or "White supremacy." This is a very common practice among higher education leaders, unless an overtly racist action is caught on film like the OU Sigma Alpha Epsilon (SAE) fraternity singing "There will never be a nigger in SAE" (Cabrera, 2015). Thus, higher education leaders tend to treat racism and Whiteness the same way that wizards in Harry Potter treat Lord Voldemort: never uttering his name (Rowling, 1999). Within colleges and universities, we Voldemort racism and White supremacy—as if not mentioning them will make these social problems magically disappear. The unintended consequence of reserving "racism" only for blatant actions is that it tends to individualize the problem of contemporary White supremacy instead of framing it as a systemic reality.

From the orientation of racism as an individual problem, the White guys I spoke with also discussed fights over campus space. Essentially, they naïvely thought that all space was open to everyone or at least should be. When they encountered space where Whiteness was not the cultural norm (e.g., Trevor in the Chicano Studies library), they tended to become very agitated. This was interesting because there were many spaces where Whiteness was the norm, which tended to produce a number of counterproductive behaviors (e.g., racist joking) that were reinforced by the White guys' underlying racial ideologies (e.g., minorities are overly sensitive). This background served as the context for mutually reinforcing conditions that function like Harro's (2000) *cycle of socialization*, but this is more a *cycle of rationalization* (see Figure 1).

Within this context, the background of hegemonic Whiteness creates the condition that normalizes the experiences and views of White people in general, and White men in particular. This, in turn, allows for racist joke telling, use of the n-word, or cultural appropriation to occur. These behaviors and environments (White space) are contextualized within an ideological orientation that blames minorities for injecting race into nonracial situations (minority sensitivity). These four mutually reinforcing spheres (background, behavior, ideology, and environment) created a cyclical logic whereby the participants believed there was no racism or minimal racism in contemporary society against People of Color because they saw none in their experiences. Noticeably unexamined by the White guys I spoke with was the role their Whiteness played in the formation of these views, hence the hegemonic or taken-for-granted nature of Whiteness in their lived realities.

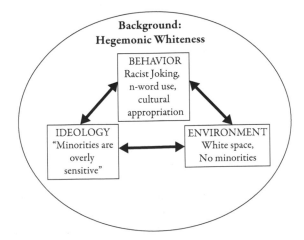

Figure 1 Cycle of rationalization

This highlights the critical need for White guys to understand three fundamental issues: (1) racism is a systemic reality that continues to structure contemporary society, (2) intent does not matter in racism (i.e., one does not have to intend to be racist), and (3) White men who allow racist practices to occur in their presence are also culpable (i.e., "racist listening" is still racism). This last point is critically important because all too often these White guys (mis)understood racism to be only the fault of an individual (e.g., telling a racist joke), and they struggled to even identify these actions as racist. Instead, O'Connor (2002) argued that those who facilitate an environment of oppression are also responsible and therefore participating in racism. Essentially, the White guys who served as the spectators for racist joke telling, n-word use, or cultural appropriation were also being racist. These performances required audiences to function, and if one removes the audience, they can also disrupt racism.

What could this look like in practice? For one example, I refer readers to the example provided by Tim Wise in *White Like Me* (2008, p. 92). As a White guy, Wise has frequently been able to be part of groups where other White guys are telling racist jokes as a form of both White bonding (Sleeter, 1994) and male bonding (Lyman, 1987). Frequently, these jokes start with, "Did you hear the one about the Black guy . . . ?" One time, Wise followed the joke with, "Did you hear the one about the white guy who told this really racist joke because he assumed everyone he was hanging out with was also white?" (p. 92). He then proceeded to say that even though he is light skinned, his mother is Black. The joke teller apologized profusely, saying he did not know, and it was at this point that Wise confessed that he was not Black. The joke teller was confused, leading Wise (2008) to publicly offer the following question: "I find it interesting that when you thought I was [Black], you apologized for the joke. In other words, you know it was wrong to say, so that if you'd been around a black person knowingly, you never would have said it. So why did you feel comfortable saying it in front of all of us?" (p. 92). This kind of critical Socratic-racial questioning offers an opportunity for people to self-interrogate and actually explore the reasoning behind their own racist actions. It is an incredibly important strategy, in particular for other White guys who have access to this backstage performance (Picca & Feagin, 2007). These approaches to racial joking require a great deal of forethought and some fortitude because this social disruption can frequently lead to social discomfort. However, Feagin and O'Brien (2003) argued, "Weighing one person's modest discomfort against another person's often substantial pain and agony [from racism], and finding the former more important, sends a troubling message about the latter's worth as a person" (p. 188). No one said that interpersonal anti-racism was going to be easy (or without agitation), and those who say we will naturally achieve racial equity probably also have some oceanfront property in Arizona to sell (nod to George Strait).

While the individuals in this study bore personal responsibility for perpetuating racism, the institutions of higher education were also culpable because on their campuses White guys were able to congregate among other White guys while thinking there was nothing wrong with this dynamic. There were massively different levels of compositional diversity, or the proportion of Students of Color on campus (Milem et al., 2005) between WU and SWU. They were in different geographic regions. One practiced affirmative action, one did not. Yet the White guys I spoke with tended to have very similar experiences with racial discomfort, beliefs about "reverse racism," and these related to their abilities to retreat into White space. The primary difference was in terms of the imagined affirmative action at WU, and this was likely a function of this institution being much more academically competitive.

Regardless, these institutions bore responsibility for fostering an ecology where White male racial comfort was centered and supported. There were times when some of the White guys I spoke with for chapters 2 through 6 were uncomfortable within racial environments where Whiteness was not the norm; however, these situations were more temporary than consistent and did not lead to meaningful developments. The White guys in these chapters, in contrast to a lot of the racial identity development literature (e.g., Helms, 1990), were in a state of either racial arrested development (Cabrera et al., 2016) or racial regression. That is, one of the key lessons many of the White guys I spoke with learned in college was that White men are the "true" victims of multiculturalism. During a time of great growth potential (Pascarella & Terenzini, 2005), these institutions of higher education tended to promote minimal or negative growth among these White guys.

It was really interesting that within these higher education environments many of the White guys I spoke with in chapters 2 through 6 were frustrated by what they saw as racial minorities assuming White guys are going to be racist against them. While it is questionable how accurate these views are, it does highlight one core issue. If Students of Color on campus are apprehensive about interacting with White guys on campus, they have ample justification for their unease. One need look no further than the very narratives of the White guys I spoke with to see how racially oblivious, and frequently racist, they were. So, what are institutions of higher education to do? Before I dive into that, I return to the underlying purpose of this book.

How These White Guys Affect Folk of Color

The White guys I spoke with in chapters 2 through 6 did not believe racism was a particularly relevant or pressing social issue; their largely White learning/living environments reinforced these views; they had only a superficial understanding of the nature of racism and rarely thought of themselves as being racist. From these experiences and beliefs, many of the White guys I spoke with openly discussed instances where they and their friends racially harassed People of Color. Ken described an incident where a friend of his called a Black guy a nigger, but did not think it was racist because the Black guys called him a cracker. Trevor openly profiled and interrogated a Chicano student in the Chicano Studies library and then tried to turn himself into the "victim" of the situation. Matt wore stereotypical "Black apparel," listened to hip-hop, "talked Black," and publicly appropriated Black culture in racist and misogynistic ways. Roger was part of the group who "took back" student council from the Student of Color slate. The point is that despite spending the bulk of their time in White racial enclaves, the White guys I talked with for chapters 2 through 6 still had interactions with People of Color. When these occurred, these White guys frequently described instances when they and their friends were being racist. I just added this brief section as a reminder: the beliefs, ideologies, and experiences the White guys described in chapters 2 through 6 are not self-contained but become the basis for anti–People of Color racism, frequently enacted without the White guys aware of the harm they caused. However, there is still some possibility for institutions of higher education and White men to be part of the larger movement promoting racial equity.

What Is Higher Education to Do?

White the narratives in chapters 2 through 6 highlighted how White guys and institutions participate in the re-creation of White supremacy, chapter 7 explored a number of ways that they can challenge it. I reiterate a number of these methods, but please understand that these do not exist in isolation. That is, there is no singular racial silver bullet, and the best strategy is multiple approaches concurrently (Milem et al., 2005). Also, I am compelled by Gillborn's (2008) argument that institutions and social policies are generally created and guided by a White supremacist logic. That is, systemic racism is so engrained in contemporary society that color-blind or "race-neutral" approaches serve only to reify racial inequality (Bonilla-Silva, 2006). Systemic racism is present, neutrality is not an option, and institutional leaders have to ask themselves if they want to be part of the solution or part of the problem. As Howard Zinn (2010) reminded us, "You can't be neutral on a moving train." The difficulty, however, is that race-conscious approaches to institutional policies frequently trigger discourses of "reverse racism" and institutional pushback from White students. Thus, institutional leaders find themselves between a racist rock and a privileged hard place, but all is not lost.

First, institutions need to disrupt the cultural hegemony of Whiteness on their campuses. That is much easier said than done, but there are a number of schools grappling with their legacy of racism. For example, Yale University has changed the name of Calhoun College (John C. Calhoun being an ardent supporter of slavery) to Grace Hopper College (Hopper a mathematician and computer scientist) in an attempt to take account of its racist past (Holden, 2017). This has been part of a larger movement to remove statues celebrating the Confederacy from public spaces. While these actions have had a predictable backlash, it is also important for institutional leaders to send clear signals to their student populations that a racist past does not determine a racist future as long as one accounts for this historical legacy instead of sweeping it under the rug (Milem et al., 2005). This is a racial/institutional version of the cliché that *those who don't learn history are doomed to repeat it.*

Cross-racial interactions were incredibly important for a number of White guys I talked with beginning to understand racism, but there are many caveats to this. First, while higher education represents an important opportunity to *break the cycle of segregation* (Saénz, 2010), neither WU or SWU had demographics that came close to matching the racial representation of their respective states. In particular, Latinx, Black, and Native American students were extremely underrepresented. I prefer to consider expanding access for these minoritized student populations as an end in and of itself, where equitable college access across racial/ethnic lines is what is owed to these students and their communities. However, a potential side benefit of this increased access is that it can be a learning opportunity for White students (Hurtado, Alvarez, Guillermo-Wann, Cuellar, & Arellano, 2012). There have to be certain conditions in place, and even then, I struggle with this approach, as I will explain.

Once students arrive on a college campus, there cannot be a laissez-faire approach to diversity because they will likely retreat to their own ethnic enclaves (antonio, 2001; Duster, 1991; Picca & Feagin, 2007). This means identifying spaces on college campuses where White students in particular are clustering, which will also mean having some uncomfortable and difficult conversations about the housed Greek system (Chang & DeAngelo, 2002; Park, 2008). The next step is to disrupt the social practices that cyclically allow these White enclaves to exist (e.g., recruitment practices). Ultimately, change requires seeing and labeling White racial segregation for what it is instead of framing it as happenstance, moving the paradigm away from *Why Are All the Black Kids Sitting Together in the Cafeteria?* (Tatum, 2003).

Additionally, institutional leaders need to structure ways for White students and Students of Color to interact across race. A really important but also problematic method of doing this is through intergroup dialogues that center issues of *immunity, privilege,* and *oppression* (Cabrera, 2017; Nagda & Zuñiga, 2003; Zuñiga, Nagda, & Sevig, 2002). This thematic focus is critically important because simply learning about cultural difference is a watered-down form of multiculturalism that does nothing to address issues of social inequality. Regardless, these structured, critical dialogues hold a great deal of promise in the sense that they offer an opportunity for White students to begin under-standing and exploring how Whiteness benefits them and harms Students of Color. In particular, it puts a human face on the issue of White supremacy. Many of the White guys in chapter 7 talked of the incredible importance of seeing, hearing, and understanding racism—not as an abstraction, but how it adversely affects actual people in their lives. This is can be a problematic approach for a few reasons.

First, it takes a great deal of mental and emotional energy for Students of Color to educate White students (Richeson & Shelton, 2007), and as Larry put it, "I don't think it's Latino or Black people's responsibility to educate White people." It is wonderful that many Students of Color are willing to help their White peers learn about the realities of racism, but please be clear that it is not their responsibility and White students are not entitled to their labor. Second, there is a debate about the nature of safe spaces. Frequently, one of the agreements set forth at the beginning of intergroup dialogues is that they will be safe spaces for an open exchange of experiences and ideas. Leonardo and Porter (2010) took issue with this and instead argued that racism is so engrained in society and microaggressions against Students of Color are so common that establishing safe spaces in practice means creating shelter for White racism.

Finally, there is a common trap where discussions of race can recenter White-ness, inadvertently re-creating the very racial dynamics these discussions are supposed to combat (Applebaum, 2010). This occurs most often when White people demand their views on race carry equal weight in the conversation, claiming some authority on the issue (Applebaum, 2008). Therefore, critical interrogations of Whiteness are necessary to help White men work through their racial issues (Ortiz & Rhoads, 2000; Zuñiga et al., 2002), but a balance is needed where White men do not dominate the conversation. In fact, this highlights the importance of skilled facilitators who stress the need for White men to truly listen to their Peers of Color on the subject of race (Applebaum, 2008). While I am very sensitive to these potential pitfalls, I do not want to throw out the baby with the bathwater. Instead, those who facilitate these dialogues have to be well trained and prepared to navigate these and many other issues that can arise when people start having open and honest conversations about race. It is an approach that holds promise, but positive outcomes are not guaranteed.

So that Students of Color do not have to bear the entire burden of educat-ing their White peers on racial oppression, providing classes on the subject can also be extremely impactful (Bowman, 2011). However, not all course offerings are equally effective. One cannot simply take out Shakespeare, insert Maya Angelou, and claim the class is meaningful ethnic studies. Rather, Sleeter (2011) offered core features of effective ethnic studies courses:

1. explicit identification of the point of view from which knowledge emanates, and the relationship between social location and perspective;
2. examination of U.S. colonialism historically, as well as how relations of colonialism continue to play out;
3. examination of the historical construction of race and institutional racism, how people navigate racism, and struggles for liberation;
4. probing meanings of collective or communal identities that people hold; and
5. studying one's community's creative and intellectual products, both historic and contemporary. (p. 3)

Within this paradigm, not all college classes that count for "diversity requirements" will meet these criteria if they are simply analyses of difference in the absence of systems of oppression. Again, the watered-down multicultural approaches of "foods and fiestas" or "heroes and holidays" simply do not work because they lack critical engagement with the underlying issue: White supremacy. Therefore, it is important for institutions of higher education to mandate a diversity requirement for graduation (Milem et al., 2005), but they also have to be discerning about what counts under this umbrella term.

The narratives of the White guys in chapter 7 provide additional guidance on how to make diversity courses effective. First, the classes seemed to be most effective when there were sustained opportunities for engagement. Two-semester or three-quarter series of classes seemed to work much better at helping the White guys understand issues of racism relative to a one-and-done course. Second, the White guys in chapter 7 continually referenced professors humanizing issues of race and racism. They talked about professors taking the time to put a human face on racial oppression, supplementing historical trends and statistical analyses. This created what Josh referred to as a sense of "linked fate" between White people and People of Color.

Ultimately, these educational opportunities were meant not for the White guys to become experts on racism, but rather to disrupt epistemologies of ignorance (Mills, 1997). What was needed was not full understanding on a subject but rather for White guys to begin understanding how much they did not know about issues of racism. No number of ethnic studies courses and *barrio* volunteering will ever allow a White man to walk in the shoes of a Person of Color in a racist society. White men can hear about the fear and pain of racial oppression, but they can never actually experience it. This leads to a strange balance that needs to be struck. On the one hand, it is incumbent on White men to educate themselves about the realities of systemic racism historically and contemporarily. Doing so requires a humility accompanying this awareness—to understand that they will never fully know or truly understand.

Student affairs can also play an important role in the development of White male racial justice allies. Many of the White guys in chapter 7 talked about having a non-racial-minority identity being critically important to their engagement with issues of racism. They understood what it felt like to be an oppressed minority (e.g., gay in a heterosexist society), and this mirrored Peggy McIntosh's personal narrative when she developed the term *White privilege* (1989). As a feminist scholar, she was perpetually frustrated by her male colleagues who "didn't get it" regarding gender. She had an "ah-ha" moment when her female colleagues of color told her that when it came to race, McIntosh also "didn't get it." That became a springboard for deeper engagement around issues of race for McIntosh as well as many of the White guys in chapter 7. They were clear that, for example, experiencing homophobia was not the same as experiencing racism. Rather, they were more open to learning about race, acknowledging they as White men played some role in the perpetuation of racial oppression, just as straight people do to gay and bisexual men. This is not to essentialize or romanticize these White guys' experiences, but rather to demonstrate that there is opportunity for student affairs engagement by understanding the multiple identities that White guys bring to the table beyond race and gender.

One interesting dynamic among the White guys in chapter 7 was that they not only were willing to identify and critique racism in society at large, but also saw it within themselves. They were willing to engage issues of racism and had more developed senses of who they were racially. Along these lines, Baldwin (1961) offered an insightful meditation on the intersection of the self and society for White men: "Trying to convey to a white man the reality of the Negro experience has nothing whatever to do with the fact of color, but has to do with this man's relationship to his own life. He will face in your life only what he is willing to face in his" (p. 175). The challenge for student affairs professionals therefore becomes working on White men's relationship to their own racial lives as a jumping off point to actually engaging issues of racism. The delicate balance becomes having White men do the self-work necessary so they can meaningfully engage race without making their experiences the star of this racial show. Rather, their self-work is the means to the end of actually engaging, challenging, and being part of transforming racism.

Taking actual racial justice actions was the area that distinguished the White guys in chapter 7 who were just *working through Whiteness* (Cabrera, 2012) from those who were engaging in allyship development (Reason & Broido, 2005). It is incredibly important for student affairs practitioners to offer opportunities for White people in general, and White men in particular, to take tangible racial justice actions. As Peet (2006) demonstrated, if students learn social justice critique without a way to channel their newfound awareness, it can actually have a counterproductive effect, fostering nihilism and frustration. The different opportunities for engagement will be determined by the local conditions, so instead I simply highlight the importance of this and leave it to the creative energy of those on the ground level to determine what this praxis might look like. I do, however, find a great deal importance in the warning of Ellsworth (1989), where a number of her students were frustrated when taking social justice actions. They continually said that contrary to the utopian promises of critical pedagogy, their actions did not "feel empowering." Racial justice work is sometimes frustrating (or most of the time frustrating), but it is still incredibly important. Practitioners, however, need to avoid false promises that social justice can imply.

These are some of the many ways institutions of higher education can promote racial justice, but please do not treat this as a checklist. Also, please do not take the suggestions as piecemeal because individual, isolated approaches to campus-based racial justice are ineffective (Hurtado et al., 2012; Milem et al., 2005). Racial justice has to be articulated as an institutional value, and then a series of mutually supportive initiatives need to be enacted concurrently to truly change the campus culture of colleges and universities, disrupting what Gusa (2010) refers to as the *White institutional presence*. Ultimately, this "requires rigorous work of informed critical introspection that sees one's performance of Whiteness, as well as sees the performance of Whiteness in the practice of others" (Gusa, 2010, p. 481). The constant analysis, action, and self-reflection is necessary because Whiteness is not only fragile (DiAngelo, 2011) but also agile (chapter 2). Thus, institutions of higher education need to be prepared to act quickly based upon the ever-changing racial terrain of contemporary American society in order to be part of disrupting White supremacy.

Actions to combat White supremacy need to be proactive and transformative, and unfortunately these are two areas where higher education is severely lacking. For example, Chang (2002) argued that colleges and universities tend to be more reactive in their approaches, and more concerned with maintaining control over their decision making instead of engaging in the process of social transformation. Regardless, these institutional efforts can be incredibly important because the process of disrupting epistemologies of ignorance (Mills, 1997) is rarely initiated by White students themselves (Reason & Evans, 2007; Reason, Millar, & Scales, 2005). Even if White men are affectively ready to receive information on racial oppression, they frequently need an opportunity and a nudge from teachers, professors, peers, and student affairs professionals. As White men begin to engage issues of racism, they need to be critically self-reflective as there are a number of pitfalls well-intentioned aspiring allies encounter.

Some Guidance and Thoughts on
White Male Aspiring Racial Justice Praxis

The path for White men challenging racism is nonlinear, complicated, and ever changing, kind of like challenging racism itself. In this journey, there are a number of issues that White men need to be aware of. For example, there is a constant debate about what to call a White person who uses his White immunity at the service of racial justice. Some prefer "racial justice ally," while others prefer to use "anti-racist." Neo-abolitionists such as Ignatiev (1997) begin with the perspective that "the point is not to interpret Whiteness, but to abolish it." From this orientation, they tend to argue that to be a "White ally" is an oxymoron. While my weak preference within this debate is "racial justice ally," the cautionary note to White men I offer is this: if you worry more about the name of your social identity than actually doing racial justice work, you are not an ally. It is action that truly defines one's relationship to systemic racism as being either complicit (Applebaum, 2010) or an ally (Cabrera, 2012). Frequently, White people trying to challenge racism traverse the line between White complicity and White allyship many times during the course of their lifetimes.

The first step toward allyship, however, tends to be moving from color-blind to color-cognizant (Reason & Evans, 2007). There is a fundamental roadblock in supporting the racial cognizance development of White men, and it can be summarized in the following (not funny) joke:

Q: How many psychiatrists does it take to change a light bulb?
A: Only one, but the light bulb has to want to change.

Given the massive amounts of resistance the bulk of the White guys I spoke with offered in terms of meaningfully engaging racism, how could they be open to actually knowing and challenging contemporary White supremacy? Why would they become involved dismantling a system from which they both benefit and contribute (Applebaum, 2010)? Pragmatically, it does not make sense because eliminating the structural disadvantages of racism for People of Color means that White folk will need to lose some of their social standing as well. Instead, the focus needs to be moral, and the good news is that at least most people today agree that racism is morally repugnant (Bonilla-Silva, 2001, 2006; Sniderman, Crosby, & Howell, 2000). The bad news is that the bulk of White Americans have no real understanding of what racism is (Applebaum, 2010; Bonilla-Silva, 2006; Feagin, 2010; Omi & Winant, 2015). While the moral charge is extremely promising, it has yet to be realized, as Baldwin (1984) so eloquently put it: "Morally, there has been no change at all, and moral change is the only real one" (p. xiii). That is, systemic racism and White supremacy remain intact, and the challenge becomes how to use a moral charge as a starting point for racial justice education.

Part of this includes the pressing importance of White people learning the history of Whiteness (Allen, 1997; Kendi, 2016; Takaki, 1993). Understanding where people come from is critically important in them developing and growing as individuals. In the larger social context, Freire (2000) argued, "Looking at the past must only be a means of understanding more clearly what and who they are so that they can more wisely build the future" (p. 83). While Freire was specifically addressing the oppressed in his analysis, a similar dynamic exists for people of the oppressor class. In this instance, White men can be part of the elimination of racism, but they need to know their racial history to more clearly "build the future." This is, in part, why I included a stronger historical analysis in my development of *White immunity* (Cabrera, 2017) than McIntosh (1989) did when offering *White privilege*. This history was not meant to be the "essential history" that White men need to know to struggle against racism. Rather, there are some important areas briefly discussed that can serve as jumping-off points for White men to explore the history of Whiteness, taking responsibility for the development of their own racial justice praxis.

While White men begin embarking on this journey, there are other issues that frequently arise. First, Reason and Broido (2005) strongly caution against people being allies as a "fad," offering that a "fair-weather ally who works only when it is convenient or easy, risks reinforcing the suspicions of target group members through more unfulfilled promises" (p. 87). The epitome of White immunity (Cabrera, 2017) is to be able to withdraw from racial justice as a matter of convenience. It is easy to profess that one values racial justice, but are they willing to continue engaging when situations become uncomfortable, trying, or tense? The test of White men's belief in racial justice truly occurs when the work becomes difficult.

A major contributing factor to people being "fair-weather allies" lies in the desire for many White men to think of themselves as "good." Larry spoke the most deeply on this subject as he, back in Oakland, did not want to be seen as one of "those White people." Instead, he wanted to be viewed as a down, politically active, cool White boy. This form of White narcissism (Matias, 2016) guided a great deal of his initial racial justice work, and he finally came to realize he had to "stop trippin'" off what other people thought of him. Instead, it was important to do the good work as an end itself. Unfortunately, a great deal of White racial justice work is done to prove how morally good an individual White person is (Reason & Broido, 2005). Instead, Jay Smooth offered an alternative approach to racial justice work during his TEDx talk: "I think we need to move away from thinking that 'being good' is a fixed, immutable characteristic, and shift towards seeing being good as a practice. And it is a practice that we carry out by engaging with our imperfections."[1] Jay Smooth argued that instead of thinking "I am a good person," we should ask, "What actions/practice would be good in this situation?" This requires a great deal of critical self-reflection as White men battle with racist imperfections that have developed over the course of their lives—frequently without their knowledge (Cabrera, 2012; Edwards, 2006; Reason & Broido, 2005). The more that White men think of themselves as good people, the more that maintaining that perception usurps actual racial justice praxis. That is, the more that White men think of themselves as "good Whites," the less likely they are to actually do the work.

In terms of doing racial justice work, White men need to remember that they are welcomed to participate, but their involvement is not essential to the advancement of this larger goal. If White men are willing to accept this, then they also need to consider the following. Racial justice actions are important, but in isolation they are not effective at promoting social equity. As Cabrera (2012) offered, "A social movement of one is not a social movement at all" (p. 396). It sometimes makes White people uncomfortable talking about social movements and activism when the subject is racism. The problem with this discomfort is that racism is a systemic reality that is able to withstand a number of individual, anti-racist actions. In the absence of being connected to a larger collective, racial justice praxis is ineffective and sometimes quixotic: doing battle with windmills but not truly advancing racial justice.

Finally, I offer a word of caution to White men beginning to engage in allyship work: stay in your lane. It is more important for you to listen, learn, and make yourself useful to the larger cause than for you to be in charge. Edwards (2006) offered a strong critique of this behavior when he said, "Some who genuinely aspire to act as social justice allies are harmful, ultimately, despite their best intentions, perpetuating the system of oppression they seek to change" (p. 39). That is, when people of a privileged social group begin engaging in allyship work, there is a tendency to turn their newfound moral outrage into overcompensation. This can lead to co-opting racial justice movements, failing to acknowledge the work that has come before their involvement, and being frustrated when their work goes unacknowledged (sometimes leaving as a result). Please remember that when it comes to racial justice, the bulk of your work will go unacknowledged. Or, as the Angry Black Woman (2008) succinctly articulated in her blog, "You don't get a cookie." If you are involved to receive recognition, find a different venue. Moving from the White men to the scholars doing this work, I have a few concluding thoughts where I hope people can learn not only from my analyses but from my methodological mistakes as well.

A Word of Caution to Scholars of Color
Doing Whiteness Work

There is a great deal more work to do in the area of studying White racism, in particular White male racism in higher education. I am not currently concerned with Whiteness research overtaking Critical Race Theory work and recentering Whiteness in racial discussions within this field. It is more of a cautionary note that anyone doing this work should be continually aware (Apple, 1998). However, I do have one very important issue that Scholars of Color either doing this work or aspiring to do this work should consider: *Please make sure that you practice appropriate self-care.* Learn from my mistakes and take care of yourself while conducting this type of research. The interviews functioned as a type of constant microaggression (Sue, 2010), but I as the interviewer had to appear unaffected by them. What I did not realize was that I frequently exceeded my daily recommended dose of microaggressions, and they adversely affected my mental and emotional health. Being a straight, cisgender male, I fell into the traps of masculinity, putting on my "man face" (Edwards & Jones, 2009). It was only when I started admitting that I was experiencing racial pain through these interviews that I was able to begin healing. It was also only at that time that I was able to actually do the work because my racial anger and frustration continually clouded my judgment. For an extended discussion of this process, please see Cabrera (2016).

Please do not misconstrue this as a narrative of "poor me"—you already know how I feel about sympathy. I signed up for this work, and it harkens back to a phrase Hunter S. Thompson was fond of saying: "Buy the ticket, take the ride" (cited in Cabrera, 2016, p. 21). This is more of a word of caution to Scholars of Color conducting this work—in particular Men of Color. It will likely be painful. Allow yourself to acknowledge the pain while making time and space to heal from it. Connect with others so you can vent your frustrations. Find productive ways to keep from slipping into nihilism (Peet, 2006), but also understand that your anger is a natural response to hearing a consistent stream of racism. As Dr. Maya Angelou so beautifully explained to Dave Chappelle on the show *Iconoclast*, it was absolutely understandable and expected for people to be angry about the numerous assassinations that occurred in the 1960s. However, she offered a word of caution:

MA: If you're not angry, you're either a stone, or you're too sick to be angry. You should be angry.

DC: But what do you do—

MA: Now mind you, there's a difference. You must not be bitter.

DC: That's a hard—[laughs]

MA: Now let me show you why. Bitterness is like cancer. It eats upon the host. It doesn't do anything to the object of its displeasure. So, use that anger, yes, you write it, you paint it, you dance it, you march it, you vote it, you do everything about it. You talk it. Never stop talking it. (Berlinger, 2006, 19:58)

Therein lies the challenge of the work. I have to allow myself to be angry at social oppression without allowing it to make me bitter in the process. Hearing these racial narratives made me very angry, so I had to find productive outlets for this frustration, lest it become bitterness. In some ways, this book is a method for allowing this to occur. To my fellow Scholars of Color doing this work, please learn from my mistakes and let the racial poison escape your body or it will eat you from the inside out. Most frustratingly, you will be hurting and you will not even know why. Please do the work, but also be careful as you are doing it. Practice the necessary self-care to sustain yourself.

Concluding Thoughts and Looking Ahead

This work is unabashedly rooted in a critical approach to the subject of race and racism in higher education, exploring different methods of promoting social justice. The term "social justice" has become another boogieman of the political right, and as previously mentioned, an Arizona legislator recently advanced a bill to ban the teaching of social justice in public education throughout the state (Roberts, 2017). This is interesting because justice is a human creation. It is not a naturally occurring state of affairs. Rather, it is a constant struggle against our collective, human imperfections and our tendency to oppress and marginalize each other. From this perspective, action is needed to promote justice, and in this instance racial justice. There is an underlying irony that I am writing this book in the state of Arizona, where public schools are required, by law, to set aside time every day for students to recite the Pledge of Allegiance at the beginning of every school day (Flag, Constitution and the Bill of Rights Display Act of 2005). When students recite the pledge, they say "with liberty and justice for all," but when people in the state actually try to promote social justice, it is seen as so threatening that a state law was proposed to ban this practice.

I have had some friends and colleagues express concern that there is a negative tone to the bulk of this book, but I think this is warranted given the extremely racist nature of the majority of the interviews. However, it is neither a pessimistic nor an optimistic text, but a hopeful one. Cornel West (2005) offered some clarity on this distinction: "This hope is not the same as optimism. Optimism adopts the role of the spectator who surveys the evidence in order to infer that things are going to get better. Yet we know that the evidence does not look good. . . . Hope enacts the stance of the participant who actively struggles against the evidence in order to change the deadly tides of wealth inequality, group xenophobia, and personal despair." Hope is eternal, and if I am not hopeful, it is because I lack the will and/or creative imagination to envision a more racially just future. To be human is to be perpetually incomplete while constantly in the process of becoming a more fully realized being (Freire, 2000). From this perpetually unfinished nature springs human potential—opportunities for growth, creation, resistance, and transformation. There is nothing easy about doing racial justice work, but that is part of the reason why it is so incredibly important. Even during some of the bleakest times in Arizona amid the anti-immigrant and anti–Mexican American Studies policies of the early 2010s, I have been able to witness and participate in some of the most beautiful examples of humanity. I was never able to be optimistic because all of the available evidence pointed to issues of race only getting worse. I would not be pessimistic because as the rapper Immortal Technique reminds in the song "Mistakes," "'Cause even when the world is falling on top of me / Pessimism is an emotion, not a philosophy" (Coronel, 2008). Instead, I remain eternally hopeful, but not in a naïve or Pollyannaish way. Rather, my hope compels me to perpetually, collectively struggle against White supremacy in society at large, and within higher education institutions in particular.

If we collectively believe that racism is evil, then we all bear responsibility for disrupting and transforming this oppressive system. People within institutions of higher education hold a greater obligation because we reap more of society's rewards. This work can be daunting given the sheer magnitude of the problem; however, this should not become an excuse for inaction. As Baldwin (1961) so forcefully and beautifully stated, "There is never a time in the future in which we will work out our salvation. The challenge is in the moment, the time is always now" (p. 106). We cannot wait until the "right time" for this work to be done because there is no perfect time and searching for it only creates *analysis paralysis*. So, go forth with love of humanity in your heart, connected to larger collectives of people doing this work, and having courage amid uncertainty. There is nothing less than our collective salvation at stake.

Appendix A
Questionnaire Results, Part I

Pseudonym	Major	Age	Year	Sexual Orientation	Political Orientation[1]
Western University					
Adam	Philosophy	21	4	Hetero	Libertarian
Andy	Material science/ engineering	20	2	Hetero	Centrist
Brandon	Business economics	19	1	Hetero	Centrist
Derek	Economics/ international studies	18	1	Hetero	Libertarian
George	Sociology	20	2	Hetero	Libertarian
Hoyt	Linguistics	21	2	Hetero	Strongly Conservative
Jeremy	English	19	2	Hetero	Democrat
Jonathan	Physiological science	21	4	Hetero	Conservative
Keith	Philosophy	22	4	Hetero	Centrist
Lance	Math/law	22	Grad	Bi	Libertarian/ objectivist
Nick	Political science	22	3	Hetero	Democrat
Robert	History	22	4	Hetero	Slightly left of center
Roger	Math/econ	22	5	Hetero	Democrat
Ryan	Economics	20	2	Hetero	Republican
Trevor[5]	Economics	22	4	Hetero	Democrat
Southwestern University					
Bernard	Political science	20	3	Hetero	Conservative
Duncan	Economics	21	3	Hetero	Centrist
Dwight	English	22	4	Hetero	Centrist
Jack	Deaf studies	20	2	Gay	Democrat
Jacob	Political science	33	4	Hetero	Democrat
Jeff	Business	19	2	Hetero	Libertarian
Joel	Economics/ international studies	20	2	Not answered	Libertarian
Justin	Mathematics	20	2	Not answered	Libertarian
Ken	Journalism	19	2	Hetero	Conservative
Kevin	Economics/political science	18	2	Hetero	Libertarian
Kirk	Undeclared	19	2	Hetero	Democrat
Kurt	Psychology	22	4	Hetero	Centrist
Martin	Spanish/economics	20	—	Hetero	Conservative
Matt	Sociology	21	—	Hetero	Democrat

[1]Response to the open-ended question: "How do you describe yourself politically?"
[2]Question reads: "Have you invited a Black, Latina/o, or Native American for lunch or dinner recently?"
[3]Question reads: "Think of your three closest friends, other than relatives. How many of these three friends are White?"
[4]Question reads: "Have you ever had a romantic relationship with a person from the following racial groups?"
[5]Trevor declined to complete the survey, and his information in this table is derived from the interview transcript.

Parental Income	Neighborhood % White	High School % White	How Often You Think about Race	Meal with/ Minority[2]	White Friends[3]	Dated Black[4]	Dated Latinx[4]
$100,000–$199,999	~50%	0–25%	Once a week	No	3	No	Yes
$80,000–$99,999	75–100%	75–100%	Once a month	Yes	2	No	No
$100,000–$199,999	75–100%	0–25%	Once a week	No	3	No	No
$40,000–$59,999	75–100%	75–100%	>Once per week	Yes	0	No	No
$100,000–$199,999	75–100%	75–100%	>Once per week	No	3	No	No
$100,000–$199,999	75–100%	75–100%	Once a week	No	3	No	Yes
$60,000–$79,999	75–100%	50–75%	>Once per week	No	3	No	No
$80,000–$99,999	75–100%	25–50%	Once a month	Yes	2	No	No
$80,000–$99,999	~50%	~50%	Once a week	No	3	No	Yes
>$200,000	50–75%	25–50%	>Once per week	Yes	3	No	No
$100,000–$199,999	75–100%	~50%	Once a week	No	3	No	Yes
$80,000–$99,999	0–25%	~50%	Once a month	No	3	No	No
$100,000–$199,999	75–100%	75–100%	>Once per week	No	3	No	No
$100,000–$199,999	50–75%	0–25%	>Once per week	Yes	3	No	No
—	—	—	—	—	—	—	—
$100,000–$199,999	75–100%	75–100%	<Once a month	Yes	2	No	No
>$200,000	0–25%	75–100%	<Once a year	Yes	3	No	Yes
$60,000–$79,999	50–75%	~50%	Once a week	Yes	1	Yes	Yes
$40,000–$59,999	50–75%	~50%	Once a week	Yes	2	No	No
$80,000–$99,999	~50%	~50%	>Once per week	No	1	No	No
>$200,000	0–25%	50–75%	<Once a year	Yes	2	No	Yes
$100,000–$199,999	0–25%	75–100%	Not answered	Yes	2	No	No
$30,000–$39,999	50 75%	50–75%	Once a week	Yes	2	No	Yes
$100,000–$199,999	75–100%	50–75%	>Once per week	No	2	No	No
>$200,000	75–100%	75–100%	Once a week	Yes	2	No	No
$100,000–$199,999	25–50%	50–75%	>Once per week	No	2	No	No
$80,000–$99,999	75–100%	75–100%	<Once a month	No	3	No	Yes
<$20,000	75–100%	75–100%	>Once per week	No	3	No	Yes
$60,000–$79,999	50–75%	~50%	<Once a year	No	3	Yes	Yes

Appendix B
Questionnaire Results, Part II

Pseudonym	Major	Age	Year	Sexual Orientation	Political Orientation[1]	Parental Income
Western University						
Alex	Global studies	19	1	Not answered	Centrist	$100,000–$199,999
Benji	History	20	3	Hetero	Democrat	$100,000–$199,999
David	Bio/Cent & East European studies	20	3	Hetero	Leftist	$60,000–$79,999
Josh	Political science/ Afro-American studies	21	3	Hetero	Socialist	>$200,000
Larry	Sociology	22	4	Hetero	Leftist	$60,000–$79,999
Mark	Political science	20	3	Hetero	Centrist	$100,000–$199,999
Zeke	History	22	4	Hetero	Democrat	$100,000–$199,999
Southwestern University						
Chad	German studies	29	4	Hetero	Leftist	$20,000–$29,999
Chris	Geography	23	5	Gay	Liberal	$100,000–$199,999
Devin	Psychology/German	22	4	Hetero	Democrat	$80,000–$99,999
Greg	Undeclared	24	3	n/a[5]	Leftist	$20,000–$29,999
Jason	Sociology	20	3	Bisexual	Democrat	$60,000–$79,999
Jay	Communication	20	3	not answered	Centrist	$80,000–$99,999
Max	Communication	31	4	Hetero	Progressive/ leftist	$60,000–$79,999

[1]Response to the open-ended question: "How do you describe yourself politically?"
[2]Question reads: "Have you invited a Black, Latina/o, or Native American for lunch or dinner recently?"
[3]Question reads: "Think of your three closest friends, other than relatives. How many of these three friends are White?"
[4]Question reads: "Have you ever had a romantic relationship with a person from the following racial groups?"
[5]This is precisely how the participant answered the question.

Neighborhood % White	High School % White	How Often You Think about Race	Meal with Minority[2]	White Friends[3]	Dated Black[4]	Dated Latinx[4]
75–100%	75–100%	>Once per week	Yes	2	No	No
50–75%	~50%	>Once per week	Yes	2	No	No
25–50%	0–25%	>Once per week	No	2	Yes	Yes
75–100%	0–25%	>Once per week	Yes	1	No	No
25–50%	25–50%	>Once per week	Yes	1	Yes	Yes
75–100%	75–100%	Once a week	No	3	No	No
75–100%	25–50%	>Once per week	Yes	3	No	No
75–100%	75–100%	Once a week	No	1	No	No
75–100%	75–100%	Once a week	Yes	1	No	Yes
50–75%	50–75%	>Once per week	No	2	Yes	No
75–100%	0–25%	>Once per week	No	3	No	No
25–50%	25–50%	Once a week	No	3	No	No
50–75%	75–100%	Once a week	No	3	No	No
75–100%	75–100%	Once a week	No	1	Yes	No

Acknowledgments

This book is the cumulation of about a decade's worth of work on Whiteness in higher education, and I have a ton of people to thank for their tireless support. First, my committee of Walter Allen, Sylvia Hurtado, Rob Rhoads, and Miguel Unzueta, were instrumental in giving this project legs. Thank you all for critical feedback and support through and through. To Sylvia in particular, thank you for chairing an admittedly risky dissertation topic! It meant a lot that you were willing to go into these uncharted waters with me.

As Whiteness is both an esoteric and controversial subject, I am incredibly indebted to the numerous scholars whose work and mentorship has been foundational in doing this work. They include, but are not limited to, Zeus Leonardo, David Gillborn, Shaun Harper, Ricky Allen, Lori Patton Davis, Jeff Chang, and Tim Lensmire. I especially want to thank my "academic twin" Cheryl Matias who has continually pushed my Whiteness work to be better ever since we were in grad school.

I am incredibly indebted to my colleagues at the University of Arizona who have also supported this work. While many Whiteness scholars are ridiculed for their research, I have received an incredible amount of interested, lively, and critical engagement. Thank you for creating such a nurturing environment, especially while I was a junior scholar, Jeff Milem, Gary Rhoades, Regina Deil-Amen, Jenny Lee, Francesca López, Jill Koyama, Cecilia Rios-Aguilar, and Ozan Jaquette.

Thanks so much to the crew at Rutgers University Press for both taking a chance on this book and working diligently to help me develop and refine the text. I especially appreciate the efforts of my editors Kimberly Guinta and Lisa Banning.

A previous version of Chapter 4 was published in the *Journal of College Student Development*: Cabrera, N. L. (2014). "But we're not laughing: White male college students' racial joking and what this says about 'post-racial' discourse." *Journal of College Student Development,* 55(1), 1–15. I would like to thank the editors of the journal for allowing me to reproduce this work in the current text.

Finally, to my family, your support throughout has been invaluable, even if you did not always understand what I was doing. Thank you, Dad, Mom and Kim, Aunt Marti, Aunt Bea, and DeMara. Paloma, you were there from the beginning, providing encouragement to keep me developing work, and frequently offering an exasperated look when I told you what I was finding—thank you! Finally, Joaquín you came into this world in the middle of this work, but you are the foundation. You, son, keep me grounded, and this book is the answer to the question you keep asking me from your favorite musical *Hamilton,* "Why do you write like you're running out of time?"

Peace, NC$_{c/s}$

Notes

Preface

1 I have not been able to find proper attribution for this quotation, hence the author is "Anonymous."
2 I wanted to include the Fighting Whites image in this book, but I was not able to secure permission in time to use it. If readers would like to see it, please visit https://en.wikipedia.org/wiki/Fighting_Whites.

Chapter 1   The Unbearable Whiteness of Being

1 Here is the clip from Fox News where Campus Reform activists reported Bebout's class to the national media: https://www.youtube.com/watch?v=607cAHlmQaw. Many other news outlets subsequently explored the issue, but this was the origin on the manufactured controversy.
2 I want to be clear about a difficult decision I made while writing this book. A number of times during the course of talking with the White guys I interviewed, they used the n-word. They were also relatively prone to using profanity in their narratives of race. Some have suggested to me that I should use asterisks to mask these words. Reading drafts where I did so, I noticed their statements were too sanitized. Therefore, when I am quoting the White guys I interviewed or media events on racial controversies, I report verbatim. I understand that these comments will likely provoke a visceral response for some readers, so please consider this my version of a trigger warning.
3 This label is frequently applied by conservative critics of U.S. higher education. For one of many examples, please see http://bernardgoldberg.com/americas-expensive-indoctrination-camps/. See also Campus Reform (https://www.campusreform.org) and The College Fix (https://www.thecollegefix.com) for other examples.
4 In this text, I tend to use *minoritized* instead of *minority* when describing People of Color or Students of Color. The reason is twofold. First, *minority* is frequently implied to mean a numerical assessment, and issues of racism are much deeper than this, as this book presents an analysis of power dynamics along racial lines.

Second, *minoritized*, as a combination of *minority* and *marginalized*, implies actions on behalf of the powerful (not necessarily numeric) majority that lead to the marginalized status of People of Color. Thus, *minoritized*, instead of being a descriptor of People of Color, is actually a verb describing the oppressive practices of the socially dominant group.

5   Here is one of the clips in which comedian Paul Mooney offers his "complexion of protection" bit: https://www.youtube.com/watch?v=wXk_DPpUFlo. Please note that my referencing of this standup routine should not be inferred as a full endorsement of the comedian or the bit because in this clip Mooney is both racially insightful and misogynistic.

Chapter 2   "Race Just Doesn't Matter That Much"

1   My dad used to humorously refer to these words as "rectal reasoning."

2   While I use transcripts from twenty-eight White guys, I have only twenty-seven questionnaires as one participant declined to complete his.

3   Compositional diversity refers to the proportion of Students of Color on a particular institution (Milem, Chang, & antonio, 2005). For close to a decade, it was referred to as "structural diversity" (Hurtado, Alvarez, Guillermo-Wann, Cuellar, & Arellano, 2012). It is, however, only one component of the larger campus racial climate, which also includes (1) an institution's historical legacy of inclusion/exclusion, (2) the behavioral dimension (i.e., quantity and quality of cross-racial interactions), (3) the psychological dimension (i.e., perceptions of a campus's racial inclusivity/exclusivity), and 4) the organizational dimension (e.g., to what degree diversity is embedded in tenure processes, hiring, and the curriculum) (Milem et al., 2005).

4   When I offer dialogue between myself and one of the White guys, I abbreviate Nolan as "N" and then use the pseudonym's first initial (in this case "K" for Kurt).

5   Objectivism is largely associated with the writings of Ayn Rand, and its central tenets include that (1) individual freedom is prized above all, (2) pursuing one's own self-interests is the highest form of human endeavor, (3) objective reality exists, (4) purely logical, rational thought is the best that humankind has to offer, and (5) laissez-faire capitalism is the most morally acceptable social structure to allow humans to pursue their individual interests.

6   The discussion of Occam's razor is part of the thirteenth episode in *Scrubs'* first season, titled "My Balancing Act" (http://scrubs.wikia.com/wiki/My_Balancing _Act). The specific quotation by the character Dr. Cox is at the end of this short clip: https://www.youtube.com/watch?v=CDY214pcbOw.

Chapter 4   "Why Can't Stevie Wonder Read? Because He's Black"

1   Lisa Lampanelli is a White insult comic who centers a lot of her work on racist stereotypes. The following is relatively emblematic of her body of work: https:// www.youtube.com/watch?v=JoucC1laFRE. The specific part I am referencing is at the 4:51 mark.

2   Moshe Kasher's full stand-up set can be found here: http://www.cc.com/episodes /p3draz/moshe-kasher—live-in-oakland-moshe-kasher—live-in-oakland-season-1 -ep-101. The specific moment I am referring to is at 0:57, but if readers continue watching the whole set, they will see a lot of very insightful and

thought-provoking racial (as opposed to racist) comedy. I personally enjoy Kasher's stand up very much, and my critique at the beginning of this chapter should not be construed as a dismissal of his body of work.

3 Some coverage of Mel Gibson's arrest can be found here: http://www.cnn.com /2006/LAW/08/02/gibson.charged/index.html?_s=PM:LAW.

Chapter 6 "They'd Never Allow a White Student Union"

1 MEChA stands for El Movimiento Estudiantil Chicanx de Aztlán, one of the oldest Chicanx student organizations in the country. It grew out of the Chicano Movement and is a very prevalent activist/social organization on college campuses (http://www.chicanxdeaztlan.org).

2 The Chicano Moratorium was one component of the larger Chicano Movement in the 1960s that was explicitly against the Vietnam War. This was in stark contrast to many in the Mexican American community who saw military service as both emblematic of masculinity and a patriotic duty. The Chicano Moratorium instead asked why so many poor Brown folk were going to Vietnam to die and what the Vietnamese had done to "provoke" such aggression. For more details on the Chicano Moratorium, please see Rodriguez (2015).

3 Proposition 209 eliminated affirmative action in the state. After it was passed, the proportion of Black, Latinx, and Native American students at WU plummeted. The student organizing that Roger referred to was in direct response to this larger policy environment.

4 LOGIC is the campus-based Objectivist student organization.

Chapter 7 "Because It's the Right Thing to Do"

1 The song "Everyone's a Little Bit Racist" can be found here: https://www.youtube .com/watch?v=RXnMiuHhsOI. My primary issue is conflating racism (system of oppression) with prejudice (individual orientation). It would be more accurate to title the song "Everyone's a Little Bit Prejudiced," although it does not have the same ring to it.

2 Jay Smooth's entire TEDx talk can be found here: https://www.youtube.com /watch?v=MbdxeFcQtaU. I highly suggest people watch the entire lecture, and the specific section I reference is at the 5:11 mark.

Chapter 8 Conclusion

1 Jay Smooth's entire Tedx TEDx talk can be found here: https://www.youtube .com/watch?v=MbdxeFcQtaU. I highly suggest people watch the entire lecture, and the specific section I reference is at the 8:55 mark.

References

Allen, T. W. (1997). *The invention of the White race*. Vol. 2: *The origin of oppression in Anglo-America*. New York, NY: Verso.

Angry Black Woman. (2008, April 29). Things you need to understand #9—You don't get a cookie. Retrieved from http://theangryblackwoman.com/2008/04/29/no-cookie/

antonio, a. l. (2001). Diversity and the influence of friendship groups in college. *Review of Higher Education, 25*(1), 63–89.

Apple, M. (1998). Foreword. In J. Kincheloe, S. Steinberg, N. Rodriguez, & R. Chennault (Eds.), *White reign: Deploying Whiteness in America* (pp. ix–xiii). New York, NY: St. Martin's Griffin.

Applebaum, B. (2008). "Doesn't my experience count?": White students, the authority of experience and social justice pedagogy. *Race Ethnicity and Education, 11*(4), 405–414.

Applebaum, B. (2010). *Being White, being good: White complicity, White moral responsibility, and social justice pedagogy*. Lanham, MD: Lexington Books.

Associated Press. (2016, December 11). Ahead of pro-Trump rally, KKK members claim they're "not White supremacists." *NBC News*. Retrieved from http://www.nbcnews.com/news/us-news/kkk-other-racist-groups claim-they-re-not-white-supremacists-n694536

Astin, A. W. (1993). *What matters in college: Four critical years revisited*. San Francisco, CA: Jossey-Bass.

Bacote, V. (2015). Erasing race: Racial identity and theological anthropology. In A. B. Bradley (Ed.), *Black scholars in White space: New vistas in African American Studies from the Christian academy* (pp. 123–138). Eugene, OR: Pickwick.

Baldwin, J. (1961). *Nobody knows my name: More notes of a native son*. New York, NY: Dell Publishing.

Baldwin, J. (1963). *The fire next time*. New York, NY: Dial Press.

Baldwin, J. (1984). *Notes of a native son*. Boston, MA: Beacon.

Bell, D. A. (1979). *Brown v. Board of Education* and the interest convergence dilemma. *Harvard Law Review, 93*(3), 518–534.

Bell, D. A. (1992). *Faces at the bottom of the well: The permanence of racism*. New York, NY: Harper Collins.

Berlinger, J. (2006, November 30). Dave Chappelle and Maya Angelou. In S. Beaumont, *Iconoclasts*. New York, NY: SundanceTV.

Blumer, H. (1958). Race prejudice as a sense of group position. *Pacific Sociological Review, 1*(1), 3–7.

Bobo, L. D., Kluegel, J. R., & Smith, R. (1997). Laissez faire racism: The crystallization of a "kinder, gentler" anti-Black ideology. In S. Tuch & J. Martin (Eds.), *Racial attitudes in the 1990s: Continuity and change* (pp. 15–42). Westport, CT: Praeger.

Bobo, L. D., & Tuan, M. (2006). *Prejudice in politics: Group position, public opinion, and the Wisconsin treaty rights dispute*. Cambridge, MA: Harvard University Press.

Bonilla-Silva, E. (2001). *White supremacy & racism in the post–civil rights era*. Boulder, CO: Lynne Rienner.

Bonilla-Silva, E. (2006). *Racism without racists: Color-blind racism and the persistence of racial inequality in the United States* (2nd ed.). Lanham, MD: Rowman & Littlefield.

Borger, J. (2006, November 27). New York on edge as police kill unarmed man in hail of 50 bullets on his wedding day. *Guardian*. Retrieved from https://www.theguardian.com/world/2006/nov/27/usa.julianborger

Boswell, A. A., & Spade, J. Z. (1996). Fraternities and collegiate rape culture: Why are some fraternities more dangerous places for women? *Gender & Society, 10*(2), 133–147.

Bourgois, P. (2003). *In search of respect: Selling crack in El Barrio* (2nd ed.). New York, NY: Cambridge University Press.

Bowen, H. R. (1977). *Investing in learning: The individual and social value of American higher education*. San Francisco, CA: Jossey-Bass.

Bowman, N. A. (2011). Promoting participation in a diverse democracy: A meta-analysis of college diversity experiences and civic engagement. *Review of Educational Research, 81*(1), 29–68.

Brodin, M. S. (2014). The fraudulent case against affirmative action: The untold story behind *Fisher v. University of Texas*. *Buffalo Law Review, 62*(2), 237–290.

Broido, E. M. (2000). The development of social justice allies during college: A phenomenological investigation. *Journal of College Student Development, 41*(1), 3–18.

Brown, M. C., II. (2001). Collegiate desegregation and the public Black college: A new policy mandate. *Journal of Higher Education, 72*, 46–62.

Brown, M. K., Carnoy, M., Currie, E., Duster, T., Oppenhiemer, D. B., Shultz, M. M., & Wellman, D. (2003). *White-washing race*. Berkeley: University of California Press.

Brown v. Board of Education of Topeka, 347 U.S. 483 (1954).

Bush, M. E. L. (2011). *Everyday forms of Whiteness: Understanding race in a "post-racial" world* (2nd ed.). Lanham, MD: Rowman & Littlefield.

Cabrera, N. L. (2009). *Invisible racism: Male, hegemonic Whiteness in higher education* (Unpublished doctoral dissertation). University of California, Los Angeles.

Cabrera, N. L. (2011). Using a sequential exploratory mixed-method design to examine racial hyperprivilege in higher education. In K. A. Griffin & S. D. Museus (Eds.), *New directions for institutional research: No. 151. Using mixed-methods approaches to study intersectionality in higher education* (pp. 77–91). San Francisco, CA: Jossey-Bass.

Cabrera, N. L. (2012). Working through Whiteness: White male college students challenging racism. *Review of Higher Education, 35*, 375–401.

Cabrera, N. L. (2014a). Beyond Black and White: How White male college students see their Asian American peers. *Equity & Excellence in Education, 47*(2), 133–151.

Cabrera, N. L. (2014b). "But I'm oppressed too": White male college students framing racial emotions as facts and recreating racism. *International Journal of Qualitative Studies in Education, 27*(6), 768–784.

Cabrera, N. L. (2014c). But we're not laughing: White male college students' racial joking and what this says about "post-racial" discourse. *Journal of College Student Development, 55*(1), 1–15.

Cabrera, N. L. (2014d). Exposing Whiteness in higher education: White male college students minimizing racism, claiming victimization, and recreating White supremacy. *Race Ethnicity and Education, 17*(1), 30–55.

Cabrera, N. L. (2015, March 18). What the Oklahoma frat video tells us about America. *Al Jazeera America*. Retrieved from http://america.aljazeera.com/opinions/2015/3/what-the-oklahoma-frat-video-tells-us-about-america.html

Cabrera, N. L. (2016). When racism and masculinity collide: Some methodological considerations from a Man of Color studying Whiteness. *Whiteness and Education, 1*(1), 15–25.

Cabrera, N. L. (2017). White immunity: Working through the pedagogical pitfalls of privilege. *Journal Committed to Social Change on Race and Ethnicity, 3*(1), 74–86.

Cabrera, N. L. (in press). Where is the racial theory in Critical Race Theory? A constructive criticism of the Crits. *The Review of Higher Education.*

Cabrera, N. L., Franklin, J. D., & Watson, J. S. (2017). *Whiteness in higher education: The invisible missing link in diversity and racial analyses.* Association for the Study of Higher Education monograph series. San Francisco, CA: Jossey-Bass.

Cabrera, N. L., & Holliday, M. R. (2017). Racial politics and racial identity: A case study of Arizona, 2010–2011. *Hispanic Journal of Behavioral Sciences, 39*(2), 131–149.

Cabrera, N. L., & Hurtado, S. (2015). The ivory tower is still White: Chicano/Latino college students on race, ethnic organizations, and campus racial segregation. In R. E. Zambrana & S. Hurtado (Eds.), *The magic key: The educational journey of Mexican Americans from K–12 to college and beyond* (pp. 145–167). Austin: University of Texas Press.

Cabrera, N. L., Watson, J. S., & Franklin, J. D. (2016). Racial arrested development: A critical Whiteness analysis of the campus ecology. *Journal of College Student Development, 57*(2), 119–134.

Capraro, R. L. (2000). Why college men drink: Alcohol, adventure, and the paradox of masculinity. *Journal of American College Health, 48*, 307–315.

Carnevale, A. P., & Strohl, J. (2013). *Separate & Unequal: How higher education reinforces the intergenerational reproduction of White racial privilege.* Washington, DC: Georgetown Public Policy Institute.

Carroll, H. (2011). *Affirmative reaction: New formations of White masculinity.* Durham, NC: Duke University Press.

Chang, J. (2014). *Who we be: The colorization of America's youth.* New York, NY: St. Martin's.

Chang, M. J. (2002). Preservation or transformation: Where's the real educational discourse on diversity? *Review of Higher Education, 25*(2), 125–140.

Chang, M. J., Astin, A. W., & Kim, D. (2004). Cross-racial interaction among undergraduates: Some consequences, causes, and patterns. *Research in Higher Education, 45*(5), 529–553.

Chang, M. J., & DeAngelo, L. (2002). Going Greek: The effects of racial composition on White students' participation patterns. *Journal of College Student Development, 43*(6), 809–823.

Cherette, M. (2010, October 30). Jon Stewart's closing rally speech: "If we amplify everything, we hear nothing." *Gawker.* Retrieved from http://gawker.com/5677453/jon-stewarts-closing-rally-speech-if-we-amplify-everything-we-hear-nothing

Chesler, M. A., Lewis, A. E., & Crowfoot, J. E. (2005). *Challenging racism in higher education: Promoting justice.* Lanham, MD: Rowman & Littlefield.

Chesler, M. A., Peet, M., & Sevig, T. (2003). Blinded by the Whiteness: The development of White college students' racial awareness. In A. W. Doane & E. Bonilla-Silva (Eds.), *White out: The continuing significance of racism* (pp. 215–230). New York, NY: Routledge.

Chou, R. S., & Feagin, J. R. (2008). *The myth of the model minority: Asian Americans facing racism.* Boulder, CO: Paradigm.

Cole, E. R. (2018). College presidents and Black student protests: A historical perspective on the image of racial inclusion and the reality of exclusion. *Peabody Journal of Education, 93*(1), 78–89.

Connell, R. W. (2005). *Masculinities.* Berkeley: University of California Press.

Coronel, F. A. (2008). Mistakes [Recorded by Immortal Technique]. On *The 3rd World.* New York, NY: Viper Records.

Coscarelli, J. (2014, May 14). Bill O'Reilly denies the existence of White privilege because he once worked at an ice cream shop. *New York.* Retrieved from http://nymag.com/daily/intelligencer/2014/05/bill-oreilly-denies-white-privilege-video.html

Crosby, F. J. (2004). *Affirmative action is dead: Long live affirmative action.* New Haven, CT: Yale University Press.

cummings. e. e. (1994). Since feeling is first. In e. e. cummings, *100 selected poems* (p. 35). New York, NY: Grove.

DiAngelo, R. (2011). White fragility. *International Journal of Critical Pedagogy, 3*(3), 54–70.

D'Souza, D. (1991). *Illiberal education.* New York, NY: Vintage.

Du Bois, W. E. B. (1935). *Black reconstruction: An essay toward a history of the part which Black folk played in the attempt to reconstruct democracy in America, 1860–1880.* New York, NY: Hardcourt, Brace.

Du Bois, W. E. B. (1969). *The souls of Black folk.* New York, NY: Signet Classic.

Du Bois, W. E. B. (1971). *The seventh son: The thought and writings of W. E. B. Du Bois* (J. Lester, Ed.). Vol. 2. New York, NY: Vintage.

Duster, T. (1991, September 25). Understanding self-segregation on the campus. *Chronicle of Higher Education,* pp. B1–B2.

Eagan, M. K., Stolzenberg, E. B., Zimmerman, H. B., Aragon, M. C., Whang Sayson, H., & Rios-Aguilar, C. (2017). *The American freshman: National norms fall 2016.* Los Angeles: University of California, Los Angeles, Higher Education Research Institute.

Edwards, K. E. (2006). Aspiring social justice ally identity development: A conceptual model. *NASPA Journal, 43*(4), 39–60.

Edwards, K. E., & Jones, S. R. (2009). "Putting my man face on": A grounded theory of college men's gender identity development. *Journal of College Student Development, 50*(2), 210–228.

Ellsworth, E. (1989). Why doesn't this feel empowering? Working through the repressive myths of critical pedagogy. *Harvard Educational Review, 59*(3), 297–325.

Eng, D. L. (2001). *Racial castration: Managing masculinities in Asian America.* Durham, NC: Duke University Press.

Ernst, D. (2015, June 20). Maher: PC "idiots" shouldn't lecture Seinfeld, Larry the Cable Guy on comedy. *Washington Times.* Retrieved from http://www .washingtontimes.com/news/2015/jun/20/bill-maher-pc-idiots-shouldnt-lecture -jerry-seinfe/

Escueta, E., & O'Brien, E. (1995). Asian Americans in higher education: Trends and issues. In D. T. Nakanishi & T. Y. Nishida (Eds.), *The Asian American educational experience: A source book for teachers and students* (pp. 259–272). New York, NY: Routledge.

Evans, N. J., Forney, D. S., Guido, F., Patton, L. D., & Renn, K. A. (2010). *Student development in college: Theory, research, and practice* (2nd ed.). San Francisco, CA: Jossey-Bass.

Feagin, J. R. (2006). *Systemic racism: A theory of oppression.* New York, NY: Routledge.

Feagin, J. R. (2010). *The White racial frame: Centuries of racial framing and counter-framing.* New York, NY: Routledge.

Feagin, J. R., & O'Brien, E. (2003). *White men on race.* Boston, MA: Beacon.

Feagin, J. R., Vera, H., & Imani, N. (1996). *The agony of education: Black students at white colleges and universities.* New York, NY: Routledge.

Feldstein, R. (1997). *Political correctness: A response from the cultural left.* Minneapolis: University of Minnesota Press.

Flag, Constitution and the Bill of Rights Display Act, Ariz. Rev. Stat. Ann. §§15–506 (2005).

Flegenheimer, M., & Haberman, M. (2017, May 1). "You're the best," Trump once told Pelosi. Can they deal again? *New York Times.* Retrieved from https://www.nytimes .com/2017/05/01/us/politics/trump-nancy-pelosi-congress.html?mcubz=0

Frankenberg, E., & Orfield, G. (Eds.). (2012). *The resegregation of suburban schools: A hidden crisis in American education.* Cambridge, MA: Harvard University Press.

Freire, P. (2000). *Pedagogy of the oppressed* (30th anniv. ed.). New York, NY: Herder and Herder.

Garcia, G. A., Johnston, M. P., Garibay, J. C., Herrera, F. A., & Giraldo, L. G. (2011). When parties become racialized: Deconstructing racially themed parties. *Journal of Student Affairs Research and Practice, 48*(1), 5–21.

Geiger, R. L. (2005). Ten generations of American higher education. In P. G. Altbach, R. O. Berdahl, & P. J. Gumport (Eds.), *American higher education in the twenty-first century: Social, political, and economic challenges* (2nd ed., pp. 38–70). Baltimore, MD: Johns Hopkins University Press.

Georgevich, M. (2007, February 15). Theme party provokes outrage. *Santa Clara.* Retrieved from http://thesantaclara.org/theme-party-provokes-outrage-2/# .Wbo08a2ZOqA

Gillborn, D. (2008). *Racism and education: Coincidence or conspiracy?* London, England: Routledge.

Gramsci, A. (1971). *Selections from the prison notebooks of Antonio Gramsci* (Q. Hoare & G. N. Smith, Eds. & Trans.). New York, NY: International.

Greer, S. (2017). *No campus for White men. The transformation of higher education into hateful indoctrination.* Washington, DC: WND Books.

Guinier, L. (2015). *The tyranny of meritocracy: Democratizing higher education in America.* Boston, MA: Beacon.

Gusa, D. L. (2010). White institutional presence: The impact of Whiteness on campus climate. *Harvard Educational Review, 80,* 464–490.

Gutmann, A. (1999). *Democratic education.* Princeton, NJ: Princeton University Press.

Han, C.-S. (2008). No fats, femmes, or Asians: The utility of Critical Race Theory in examining the role of gay stock stories in the marginalization of Asian men. *Contemporary Justice Review, 11*(1), 11–22.

Haney-López, I. (2006). *White by law: The legal construction of race.* New York, NY: New York University Press.

Harper, S. R. (2012). Race without racism: How higher education researchers minimize racist institutional norms. *Review of Higher Education, 36*(1), 9–29.

Harper, S. R., & Harris, F., III. (2010). *College men and masculinities: Theory, research, and implications for practice.* San Francisco, CA: Jossey-Bass.

Harper, S. R., Harris, F., III, & Mmeje, K. C. (2005). A theoretical model to explain the overrepresentation of college men among campus judicial offenders: Implications for campus administrators. *NASPA Journal, 42*(4), 565–588.

Harper, S. R., Patton, L. D., & Wooden, O. S. (2009). Access and equity for African American students in higher education: A critical race historical analysis of policy efforts. *Journal of Higher Education, 80*(4), 389–414.

Harris, C. I. (1993). Whiteness as property. *Harvard Law Review, 106,* 1707–1791.

Harro, B. (2000). The cycle of socialization. In M. Adams, W. J. Blumenfeld, R. Castaneda, H. W. Hackman, M. L. Peters, & X. Zuñiga (Eds.), *Reading for diversity and social justice: An anthology on racism, anti-Semitism, sexism, heterosexism, ableism, and classism* (pp. 79–82). New York, NY: Routledge.

Helms, J. E. (1990). *Black and White identity: Theory, research, and practice.* Westport, CT: Praeger.

Holden, T. (2017, February 10). The right call: Yale removes my racist ancestor's name from campus. *New York Times.* Retrieved from https://www.nytimes.com/2017/02/10/opinion/get-my-racist-ancestors-name-off-of-yales-campus.html?mcubz=0

hooks, b. (1995). *Killing rage: Ending racism.* New York, NY: Henry Holt.

Hurtado, S. (1992). The campus racial climate: Contexts of conflict. *Journal of Higher Education, 63*(5), 539–569.

Hurtado, S., Alvarez, C. L., Guillermo-Wann, C., Cuellar, M., & Arellano, L. (2012). A model for diverse learning environments: The scholarship on creating and assessing conditions for student success. In J. C. Smart & M. B. Paulsen (Eds.), *Higher education: Handbook of theory and research* (Vol. 27, pp. 41–122). Dordrecht, The Netherlands: Springer.

Hurtado, S., Maestas, R., Hill, L., Inkelas, K., Wathington, H. D., & Waterson, E. (1998). *Perspectives on the climate for diversity: Findings and suggested recommendations for the Texas A&M University campus community.* Ann Arbor, MI: Center for the Study of Higher and Postsecondary Education.

Ignatiev, N. (1995). *How the Irish became White.* New York, NY: Routledge.

Ignatiev, N. (1997). The point is not to interpret Whiteness but to abolish it. *Race Traitor.* Retrieved from http://racetraitor.org/abolishthepoint.html

Jaschik, S. (2015, August 24). Saida Grundy, moving forward. *Inside Higher Ed.* Retrieved from https://www.insidehighered.com/news/2015/08/24/saida-grundy-discusses-controversy-over-her-comments-twitter-her-career-race-and

Johansen, B. E. (2010). Putting the moccasin on the other foot: A media history of the "Fighting Whities." In C. R. King (Ed.), *The Native American mascot controversy: A handbook* (pp. 163–178). Lanham, MD: Scarecrow.

Johnson, A. (2001). *Power, privilege, and difference.* Mountain View, CA: Mayfield.

Johnson, A. (2005). *The gender knot: Unraveling our patriarchal legacy.* Philadelphia, PA: Temple University Press.

Jordan, B., King, D., Dennis, W., & GTA. (1991). Mind playing tricks on me [Recorded by Geto Boys]. On *We Can't Be Stopped.* Houston, TX: Rap-A-Lot Records.

Kantrowitz, M. (2011, September 2). *The distribution of grants and scholarships by race.* Skokie, IL: FinAid. Retrieved from http://www.finaid.org/scholarships/20110902racescholarships.pdf

Karabel, J. (2005). *The chosen: The hidden history of admission and exclusion at Harvard, Yale, and Princeton.* Boston, MA: Houghton Mifflin.

Keene, A. (2015). Representations matter: Serving Native students in higher education. *Journal Committed to Social Change on Race and Ethnicity, 1*(1), 102–111.

Kendall, F. E. (2006). *Understanding White privilege: Creating pathways to authentic relationships across race.* New York, NY: Routledge.

Kendi, I. X. (2016). *Stamped from the beginning: The definitive history of racist ideas in America.* New York, NY: Nation Books.

Kerr, C. (1995). *The uses of the university* (4th ed.). Cambridge, MA: Harvard University Press.

Kim, C. J. (1999). The racial triangulation of Asian Americans. *Politics & Society, 27*(1), 105–138.

Kimmel, M. S. (2013). *Angry white men: American masculinity at the end of an era.* New York, NY: Nation Books.

Kimmel, M. S., & Ferber, A. L. (Eds.). (2017). *Privilege: A reader* (4th ed.). Boulder, CO: Westview Press.

Kimmel, M. S., & Messner, M. A. (2004). *Men's lives* (6th ed.). Boston, MA: Pearson.

Kindlon, D. J., & Thompson, M. (2000). *Raising Cain: Protecting the emotional life of boys.* New York, NY: Ballantine Books.

Klyde-Silverstein, L. (2012). The "Fighting Whites" phenomenon: An interpretive analysis of media coverage of an American Indian mascot issue. In M. G. Carstarphen & J. P. Sanchez (Eds.), *American Indians and the mass media* (pp. 113–127). Norman: University of Oklahoma Press.

Laker, J. A., & Davis, T. (2011). *Masculinities in higher education: Theoretical and practical considerations.* New York, NY: Routledge.

Lee, S. (2000). *Bamboozled.* Retrieved from http://nldslab.soe.ucsc.edu/charactercreator/film_corpus/film_2012xxxx/imsdb.com/Bamboozled.html

Lemons, S. (2015, February 17). White supremacists target ASU professor and his family over "Whiteness" course. *Phoenix New Times.* Retrieved from http://www.phoenixnewtimes.com/news/white-supremacists-target-asu-professor-and-his-family-over-whiteness-course-6636554

Lensmire, T. J., McManimon, S. K., Tierney, J. D., Lee-Nichols, M. E., Casey, Z. A., Lensmire, A., & Davis, B. M. (2013). McIntosh as synecdoche: How teacher education's focus on white privilege undermines antiracism. *Harvard Educational Review, 83*(3), 410–431.

Leonardo, Z. (2005). Through the multicultural glass: Althusser, ideology and race relations in post–civil rights America. *Policy Futures in Education, 3*, 400–412.

Leonardo, Z. (2009). *Race, whiteness, and education*. New York, NY: Routledge.

Leonardo, Z., & Porter, R. K. (2010). Pedagogy of fear: Toward a Fanonian theory of "safety" in race dialogues. *Race, Ethnicity, and Education, 13*(2), 139–157.

Lewis, A. (2004). *Race in the schoolyard: Negotiating the color line in classrooms and communities*. New Brunswick, NJ: Rutgers University Press.

Linder, C. (2015). Navigating guilt, shame, and fear of appearing racist: A conceptual model of antiracist White feminist identify development. *Journal of College Student Development, 56*(6), 535–550.

Lipsitz, G. (2006). *The possessive investment in Whiteness: How White people profit from identity politics*. Philadelphia, PA: Temple University Press.

Lipsitz, G. (2011). *How racism takes place*. Philadelphia, PA: Temple University Press.

Lukes, S. (2005). *Power: A radical view* (2nd ed.). New York, NY: Palgrave.

Lyman, P. (1987). The fraternal bond as a joking relationship: A case study of the role of sexist jokes in male group bonding. In M. S. Kimmel (Ed.), *Changing men: New directions in research on men and masculinity* (pp. 148–163). Thousand Oaks, CA: Sage.

Macalpine, M., & Marsh, S. (2005). "On being White: There's nothing I can say": Exploring Whiteness and power in organizations. *Management Learning, 36*(4), 429–450.

MacMullan, T. (2009). *Habits of Whiteness: A pragmatist reconstruction*. Bloomington: Indiana University Press.

Matias, C. E. (2016). *Feeling white: Whiteness, emotionality, and education*. Boston, MA: Sense.

Maynard, J. (2004, October 29). Professor says racism is subconscious, but present. *The Battalion*.

Mazza, E. (2017, May 3). Bill Maher warns Democrats: "Ease up on the identity politics." *Huffington Post*. Retrieved from http://www.huffingtonpost.com/entry/bill-maher-democrats_us_59093dbfe4b0bb2d08731eed

McElroy, E. (2018). Postsocialism and the Tech Boom 2.0: Techno-utopics of racial/spatial dispossession. *Social Identities, 24*, 206–221.

McIntosh, P. (1989, July/August). White privilege: Unpacking the invisible knapsack. *Peace and Freedom*, pp. 10–12.

McPherson, M., Smith-Lovin, L., & Cook, J. M. (2001). Birds of a feather: Homophily in social networks. *Annual Review of Sociology, 27*(1), 415–444.

Milem, J. F., Chang, M. J., & antonio, A. L. (2005). *Making diversity work on campus: A research-based perspective*. Washington, DC: Association of American Colleges and Universities.

Mills, C. W. (1997). *The racial contract*. Ithaca, NY: Cornell University Press.

Morrison, T. (1992). *Playing in the dark: Whiteness and the literary imagination*. Cambridge, MA: Harvard University Press.

Multicultural, social justice educator to speak at Misericordia University. (2015, September 16). *Dallas Post*. Retrieved from http://mydallaspost.com/news/local/12126/multicultural-social-justice-educator-to-speak-at-misericordia-university

Museus, S. D., & Kiang, P. N. (2009). Deconstructing the model minority myth and how it contributes to the invisible minority reality in higher education. *New Directions for Institutional Research, 142*, 5–15.

Mustaffa, J. B. (2017). Mapping violence, naming life: A history of anti-Black oppression in the higher education system. *International Journal of Qualitative Studies in Education, 30*(8), 711–727.

Nagda, B. A., & Zuñiga, X. (2003). Fostering meaningful racial engagement through intergroup dialogues. *Processes & Intergroup Relations, 6*(1), 111–128.

Norton, M. I., & Sommers, S. R. (2011). Whites see racism as a zero-sum game that they are now losing. *Perspectives in Psychological Science, 6*, 215–218.

O'Connor, P. (2002). *Oppression and responsibility: A Wittgensteinian approach to social practice and moral theory.* University Park: Penn State University Press.

Oliver, M. L., & Shapiro, T. M. (2006). *Black wealth, White wealth: A new perspective on racial inequality.* Oxford, England: Taylor & Francis.

Omi, M., & Winant, H. (2015). *Racial formation in the United States* (3rd ed.). New York, NY: Routledge.

Orfield, G., & Eaton, S. E. (1997). *Dismantling desegregation: The quiet reversal of* Brown v. Board of Education. New York, NY: New Press.

Orozco, R. (2013). White innocence and Mexican Americans as perpetrators in the school-to-prison pipeline. *Association of Mexican-American Educators, 7*(3), 75–84.

Ortiz, A. M., & Rhoads, R. A. (2000). Deconstructing Whiteness as part of a multicultural educational framework: From theory to practice. *Journal of College Student Development, 41*, 81–93.

Park, J. (2008). Race and the Greek system in the 21st century. Centering the voices of Asian American women. *NASPA Journal, 45*(1), 103–132.

Pascarella, E. T., & Terenzini, P. T. (2005). *How college affects students: A third decade of research* (Vol. 2). San Francisco, CA: Jossey-Bass.

Patton, L. D. (2010). *Culture centers in higher education: Perspectives on identity, theory, and practice.* Sterling, VA: Stylus.

Peet, M. R. (2006). *We make the road by walking it: Critical consciousness, structuration, and social change* (Unpublished doctoral dissertation). University of Michigan, Ann Arbor.

Picca, L., & Feagin, J. (2007). *Two-faced racism: Whites in the backstage and frontstage.* Oxford, England: Taylor & Francis.

Pierce, J. L. (2012). *Racing for innocence: Whiteness, gender, and the backlash against affirmative action.* Stanford, CA: Stanford University Press.

Plessy v. Ferguson, 163 U.S. 537 (1896).

Polleta, M. (2017, January 13). Divisive or empowering? New Arizona ethnic studies ban to universities. *Arizona Republic.* Retrieved from http://www.azcentral.com/story/news/politics/arizona-education/2017/01/13/divisive-empowering-new-arizona-bill-would-extend-ethnic-studies-ban-universities/96532726/

Posselt, J. R., Jaquette, O., Bielby, R., & Bastedo, M. (2012). Access without equity: Longitudinal analyses of institutional stratification by race and ethnicity, 1972–2004. *American Educational Research Journal, 49*(6), 1074–1111.

Reason, R. D., & Broido, E. M. (2005). Issues and strategies for social justice allies (and the student affairs professionals who hope to encourage them). In R. D. Reason, E. M. Broido, T. L. Davis, & N. J. Evans (Eds.), *New directions for student services: No. 110. Developing social justice allies* (pp. 81–89). San Francisco, CA: Jossey-Bass.

Reason, R. D., & Evans, N. J. (2007). The complicated realities of Whiteness: From color-blind to racially cognizant. In S. R. Harper & L. D. Patton (Eds.), *New directions for student services: No. 120. Responding to the realities of race on campus* (pp. 67–75). San Francisco, CA: Jossey-Bass.

Reason, R. D., Millar, E. A. R., & Scales, T. C. (2005). Toward a model of racial justice ally development. *Journal of College Student Development, 46*(5), 530–546.

Richeson, J. A., & Shelton, J. N. (2007). Negotiating interracial interactions: Costs, consequences, and possibilities. *Current Directions in Psychological Science, 16*(6), 316–320.

Roberts, L. (2017, January 13). Arizona legislator: No more teaching about "social justice." *Arizona Republic.* Retrieved from http://www.azcentral.com/story /opinion/op-ed/laurieroberts/2017/01/13/roberts-arizona-legislator-no-more -teaching-social-justice/96512134/

Rodriguez, M. S. (2015). *Rethinking the Chicano Movement.* New York, NY: Routledge.

Roebuck, J. B., & Murty, K. S. (1993). *Historically Black colleges and universities: Their place in American higher education.* Westport, CT: Praeger.

Roediger, D. R. (1991). *The wages of Whiteness.* London, England: Vasso.

Roediger, D. R. (Ed.). (1998). *Black on White: Black writers on what it means to be White.* New York, NY: Pantheon Books.

Ross, L. (2015). *Blackballed: The Black and White politics of race on America's campuses.* New York, NY: St. Martin's.

Rothenberg, P. S. (2005). *White privilege: Essential readings on the other side of racism* (2nd ed.). New York, NY: Worth.

Rothenberg, P. S. (2016). *Race, class, and gender in the United States: An integrated study* (10th ed.). New York, NY: Worth.

Rowling, J. K. (1999). *Harry Potter and the chamber of secrets.* New York, NY: Scholastic.

Ryan, W. (1976). *Blaming the victim.* New York, NY: Random House.

Sacks, K. B. (1994). How Jews became White. In S. Gregory & R. Sanjek (Eds.), *Race* (pp. 78–102). New Brunswick, NJ: Rutgers University Press.

Saénz, V. B. (2010). Breaking the cycle of segregation: Examining students' precollege racial environments and college diversity experiences. *Review of Higher Education, 34*(1), 1–37.

Santos, J. L., Cabrera, N. L., & Fosnacht, K. J. (2010). Is "race-neutral" really race-neutral? Adverse impact towards underrepresented minorities in the UC system. *Journal of Higher Education, 81*(6), 675–701.

Schuman, H., Steeh, C., Bobo, L., & Krysan, M. (1997). *Racial attitudes in America: Trends and interpretations.* Cambridge, MA: Harvard University Press.

Sears, D. O. (1988). Symbolic racism. In P. A. Katz & D. A. Taylor (Eds.), *Eliminating racism: Profiles in controversy* (pp. 53–84). New York, NY: Plenum.

Sidanius, J., Van Laar, C., Levin, S., & Sinclair, S. (2004). Ethnic enclaves and the dynamics of social identity on the college campus: The good, the bad, and the ugly. *Journal of Personality and Social Psychology, 87*(1), 96–110.

Singleton-Jackson, J. A., Jackson, D. L., & Reinhardt, J. (2010). Students as consumers of knowledge: Are they buying what we're selling? *Innovative Higher Education, 35*(5), 343–358.

Sleeter, C. E. (1994). White racism. *Multicultural Education, 1*(4), 5–8.

Sleeter, C. E. (2011). *The academic and social value of ethnic studies: A research review.* Washington, DC: National Education Association.

Smith, W. A., Allen, W. R., & Danley, L. L. (2007). "Assume the position . . . you fit the description": Psychosocial experiences and racial battle fatigue among African American male college students. *American Behavioral Scientist, 51*(4), 551–578.

Sniderman, P., Crosby, G., & Howell, W. (2000). The politics of race. In D. O. Sears, J. Sidanius, & L. Bobo (Eds.), *Racialized politics: The debate about racism in America* (pp. 236–279). Chicago, IL: University of Chicago Press.

Spero, R. A. (2017, January 13). Political correctness: A tool of liberal coercion—A most un-American development. *CNSNews*. Retrieved from https://www.cnsnews.com/commentary/rabbi-aryeh-spero/political-correctness-tool-liberal-coercion-most-un-american

Sue, D. W. (2010). *Microaggressions in everyday life: Race, gender, and sexual orientation*. Hoboken, NJ: Wiley.

Sulé, V. T. (2016). Hip-hop is the healer: Sense of belonging and diversity among hip-hop collegians. *Journal of College Student Development, 57*(2), 181–196.

Sullivan, S. (2006). *Revealing Whiteness: The unconscious habits of racial privilege*. Bloomington: Indiana University Press.

Suzuki, B. (2002). Revisiting the model minority stereotype: Implications for student affairs practice and higher education. In M. McEwen, C. Kodama, A. Alvarez, & C. Liang (Eds.), *Working with Asian American college students* (pp. 21–32). San Francisco, CA: Jossey-Bass.

Syrett, N. L. (2009). *The company he keeps: A history of White college fraternities*. Chapel Hill: University of North Carolina Press.

Takaki, R. (1993). *A different mirror: A history of multicultural America*. Boston, MA: Back Bay Books.

Tate, G. (Ed.). (2003). *Everything but the burden: What White people are taking from Black culture*. New York, NY: Broadway Books.

Tatum, B. D. (1992). Talking about race, learning about racism: The applications of racial identity development theory. *Harvard Educational Review, 62*, 1–24.

Tatum, B. D. (2003). *"Why are all the Black kids sitting together in the cafeteria?" And other conversations about race*. New York, NY: Basic Books.

Thelin, J. R. (2004). *A history of American higher education*. Baltimore, MD: Johns Hopkins University Press.

Tierney, W. G. (1992). An anthropological analysis of student participation in college. *Journal of Higher Education, 63*(6), 603–618.

Tinto, V. (1987). *Leaving college: Rethinking the causes and cures of student attrition*. Chicago, IL: University of Chicago Press.

Trepagnier, B. (2006). *Silent racism: How well-meaning White people perpetuate the racial divide*. Boulder, CO: Paradigm.

Trow, M. (1970). Reflections on the transition from mass to universal higher education. *Daedalus, 99*(1), 1–42.

Unzueta, M. M., Gutiérrez, A. S., & Ghavami, N. (2010). How believing in affirmative action quotas affects White women's self-image. *Journal of Experimental Psychology, 46*, 120–126.

Unzueta, M. M., & Lowery, B. S. (2008). Defining racism safely: The role of self-image maintenance on White Americans' conceptions of racism. *Journal of Experimental Social Psychology, 44*(6), 1491–1497.

Unzueta, M. M., Lowery, B. S., & Knowles, E. B. (2008). How beliefs about affirmative action as quotas protects White men's self-esteem. *Organizational Behavior and Human Decision Processes, 105*(1), 1–13.

Wallace, C., Combs, S., Jordan, S., & Betha, M. (1997). Mo money mo problems [Recorded by The Notorious B.I.G. featuring Puff Daddy and Mase]. On *Life after death*. New York, NY: Bad Boy Records.

Wander, P. C., Martin, J. N., & Nakayama, T. K. (2005). The roots of racial classification. In P. S. Rothberg (Ed.), *White privilege: Essential readings on the other side of racism* (2nd ed., pp. 29–34). New York, NY: Worth.

Warren, M. R. (2010). *Fire in the heart: How White activists embrace racial justice.* New York, NY: Oxford University Press.

West, C. (2005, January 13). Prisoners of hope. *Alternet.* Retrieved from http://www.alternet.org/story/20982/prisoners_of_hope

Wilson, J. K. (1995). *The myth of political correctness: The conservative attack on higher education.* Durham, NC: Duke University Press.

Wilson, W. J. (1980). *The declining significance of race* (2nd ed.). Chicago, IL: University of Chicago Press.

Wise, T. (2006, April 24). What kind of card is race? *Counterpunch.* Retrieved from https://www.counterpunch.org/2006/04/24/what-kind-of-card-is-race/

Wise, T. (2007, June 22). Majoring in minstrelsy: White students, Blackface and the failure of mainstream multiculturalism. Retrieved from http://www.timwise.org/2007/06/majoring-in-minstrelsy-white-students-blackface-and-the-failure-of-mainstream-multiculturalism/

Wise, T. (2008). *White like me: Reflections on race from a privileged son.* Berkeley, CA: Soft Skull.

Yancy, G. (Ed.). (2012). *Christianity and Whiteness: What would Jesus do?* New York, NY: Routledge.

Yosso, T. J., Smith, W. A., Ceja, M., & Solórzano, D. G. (2010). Critical Race Theory, racial microaggressions, and the campus racial climate for Latina/o undergraduates. *Harvard Educational Review, 79,* 659–691.

Zinn, H. (2010). *You can't be neutral on a moving train: A personal history of our times.* Boston, MA: Beacon.

Zuñiga, X., Nagda, B. A., & Sevig, T. D. (2002). Intergroup dialogues: An educational model for cultivating engagement across difference. *Equity & Excellence in Education, 35*(1), 7–17.

Index

Page number in *italics* represents figure.

About the Author

NOLAN L. CABRERA is an associate professor in the Center for the Study of Higher Education at the University of Arizona. He is the author of over fifty scholarly publications, studying the racial dynamics on college campuses, with a particular focus on Whiteness. He was the only academic featured in the MTV documentary *White People*, and was also an expert witness for the plaintiffs in Tucson Unified Mexican American Studies federal case (*Arce v. Douglas*).